MW00340064

# spend with pennies

# Everyday Comfort

# spend with pennies

# Everyday Comfort

**Family Dinner Recipes from Fresh to Cozy**

**HOLLY NILSSON**

**Publisher** Mike Sanders
**Art & Design Director** William Thomas
**Editorial Director** Ann Barton
**Designer** Joanna Price
**Food Photographer** Joanie Simon
**Lifestyle Photographer** Tracey Jazmin
**Food Stylist** Brendan McCaskey
**Copy Editor** Monica Stone
**Proofreaders** Claire Safran, Lisa Starnes
**Indexer** Celia McCoy

First American Edition, 2024
Published in the United States by DK Publishing
1745 Broadway, 20th Floor, New York, NY 10019

The authorized representative in the EEA is Dorling Kindersley
Verlag GmbH. Arnulfstr. 124, 80636 Munich, Germany

Copyright © 2024 by Holly Nilsson
DK, a Division of Penguin Random House LLC
24 25 26 27 28   10 9 8 7 6 5 4 3 2 1
001–337543–SEP2024

All rights reserved.
Without limiting the rights under the copyright
reserved above, no part of this publication may be reproduced,
stored in or introduced into a retrieval system, or transmitted,
in any form, or by any means (electronic, mechanical,
photocopying, recording, or otherwise), without the prior
written permission of the copyright owner.

A catalog record for this book
is available from the Library of Congress.
ISBN 978-0-7440-8794-9

DK books are available at special discounts when purchased
in bulk for sales promotions, premiums, fundraising, or
educational use. For details, contact SpecialSales@dk.com

Printed and bound in China

www.dk.com

MIX
Paper | Supporting
responsible forestry
FSC™ C018179

This book was made with Forest
Stewardship Council™ certified
paper – one small step in DK's
commitment to a sustainable future.
Learn more at
www.dk.com/uk/information/sustainability

To my loves Ken, Ayla, Tyler, Maddy, Kailey, Jaxson, Chris, and Colton, and to the Spend with Pennies community— you inspire me every day.

# Contents

11 Introduction

15 Recipes for Real Life

18 Homemade Seasoning Mixes

## 21 Weeknight Quick Fixes

22 Tastes-Like-All-Day Quick Ham & Bean Soup

25 Secret Sauce Orange Ginger Beef

26 Seared Pork Medallions with Creamy Cracked Pepper Sauce

29 Root Beer BBQ Pulled Chicken Sliders

30 20-Minute Broccoli Cheese Soup

33 Egg Roll in a Bowl

34 Clean-Out-the-Fridge Pot Sticker Soup

37 Easiest Ever Tomato Soup with Cheesy Basil Toasts

38 Busy Day Parmesan Mushroom Toasts

41 Avocado Tuna Bowl with Sriracha Mayo

42 Fast & Fancy Weeknight Shrimp Piccata

45 Six-Ingredient, One-Pot Tortellini Alfredo

## 47 Skillet Suppers

48 Maple Sesame Salmon Bites with Broccoli & Peppers

51 Seared Pork Chops with Creamy Spinach Gnocchi

52 Crispy Rosemary Chicken Thighs with Root Veggies

55 Cheesy Beef & Salsa Burrito Supreme

56 Easy Fried Rice

59 Herbed Ground Beef & Rice Stroganoff Skillet

60 Crispy Chicken & Potato Patties with Creamy Corn

63 Cabbage Roll Skillet with Garlic Butter Dill Rice

64 Beef & Asparagus Roll-Ups with Tarragon Sauce

67 30-Minute Creamy Dijon Chicken

68 Moroccan-Spiced Chicken Couscous Bowls

## 71 Comforting Classics with a Twist

72 Chicken Pot Pie–Stuffed Shells with Herb Butter Crumbs

75 Hearty Ground Beef Stew with Rosemary Dumplings

76 My Mom's Hoisin Pork Tenderloin Sammies

79 Spicy Sausage Pimento Mac & Cheese

80 Lentil Shepherd's Pie

83 Flaky Broccoli Cheddar Chicken Pockets

84 Zesty Unstuffed-Shells Soup with Basil Ricotta

87 BLT Baked Chicken Burgers with Chipotle Mayo

88 Crispy Oven Chicken with Savory Cheddar Waffles

91 Must-Make Pizza Meatballs & Spaghetti

## 93 Fresh & Nourishing

94   Steakhouse Surf 'n' Turf Salad

97   No-Roll Mini-Meatball Cabbage Soup

98   Flaky Fish Tacos with Lime Crema

101   Honey Dijon–Glazed Pork Tenderloin with Roasted Sweet Potatoes & Apples

102   Stuffed Spaghetti Squash with Zesty Turkey Sauce

105   Skillet Shrimp Fajitas with Corn Cucumber Salsa

106   Herb-Roasted Chicken Pasta Primavera

109   Hasselback Chicken Cordon Bleu with Skinny Dijon Sauce

110   Pan-Seared Cod with Fresh Mango Salsa

113   Cheesy Ratatouille Roll-Ups with Meat Sauce (or Not)

## 115 Cozy Pasta Favorites

116   Gonna-Want-Seconds Cheesesteak Pasta

119   Weeknight Spinach, Artichoke & Sundried Tomato Rigatoni

120   My All-Time Favorite Mac & Cheese

123   Lemon-Pesto Shrimp Pasta with Pepper Parm Crumbs

124   One-Pan Sausage & Penne in Creamy Rose Sauce

127   Kailey's Roasted Balsamic Cherry Tomato Pasta

128   Fast! Homemade Alfredo Sauce

131   Spicy-as-You-Like-It Shrimp Peanut Noodles

132   Roasted Red Pepper Pasta with Crispy Parmesan Chicken

135   All-Purpose Meaty Pasta Sauce

## 137 Sheet Pan Dinners

138   Sticky Honey-Garlic Drumsticks with Peppers & Snap Peas

141   Crispy Oven Schnitzel Burgers with Zesty Dill Pickle Slaw

142   Sheet Pan Steak with Warm Potato Salad & Horseradish Sauce

145   Bacon-Wrapped Pork Tenderloin with Roasted Brussels Sprouts

146   Sheet Pan Cheeseburgers with Crispy Potato Wedges

149   One-Pan Smoked Sausage & Roasted Veggies

150   Lemon Herb-Crusted Salmon with Garlic Green Beans

153   Zucchini Turkey Meatballs with Roasted Tomato Sauce

154   Breakfast-for-Dinner Sheet Pan Chorizo Hash

157   Crunchy Pecan Chicken with Honey-Roasted Sweet Potatoes

## 159 Casseroles Bring the Comfort

160 Three-Cheese Scalloped Potato & Beef Gratin

163 Melt-in-Your-Mouth Pork Steaks in Creamy Mushroom Sauce

164 Salsa Verde Chicken Enchilada Casserole

167 Savory Ham & Cheese Bread Pudding

168 Baked Chicken Spaghetti

171 Lazy Day Bacon & Pea Oven Risotto

172 From-Scratch Tuna Casserole

175 Cozy Chicken, Broccoli & Wild Rice Casserole

176 Hearty Baked Chili with Cornmeal Drop Biscuits

179 Cheesy Herbed-Ricotta Baked Ziti

## 181 Slow Down Sunday Suppers

182 Grandma Mary's Pierogi

185 My Mom's Best Ever Pork Roast & Gravy

188 Homestyle Roast Chicken Dinner

190 The Best Ever Meatloaf

193 Grandma Mary's Rouladen with Mushroom Gravy

194 Creamy Clam Chowder with Mini Cheddar Biscuits

197 Slow Cooker Pot Roast with Root Veggies & Gravy

198 Three-Cheese Creamy Chicken & Mushroom Lasagna

201 Rustic Beef & Veggie Pot Pie

202 Slow Cooker Sticky Honey-Garlic Ribs

## 205 What to Do with Ground Beef

206 Beefed-Up Busy Day Lasagna

209 Better-Than-Take-Out Cheeseburger Sloppy Joes

210 Spicy Hoisin Beef with Garlic Ramen Noodles

213 Baked Beef Pinwheels

214 Feta Meatballs with Lemon Orzo & Cucumber Salsa

217 Mushroom & Swiss–Stuffed Mini Meatloaf

218 Ground Beef Barley Soup

221 Melty French Onion Meatballs

222 Layered Tex-Mex Tortilla Bake

225 Hearty Homemade Goulash

## 227 When All You Have Is Chicken

228 One-Pan Chicken Pomodoro Skillet

231 Choose-Your-Own-Adventure Chicken Stir-Fry

232 Slow Cooker Homestyle Chicken & Vegetable Chowder

235 Pimento Cheese–Stuffed Chicken Breasts with Honey Corn

236 Grilled Greek Chicken Wraps with Feta Mint Sauce

239 Easy Salsa Chicken Power Bowls

240 Skillet Chicken & Gravy

243 Cozy Chicken, Mushroom & Rice Soup

244 Cowboy Chopped Chicken Salad

247 Perfect Baked Chicken Breasts

## 249 Simply Perfect Sides

250 Dill Pickle Pasta Salad

252 The Everyday Salad Dressing

252 My All-Time Favorite Yogurt-Ranch Dressing

255 Quick Tomato Cucumber Salad

255 Garlic Herb Bread

256 Skillet Onions & Potatoes

256 Garlicky Mashed Potatoes

259 Simply Seasoned Garlic Rice

259 Creamy, Cheesy Crowd-Pleasin' Rice

260 Soul-Soothing Buttered Noodles

262 Roasting Vegetables in the Oven

264 Cooking Vegetables on the Stovetop

## 267 Sweet Endings

268 Creamy Rice Pudding

271 Anything Goes Fruit Crisp

272 No-Bake Cheesecake

275 Magic Lemon Pudding Cake

276 Grandpa Z's Banana Cupcakes

279 Better-Than-Anything Chocolate Cake

280 Chocolate Chip Pecan Cookies

282 Acknowledgments

284 Index

# Introduction

I'M HOLLY, the food lover and recipe creator behind the food blog Spend with Pennies, where I create easy-to-make recipes that bring families together. Feeding my family is one of my favorite things to do, and at a very young age, I learned that you don't need fancy ingredients, difficult techniques, or countless hours to create something amazing—in fact, just the opposite. For me, the best part of cooking is turning humble ingredients into a heartwarming meal as my family gathers around the table.

Sharing this book with you is a dream come true. It's packed with family favorites from my grandma's kitchen, reader favorite recipes from my blog, and a collection of new delicious dinner ideas. I hope it brings you as much joy in the kitchen as it brought me creating it.

## The Joy of Sharing a Family Meal

When I was growing up, my parents, my two sisters, and I ate dinner as a family every night of the week. Food has a magical way of bringing people together, and our time around the dinner table did just that; it truly bonded us as a family. My mom is an amazing cook, and she made mealtime feel special with family favorites like meatloaf or stew—often served with flaky biscuits—while Dad made the best steaks. My dad was a Realtor and he worked long hours, but he never missed our family dinners. Those moments were more than just meals; they were the heart of our family: filled with chatter, laughter, and usually a dose of playful teasing from my dad. They sparked my love

of a home-cooked meal and established a tradition of family dinners that I was determined to continue with my own family one day.

Food and cooking was a tradition among my extended family as well. Each summer, we would drive fourteen hours across western Canada to visit my grandma and grandpa. Grandma Mary's house always smelled of cabbage, and her basement smelled of pickles. She had a huge garden filled with carrots and peas that we could pick to our hearts' content. There was a cupboard filled with the best fancy cereals, and we were allowed to eat dill pickles and Popsicles for breakfast. This month-long visit each year also meant huge family meals with cucumber salads, fried Spam sandwiches, and her Polish specialties—homemade cabbage rolls, pierogi, and borscht.

It was here that my love for home cooking flourished. My Grandma Mary taught me to make the best Christmas cookies, my favorite rouladen (page 193), and, of course, pierogi (page 182). All the grandchildren coveted her pierogi, which were always made the old-fashioned way with a wooden spoon and no recipe—just adding more of this or that until it felt right. Pounds of potatoes magically transformed into trays and trays of hand-pinched pierogi. We'd spoon golden buttery onions over the browned pierogi and smother them in sour cream. Those moments in the kitchen are some of my favorite memories of Grandma Mary as she shared her love with us through her meals, and to this day, enjoying a plate of pierogi feels like a warm hug in grandma's kitchen.

Grandma Mary in her kitchen

## The Comfort of Simple Cooking

At the young age of nineteen, I had my daughter Ayla and began to cook for my own family. My meals were very simple, often meatballs with a sauce made from cream of mushroom soup and some green peppers or a basic stir-fry. I loved every moment of it. In my late twenties, I found myself as a single mom with three young kids, Ayla, Tyler, and Madisyn. Our free time was spent feeding the ducks, going to the playground, and picking wild blackberries to bake pies for dessert. Although we had simple pleasures, the days were tough and finances were even tougher. I learned to cook with very little, working with only the most basic of ingredients. I pared down my grocery lists to only what I could actually afford or what was on sale—this quickly taught me what ingredients gave big flavor and what was fluff. By starting with near zero, I learned that simple and comfort go hand in hand, and to this day, that lesson remains the foundation of every dish I make. I learned how to transform humble ingredients into something memorable and delicious. And I learned that even when it felt like I was standing at the bottom of a mountain, there was true happiness found in the everyday moments: my little family around the dinner table sharing a meal. That ideal of everyday comfort remains my guiding principle and provided the inspiration for this cookbook.

When I met my husband, Ken, my kids and I moved to a new city, leaving my parents and sisters behind. Ken's family has roots in farming and ranching, and they immediately welcomed us with open arms. Ken and I started our own fairy tale together, getting married and soon after being blessed with our daughter, Kailey. I was now cooking for our growing family, including my husband, who was off to the office early in the morning, working to take care of us. I was inspired by the simple country comfort meals my mother-in-law, Ruby, had made to serve her own family of seven.

Some of my fondest memories are of family gatherings during the holidays, everyone coming together in the kitchen to create a holiday feast. As many as thirty of us would join at a long table and enjoy the special meal together, melding our family traditions to create new ones, as we were now part of another warm and welcoming family.

## Growing My Love of Food, Family, and Community

I've always had an entrepreneurial spirit (thanks, Dad!), and once my kids were in school, I spent a few years with creative ventures of my own, like selling my hand-painted glassware to gift shops. I eventually went back to school, and I graduated top of my class in biological technology.

In 2012, fresh out of school, I joined the blogging world with Spend with Pennies, offering tips on saving money and helping readers find deals on everything from groceries to diapers. I also started sharing my recipes online, and the most amazing thing happened—people started making my recipes, bringing me into their homes by sharing my food with their own families. I knew I had found my true purpose and my passion.

Although I'd been cooking for my own family for years, I was eager to learn more. I wanted to create recipes that were not only tasty but also fail-safe. I soaked up everything culinary I could, including cooking classes and a boot camp at our local culinary school, and I added food tours and cooking schools to my travel itineraries. I traveled to California several times to learn food photography and absorbed as much technical food knowledge as I possibly could.

I learned the fundamentals, and I mastered some fancy techniques and dishes; however, as a busy mom of four and now a business owner, I usually found myself gravitating to a bowl of something easy and comforting at the end of the day. That's when it clicked: If this was what I needed, it was probably exactly what my readers needed too.

## From Our Family Kitchen to Yours

During a pivotal moment in 2016, I taught myself to film and edit food videos and began posting them on social media. I worked tirelessly, often 80 hours per week, with the unwavering support of my husband who was now helping run the house, driving kids to practices, picking up groceries, and washing mountains of dishes. The Spend with Pennies community grew beyond anything I could have imagined. I personally read every single review and comment on the site, celebrating in your successes in the kitchen, answering questions, testing substitutions, and most of all, being thankful to have a space at your table and attend your most cherished family events by way of my food.

As Spend with Pennies grew, I knew I needed some extra hands to help me keep up. I feel so blessed every day to work side by side with my sister Candace and my daughter Ayla. We are surrounded by the most incredible team, who feel just like family to me. The team works hard to make Spend with Pennies the best it can be, and I'm proud of what we achieve together.

Now that my kids are grown, I sit back in awe as I think back to my beginnings—my mom who made meals so special, my dad who always put food on our table, my sisters who have been there for me through thick and thin. To this day, there is nothing anyone in my family loves more than a homemade meal from my mom because you can feel love in every bite. I continue to make a point of filling my table with the people who mean the most to me—my husband, our four kids, our sons-in-law, and the light of our lives, our grandson Jaxson. (As well as a new granddaughter who will soon join our table!)

I'm excited to share my journey and love for family through this cookbook. From my kitchen to yours— Happy Cooking ♥

# Recipes for *Real Life*

**THIS BOOK IS FILLED** with my favorite recipes—all designed for real life! No fancy techniques, no special tools, and no hard-to-find ingredients. It's okay to cook just the way you do—the way most of us do—preparing a meal after getting home from a long day in a kitchen filled with happy chaos.

To me, preparing dinner is as much about what I need in that moment as it is about what's for dinner. I think of it as self-care in action. Some days are rushed and exhausting, and I need something tasty on the table fast. That's when my Weeknight Quick Fixes (page 21) come to the rescue. Other days, I just want to slow down and reminisce about being in my grandma's kitchen. For these times, Slow-Down Sunday Suppers (page 181) are just the thing. Craving something fresh and nutritious or in need of a big ol' cozy hug in a bowl? They're all here too.

In addition to a big dose of deliciousness in every recipe, this book is packed with lots of shortcuts, ingredient swaps, and tips for success.

## Setting Up for Success

I am a big fan of simplifying, both in my cooking and in my kitchen, so I tend to skip most kitchen gadgets and opt for a few timeless essentials that streamline my time and ensure my dishes always turn out as expected.

**Instant Read Thermometer** This inexpensive tool is the number one item I recommend in the kitchen. Ingredients, particularly meat, are costly, so cooking them to the right temperature ensures that the meat is tender and juicy every time (and safe for consumption).

**Ovenproof Skillet** This is a go-to for many recipes in this book. I love taking pans from stove to oven to table for fewer dishes to wash. My preference is a 12-inch (30cm) nonstick ovenproof skillet; it's a workhorse in my kitchen.

**A Good Chef's Knife** My 8-inch (30cm) chef's knife is a favorite in my kitchen. It's great for chopping, dicing, and general prep. A sharp knife makes recipe prep a breeze, and it is much less likely to slip than a dull knife. Sharpen your knives often!

**Dutch Oven** I use a Dutch oven for everything from soups and stews to braising and cooking roasts. While an enameled cast-iron Dutch oven is an investment, it conducts heat evenly and will last for years.

**Air Fryer** I use my air fryer for everything from "roasting" vegetables to reheating pizza or making perfectly juicy chicken breasts. (See page 109 for Hasselback Chicken Cordon Bleu.) I love that it preheats in less than 5 minutes, cooks in a fraction of the time, and creates a crispy crust on so many items.

**Parchment Paper** I use parchment paper for lining pans and food prep; almost nothing sticks to it, and it makes cleanup a breeze.

## A Little Prep Goes a Long Way

Start with a simple plan. I love to start each week with an overview of my dinner plans; it doesn't have to be extensive or fancy. It could be as simple as jotting down two or three dinners you'd like to make, or it might mean a full week's worth of dinners plus planned leftovers. There are no rules here—do what works for you—but just jot it down on a piece of paper. This little meal plan list, or full meal plan if you prefer, will act as a quick reference guide when you're not sure what's for dinner.

Make a list. Use your meal plan to create a grocery list so you're ready for the week. Shopping with a grocery list reduces food waste, saves money, and more importantly, ensures you have everything on hand.

Prep ahead. I like to wash and chop veggies on the weekend for quicker weekday meals. I also make a batch of My All-Time Favorite Yogurt-Ranch Dressing (page 252) for salads and veggie dip.

Use shortcuts when needed. Give yourself permission to do a little less—it's totally okay! I've included shortcuts in the recipes where possible, and I fully encourage you to find shortcuts at the grocery store that help make your life a little easier.

- **Vegetables** Look for prepped raw vegetables like chopped peppers, broccoli, and prewashed greens. Check the produce area for raw veggie stir-fry mixes and chopped or washed vegetables for roasting, air-frying, or swapping into recipes.
- **Aromatics** Many stores sell fresh chopped onions or bags of frozen chopped onions (found with the frozen veggies) that can be used right from the freezer. Grab jars of minced garlic or ginger to save on prep time.
- **Sides** Many grains and even mashed potatoes can be purchased precooked for a quick side dish on busy weekdays. Sprinkle in some fresh herbs if you have them!

## PREP-AHEAD TIPS

| | |
|---|---|
| **Firm veggies** | Most sturdy vegetables like carrots, onions, celery, broccoli, cauliflower, and Brussels sprouts can be rinsed, chopped, and prepared for snacking or recipes. They will last a minimum of 1 week in the refrigerator in an airtight container. |
| **Delicate veggies** | More delicate vegetables like asparagus, green onions, bell peppers, and zucchini can be prepared about 3 days in advance. |
| **Leafy greens** | Washing heads of lettuce or stalks of kale ahead of time will keep them extra crisp and fresh. Rinse in cool water, spin to dry, and store in a container or plastic bag with a piece of paper towel to absorb moisture. Most greens will keep for up to 1 week. |
| **Aromatics** | Garlic and ginger can be prepared in bulk. Peel the garlic cloves or ginger root and finely mince in a food processor. Freeze flat in a freezer bag for up to 6 months, and break off pieces to use right from frozen. Onions can be chopped and frozen on a sheet pan. Once frozen, transfer to a freezer bag for up to 6 months. |
| **Meats** | Check the best-before date on packages of fresh meat, and freeze them if needed. I like to package meats to fit within the recipes I'm making, which means I usually prepare 1-pound (454g) packages. Chicken parts (including boneless breasts, thighs, or whole chicken) and whole cuts of beef, pork, or lamb can be tightly sealed and frozen for 9 to 12 months. Ground beef, turkey, chicken, or pork can be tightly sealed and frozen for up to 4 months. |
| **Seafood** | Check the best-before date on any fresh seafood items. Fattier fish like salmon or tuna can be sealed and frozen for up to 3 months while leaner fish such as cod or halibut can be frozen for up to 8 months. Shrimp can be frozen for up to 12 months. |

## Mise en Place for Real Life

Being prepared makes cooking dinner both easier and a whole lot more enjoyable! Professional chefs follow a practice known as *mise en place*, which means having everything in place and all ingredients chopped, prepped, and measured before starting the cooking process. This makes sense in a commercial kitchen and some aspects of this make sense when cooking at home too.

Prep ahead for faster cooking—*sometimes!* For recipes that come together quickly, like a stir-fry, having everything prepared ahead of time helps ensure the cooking time is just right so the chicken isn't overcooking while you're chopping vegetables. However, prepping ahead is not always the best use of your time; sometimes a recipe comes together faster if the onion is diced while waiting for the chicken to brown and the peppers are sliced while the sauce is thickening.

## About the Recipes

The recipes in this book were designed for everyday meals and offer many tips, swaps, and suggestions. Here are a few tips to set yourself up for success!

**Read the recipe before cooking.** This will help you budget your time and ensure your ingredients are ready when you need them. Recipes use salted butter and table salt unless otherwise noted.

**Review prep time and total time.** The preparation time is an estimate of how much hands-on time is needed for each recipe after you have set out all of your ingredients. It will vary slightly based on your individual skills and tools but should give you a basic idea of timing. The total time is approximately how long you can expect a dish to take from the moment you begin preparation until it is ready to put on the table.

**Look for QR codes.** A handful of recipes have QR codes that can be used to access additional information for the recipe. (Don't worry, every recipe can be prepared without using a QR code; these are just for a few extras.) QR codes include tips, alternative cooking methods, or variations. You can easily access these with the camera on any smartphone.

## Icons to Look For

 **Tips** This is where you'll find specific information about ingredients, my favorite ways to save time on prep, and any special recipe notes.

 **Serving Suggestions** Here you'll find my favorite sides and garnishes to round out the meal.

 **Hey! It's Okay to. . .** This is a permission slip to cook for real life—totally guilt free. It's okay to swap homemade meatballs for frozen or replace the from-scratch sauce with my shortcut version.

 **Feeling Fancy?** These are my favorite simple ways to elevate and impress. Drizzle with a little truffle oil or add some pan-seared scallops for a next-level version of a delicious favorite.

 **Love Your Leftovers** Cook once, eat twice—instead of reheating leftovers, turn them into a completely new meal.

 **Make Ahead** If you're looking to gain a little bit of time in the future, these are meals that can be made in advance.

 **Variations** I love recipes that are versatile and work for real life. Check the variations to change up the protein or veggies, or for ways to incorporate new flavors.

 **Something on the Side** This indicates a quick and easy side that pairs well with the recipe to round out the meal.

# Homemade **Seasoning Mixes**

Seasoning mixes add a bit of magic to your everyday meals. They're surprisingly simple, and you likely have most of the ingredients already on hand to create them! Adjust the ingredients to suit your taste. Skip what you don't like, and adjust the salt and heat levels to what you do like. Save money while spicing up your food with the freshest seasonings.

### CAJUN SEASONING

**Makes:** 6 tablespoons

2 tablespoons **paprika**
1½ tablespoons **salt**
1 tablespoon **garlic powder**
2 teaspoons **onion powder**
1½ teaspoons **dried oregano**
1½ teaspoons **dried thyme leaves**
1¼ teaspoons **cayenne pepper**
1 teaspoon freshly ground
   **black pepper**

1. Combine all ingredients in a small bowl.
2. Store in an airtight container up to 6 months.

### GARLIC-HERB SEASONING

**Makes:** 2 tablespoons

1½ teaspoons **garlic powder**
1 teaspoon **salt**
1 teaspoon **dried parsley**
¾ teaspoon **dried basil**
¾ teaspoon **dried oregano**
½ teaspoon **paprika**
¼ teaspoon crushed **dried rosemary**
¼ teaspoon freshly ground
   **black pepper**

1. Combine all ingredients in a small bowl.
2. Store in an airtight container up to 6 months.

### ITALIAN SEASONING

**Makes:** 8 tablespoons

2 tablespoons **dried basil**
2 tablespoons **dried oregano**
2 tablespoons **dried parsley**
1 tablespoon crushed **dried rosemary**
1 tablespoon **dried thyme leaves**
1 tablespoon **red pepper flakes**
1 teaspoon **garlic powder**

1. Combine all ingredients in a small bowl.
2. Store in an airtight container up to 6 months.

### POULTRY SEASONING

**Makes:** 2½ tablespoons

5 teaspoons **rubbed sage**
4 teaspoons **dried thyme leaves**
2 teaspoons **dried rosemary**
1½ teaspoons **dried oregano**
¼ teaspoon **white pepper**
Pinch **ground nutmeg**

1. Combine all ingredients in a spice grinder and grind for 30 seconds.
2. Store in an airtight container up to 6 months.

### TACO SEASONING

**Makes:** 2½ tablespoons

1 tablespoon **chili powder**
1½ teaspoons **ground cumin**
1 teaspoon freshly ground **black pepper**
½ teaspoon **onion powder**
½ teaspoon **dried oregano**
½ teaspoon **salt**
¼ teaspoon **garlic powder**
¼ teaspoon **red pepper flakes**
Pinch **cayenne pepper** (optional)

1. Combine all ingredients in a small bowl.
2. Store in an airtight container up to 6 months.

**TIP**
If you don't have a spice grinder, blend the mixture in a blender for 30 to 60 seconds or until finely ground. This spice mixture can also be crushed using a mortar and pestle.

**TIPS**
- Replace a packet of taco seasoning with 2½ tablespoons homemade taco seasoning.
- To make taco meat, use 2½ tablespoons homemade taco seasoning for 1 pound (454g) browned ground beef or ground turkey. Add ½ cup (120ml) water with the seasoning and let it simmer. Stir in a tablespoon of tomato paste or a diced tomato if you'd like.

Garlic-Herb Seasoning

Taco Seasoning

Cajun Seasoning

Italian Seasoning

Poultry Seasoning

# **Weeknight**
## *Quick Fixes*

22     Tastes-Like-All-Day Quick Ham & Bean Soup

25     Secret Sauce Orange Ginger Beef

26     Seared Pork Medallions with Creamy Cracked Pepper Sauce

29     Root Beer BBQ Pulled Chicken Sliders

30     20-Minute Broccoli Cheese Soup

33     Egg Roll in a Bowl

34     Clean-Out-the-Fridge Pot Sticker Soup

37     Easiest Ever Tomato Soup with Cheesy Basil Toasts

38     Busy Day Parmesan Mushroom Toasts

41     Avocado Tuna Bowl with Sriracha Mayo

42     Fast & Fancy Weeknight Shrimp Piccata

45     Six-Ingredient, One-Pot Tortellini Alfredo

**Prep Time:** 10 minutes
**Total Time:** 35 minutes
**Serves** 4

---

2 tablespoons butter
1 small **yellow onion**, chopped
2 ribs **celery**, chopped
1 large **carrot**, chopped
1 tablespoon **all-purpose flour**
¾ teaspoon **poultry seasoning**
(for homemade, see page 18)
½ teaspoon **garlic powder**
¾ teaspoon freshly ground **black pepper**, divided
3¼ cups (780ml) **reduced-sodium chicken broth**
3 (15.5oz / 425g) cans **great northern beans**, drained and rinsed
1 tablespoon **tomato paste**
½ teaspoon **salt**
1 cup (138g) diced **cooked ham**

---

**Ingredient Swap**
You can substitute canned **pinto beans** or any variety of canned **white beans**, such as cannellini or navy beans, for the great northern beans in this recipe.

# Tastes-Like-All-Day
# Quick Ham & Bean Soup

With a perfect blend of seasonings, this soup tastes like it's been simmering all day long. Canned beans are the hero of this recipe because you can skip the hours of soaking and simmering and have dinner on the table in about 30 minutes. Plus, this recipe is a perfect way to use up those few leftover veggies in the produce drawer.

1. In a 2-quart (1.9L) saucepan, melt the butter over medium heat. Add the onion and cook for 2 to 3 minutes or until it begins to soften. Stir in the celery and carrot and cook for 2 minutes more.
2. Add the flour, poultry seasoning, garlic powder, and ½ teaspoon pepper, and cook for 1 minute.
3. Add the broth, beans, tomato paste, salt, and remaining ¼ teaspoon pepper. Bring to a boil over medium-high heat and simmer uncovered for 10 to 15 minutes or until the carrots are tender.
4. Use a potato masher to mash a few of the beans slightly to thicken the soup. Stir in the ham and simmer for 2 minutes more.
5. Season with additional salt and pepper to taste.

 **SERVING SUGGESTIONS**
This recipe is delicious with biscuits, toast and butter, or my Mini Cheddar Biscuits (page 194).

 **TIP**
Additional vegetables can be chopped and added to the soup along with the carrots and celery.

 **MAKE AHEAD**
This recipe doubles easily and freezes well. Prepare as directed, cool the soup, then ladle it into a zipper-lock freezer bag or an airtight freezerproof container, leaving 1 inch (2.5cm) of space at the top. Freeze for up to 4 months. Thaw the soup in the fridge overnight, and heat it on the stovetop, adding a bit of water or broth as needed.

**Prep Time:** 10 minutes
**Total Time:** 25 minutes
**Serves** 4

2 large **navel oranges**
1lb (454g) **lean ground beef**
⅓ cup (106g) **orange marmalade**
3½ tablespoons **soy sauce**
1 tablespoon **cornstarch**
1 teaspoon **garlic-chili paste**,
    or more to taste
2 cloves **garlic**, minced
1 tablespoon grated **fresh ginger**
**Cooked rice** or cooked noodles,
    to serve

### Ingredient Swaps

- Freshly grated ginger is best in this recipe, but it can be replaced with ¼ teaspoon **ground ginger** in a pinch.
- If you don't have orange marmalade, **apricot jam** or **apple jelly** are great replacements for it.
- Replace the ground beef with **ground chicken** or **ground turkey.**

# Secret Sauce
# Orange Ginger Beef

Skip the hefty restaurant bill and delivery time with this easy take-out fake-out. Ground beef is always in my freezer, making this a quick, anytime kind of recipe. The secret to the huge flavor in this gingery sauce is lots of fresh orange zest, and I add a touch of heat. (If you like it spicy, double up on the chili paste!) It comes together so fast you'll have dinner in your bowl in literally minutes!

1. Zest 1 teaspoon of orange zest, and juice ½ cup (120ml) of orange juice. Set the zest and juice aside.
2. Heat a large skillet over medium-high heat. Add the beef and cook, breaking up the meat with a spoon, for 5 to 6 minutes or until no pink remains. Drain any fat.
3. Meanwhile, in a small bowl, combine the orange zest, freshly squeezed orange juice, orange marmalade, soy sauce, cornstarch, and garlic-chili paste.
4. Add the garlic and ginger to the browned beef and cook for 2 minutes or until fragrant. Stir in the orange sauce and simmer, stirring occasionally, until thickened.
5. Serve over rice or noodles.

**SERVING SUGGESTIONS**
This saucy beef is great served over cooked lo mein noodles and topped with thinly sliced green onions, sesame seeds, or some red pepper flakes for a little kick.

**Prep Time:** 10 minutes
**Total Time:** 25 minutes
**Serves** 4

_____

1 **pork tenderloin**, about 1lb (454g)
1½ teaspoons freshly ground
   **black pepper**, divided
¾ teaspoon **salt**, divided
1 tablespoon **olive oil**
1 tablespoon **butter**
1 cup (240ml) **heavy**
   **whipping cream**
¼ cup (60ml) **chicken broth**
1 teaspoon **Dijon mustard**

---

**Ingredient Swap**
**Chicken cutlets** cut ¼ inch (0.6cm)
thick may be used in place of pork.
Cook the chicken for 2 to 3 minutes
per side or until it reaches an internal
temperature of 165°F (74°C).

# Seared Pork Medallions with Creamy Cracked Pepper Sauce

This is definitely a secret-weapon type of recipe, and nobody will ever guess how fast it is to make. Cutting the pork into thick pieces and pounding those into medallions ensures not only that the pork is extra tender, but also that it cooks in less than 5 minutes! The cracked pepper sauce? It's rich and decadent, turning dinner into a gourmet meal in minutes.

1. Cut the pork tenderloin into 8 pieces, each about 1 inch (2.5cm) thick.
2. Place the pork pieces on a cutting board, cut side up. Using the flat side of a meat mallet, pound the pieces to an even thickness of ¼ inch (0.6cm). Season the medallions with ¼ teaspoon pepper and ½ teaspoon salt.
3. In a 10-inch (25cm) nonstick skillet, heat the oil over medium-high heat.
4. Add the pork medallions to the skillet in batches, four at a time, and cook for 2 minutes per side or until browned. Remove each batch from the pan and set aside, lightly covered with foil.
5. Add the butter and remaining 1¼ teaspoons pepper to the skillet and cook for 1 to 2 minutes or until fragrant.
6. Whisk in the cream, broth, mustard, and remaining ¼ teaspoon salt, scraping up any browned bits in the skillet as you stir. Simmer until thickened, about 4 to 5 minutes.
7. Add the pork, along with any juices, back into the skillet. Simmer for 1 to 2 minutes or until the pork is heated through.
8. Taste and season with additional salt and pepper, if desired.

---

**SERVING SUGGESTIONS**
The sauce in this dish is great served over white or brown rice with a side of broccoli or asparagus (page 264).

**TIP**
Pork should be a little bit pink in the middle and cooked to an internal temperature of 145°F (63°C). These thin pieces of pork need just a couple of minutes to cook; be sure not to overcook them.

**VARIATION**
For a lighter sauce, replace heavy whipping cream with 1 cup (240ml) evaporated milk whisked with 1 tablespoon cornstarch. (Keep all remaining ingredients the same.) Add to the skillet in place of the heavy whipping cream and simmer the mixture just until thickened.

**Prep Time:** 10 minutes
**Total Time:** 25 minutes
**Serves** 4

---

1lb (454g) **chicken cutlets**,
   ¼ inch (0.6cm) thick
½ teaspoon **salt**
½ teaspoon freshly ground
   **black pepper**
½ teaspoon **garlic powder**
1 cup (240ml) **root beer**
¾ cup (180ml) **barbecue sauce**

**FOR SERVING**
12 **slider buns**
2 cups (130g) **coleslaw mix** or
   shredded green cabbage
¼ cup (56g) **mayonnaise**

### Ingredient Swaps

- **Boneless, skinless chicken breasts** can be used in place of chicken cutlets. Pound to ½-inch (1.5cm) thickness and increase simmering time to 9 to 12 minutes.
- **Diet soda** will work in this recipe too. Any dark soda can be substituted for root beer, such as cola or Dr. Pepper.
- Coleslaw mix and mayonnaise can be replaced with 2 cups (440g) **prepared coleslaw.**

# Root Beer BBQ
# Pulled Chicken Sliders

Saucy, sweet, and savory, this pulled chicken is on the table faster than you can hit up a drive-thru! The secret to this speedy supper is thin chicken cutlets that literally cook in minutes. Simmer until thick and saucy, shred, and pile it high on fluffy slider rolls for a family-pleasin' kind of meal.

1. Season the chicken cutlets with the salt, pepper, and garlic powder.
2. In a medium saucepan over medium-high heat, bring the root beer to a boil. Add the seasoned chicken cutlets, reduce the heat to a simmer, cover, and let cook for 5 to 7 minutes or until the chicken is cooked through and reaches an internal temperature of 165°F (74°C). Skim off any foam that forms on the surface of the liquid.
3. Remove the chicken and the cooking liquid from the saucepan. Place the chicken in a medium bowl, and reserve the liquid in a separate bowl.
4. Shred the chicken with two forks.
5. Add the shredded chicken, barbecue sauce, and ¼ cup (60ml) of the reserved cooking liquid back to the saucepan. Reduce the heat to medium, stir, and simmer for 3 to 5 minutes or until the chicken is heated through and the sauce has thickened.
6. Wrap the slider buns in a damp paper towel and microwave for 15 to 20 seconds or until warm.
7. To serve, spread the bun halves with mayonnaise and top each bun with coleslaw mix and ¼ cup (35g) shredded chicken.

---

**TIP**
To shred the chicken quickly, transfer the warmed chicken to a bowl. Place the beaters of a hand mixer into the chicken and turn the mixer to medium-low speed. Mix until shredded.

**LOVE YOUR LEFTOVERS**
Leftover pulled chicken makes great nachos, no measuring required! Place tortilla chips on a rimmed baking sheet. Top with leftover chicken, shredded cheddar cheese blend, sliced jalapeños, and sliced green onions. Bake at 375°F (190°C) for 8 to 10 minutes or until the cheese is melted and bubbly. Serve with sour cream and salsa.

**Prep Time:** 5 minutes
**Total Time:** 20 minutes
**Serves** 4

---

1 tablespoon **butter**
1 small **yellow onion**, diced
1 cup (142g) roughly
   chopped **carrot**
3 cups (225g) **fresh
   broccoli florets**
2 cups (480ml) **chicken broth**
½ teaspoon chopped **fresh
   thyme**
½ teaspoon **garlic powder**
¼ teaspoon **salt**
¼ teaspoon freshly ground
   **black pepper**
2 tablespoons **all-purpose flour**
1½ cups (360ml) **half-and-half** or
   light cream
1 cup (113g) shredded **sharp
   cheddar cheese**
⅓ cup (33g) shredded
   **Parmesan cheese**

# 20-Minute
# Broccoli Cheese Soup

This fast and fresh broccoli cheese soup has been a longtime favorite on Spend with Pennies and for good reason. It has a rich and creamy texture, a cheesy flavor, and a superfast prep that makes it hard to believe it's actually this easy. Start to finish, this recipe is ready in about 20 minutes, making it a quick lunch or dinner.

1. In a large saucepan, melt the butter over medium heat. Add the onion and carrot and cook until the onion is softened, about 3 minutes.
2. Add the broccoli, chicken broth, thyme, garlic powder, salt, and pepper. Bring to a boil over medium-high heat, reduce the heat to medium, and simmer uncovered until the broccoli is softened, about 8 minutes.
3. With a slotted spoon, remove 1 cup of vegetables from the soup, coarsely chop, and set aside.
4. Using an immersion blender, blend the remaining vegetables and broth in the saucepan.
5. Place the flour in a small bowl. Add the half-and-half, a little at a time, stirring until smooth to create a slurry.
6. Bring the blended vegetable mixture to a boil over medium-high heat. Whisk in the slurry. Continue whisking until the soup is thick and bubbling, about 3 to 4 minutes. Let boil for 1 additional minute.
7. Remove the soup from the heat and stir in the cheddar and Parmesan cheeses along with the reserved chopped vegetables. Taste and season with additional salt and pepper, if desired.

---

 **SERVING SUGGESTIONS**
For some extra cheesy goodness, sprinkle additional shredded sharp cheddar or Parmesan on top for serving. Pair this soup with crusty bread or Garlic Herb Bread (page 255) for dipping and dunking.

 **FEELING FANCY?**
Check your local bakery for small, round loaves and serve this soup in 4 individual bread bowls!

# Egg Roll in a Bowl

**Prep Time:** 5 minutes
**Total Time:** 20 minutes
**Serves** 4

1lb (454g) **ground pork**
1lb (454g) **coleslaw mix**
4 **green onions**, sliced, white and green parts separated
4 cloves **garlic**, minced
2 teaspoons grated **fresh ginger**
3 tablespoons **soy sauce**
1 teaspoon **toasted sesame oil**
**Fresh cilantro leaves** (optional), to garnish

### Ingredient Swap
The ground pork can be replaced with **ground chicken** or **ground turkey**.

I make a version of this stir-fry almost every week and could happily eat it on repeat every day. With just a handful of ingredients, this dish packs all the flavors from your favorite eggroll into a quick and healthy bowl. It's one of the fastest ways to get dinner (or lunch!) on the table, and it reheats like a dream.

1. In a 12-inch (30 cm) skillet over medium-high heat, cook the ground pork, breaking it up with a spoon, until no pink remains. Drain any fat.
2. Add the coleslaw mix, whites of the green onions, garlic, and ginger. Cook the mixture until the coleslaw becomes tender, about 5 minutes.
3. Stir in the soy sauce and sesame oil and cook for 1 minute more.
4. Divide into bowls and garnish with the remaining green onion and cilantro, if using.

 **SERVING SUGGESTIONS**
- Top your bowls with a drizzle of sriracha, fresh bean sprouts, or sesame seeds.
- Tuck the meat mixture into fresh lettuce leaves and serve lettuce-wrap style.

 **TIP**
Stretch this meal even further by adding a few cups of bean sprouts, cauliflower rice, or very finely chopped vegetables (broccoli, celery, or carrots) when adding the coleslaw mix to the skillet.

 **SOMETHING ON THE SIDE**
For some added crunch, prep a batch of Sesame Wonton Crisps. Cut 10 wonton wrappers diagonally into four triangles each. Brush the wrappers with egg white, sprinkle with sesame seeds, and bake at 400°F (200°C) for 6 to 8 minutes or air-fry at 370°F (190°C) for 3 to 4 minutes.

**Prep Time:** 5 minutes
**Total Time:** 25 minutes
**Serves** 4

---

8 cups (1.9L) **chicken broth**
2 tablespoons **soy sauce**
2 cloves **garlic**, minced
1 tablespoon grated **fresh ginger**
1lb (454g) **frozen pot stickers**
4 cups (575g) **mixed fresh
    vegetables**, cut into
    bite-size pieces
1 teaspoon **toasted sesame oil**
2 **green onions**, thinly sliced,
    to garnish

# Clean-Out-the-Fridge
# Pot Sticker Soup

I make this soup frequently as a speedy, last-minute meal—it's easy, healthy, and super satisfying! A delicious ginger broth is filled with veggies and pot stickers, and it needs just minutes on the stovetop. This is the perfect soup to clean out the produce drawer (or freezer), since almost any veggie in the crisper will work. Feel free to toss in leftover pork, shrimp, or chicken for a bit of added protein.

1. In a large saucepan, combine the broth, soy sauce, garlic, and ginger. Bring to a boil over high heat, reduce the heat to medium, and let simmer for 5 minutes.
2. Stir in the pot stickers and vegetables and simmer for 4 to 6 minutes or until the pot stickers are cooked through and the vegetables are tender.
3. Stir in the sesame oil and garnish with green onions.

---

 **SERVING SUGGESTIONS**
This soup can be garnished with fresh, crisp bean sprouts; sriracha; or a sprinkle of fresh herbs, like cilantro or basil.

 **HEY! IT'S OKAY TO . . .**
Skip the chopping and use a fresh or frozen prepped-for-you stir-fry mix! Check the produce area of the grocery store for a fresh stir-fry mix or even use frozen stir-fry vegetables.

 **MAKE AHEAD**
If you're preparing ahead for lunches or saving leftovers, remove the pot stickers from the broth and store them separately so they don't get mushy.

 **TIPS**
- Any type of vegetable can be added to this recipe. Our favorites include cabbage, thinly sliced carrots, celery, snap peas, bok choy, and bell peppers.
- Fresh ginger packs a ton of flavor that can't be matched with dried or powdered. Buy a small root (it's super cheap!) and store it in the freezer. When needed, grate it right from frozen using a cheese grater—no need to peel it first. Add it to soups, stir-fries, or dressings for a flavor punch!

**Prep Time:** 10 minutes
**Total Time:** 20 minutes
**Serves** 4

## FOR THE SOUP

1 (24 oz / 710ml) jar **marinara sauce**

1 (14.5 oz / 411g) can **petite-diced tomatoes,** with juices

1 cup (240ml) **heavy whipping cream**

1½ cups (360ml) **chicken broth**

1 teaspoon **onion powder**

½ teaspoon **salt**

¼ teaspoon freshly ground **black pepper**

½ teaspoon **granulated sugar,** if needed

## FOR THE TOAST

½ cup (57g) shredded **mozzarella cheese**

2 tablespoons freshly grated **Parmesan cheese**

1 teaspoon **dried basil**

½ teaspoon **garlic powder**

12 slices **baguette,** cut ½ inch (1.5cm) thick

# Easiest Ever Tomato Soup
## with Cheesy Basil Toasts

Tomato soup is a childhood favorite for my daughter Kailey because her grandma, Ruby, always served it for lunch. This simple, elevated version is rich and creamy and incredibly easy. Using jarred marinara sauce in place of canned tomatoes keeps the prep extra fast because it's already perfectly seasoned, and no blending is required. It's a homestyle soup so good that it's hard to believe how quickly it comes together.

1. Preheat the broiler to 500°F (260°F).
2. **To make the soup,** in a 3-quart (2.8L) saucepan, combine the marinara sauce, diced tomatoes with juices, heavy cream, broth, onion powder, salt, and pepper. Bring to a boil over medium-high heat, reduce the heat to medium, and simmer for 10 minutes uncovered, stirring occasionally.
3. Meanwhile, **to make the toast,** in a small bowl, mix the mozzarella, Parmesan, basil, and garlic powder.
4. Place the baguette slices on a baking sheet and divide the mozzarella mixture evenly over the slices. Place under the broiler about 6 inches (15cm) from the heat, and broil until golden and bubbly, about 2 to 3 minutes.
5. Taste the soup, and if it is tart, stir in the sugar to balance the acidity. Season with additional salt and pepper to taste. Serve warm with cheesy basil toasts.

**TO PREPARE IN AN AIR FRYER**
Instead of broiling the basil toast, place the bread in a single layer in the air-fryer basket and top with the cheese mixture. No need to preheat; simply air-fry at 400°F (200°C) for 2 to 3 minutes or until the cheese is browned and bubbly.

**TIPS**
- It's important to use heavy whipping cream in this recipe. Lighter cream can curdle from the acidity of the tomatoes.
- For a smooth soup, use an immersion blender and pulse the soup.
- The sauce is the base for the flavor of this recipe, so choose a high-quality one. You can use any variety of marinara or tomato pasta sauce you'd like; tomato basil is our favorite.

**HEY! IT'S OKAY TO . . .**
Use preshredded cheese for the toast in this recipe; it broils perfectly! You can skip the basil toast and serve this soup with a traditional grilled cheese sandwich, a stack of crackers, or crusty bread if you'd prefer.

**MAKE AHEAD**
This soup can be refrigerated for up to 4 days, and it freezes beautifully! Ladle the cooled soup into zipper-lock freezer bags or airtight freezerproof containers, and freeze for up to 4 months. Reheat from frozen on the stovetop over medium-low heat, stirring occasionally.

**Prep Time:** 10 minutes
**Total Time:** 25 minutes
**Serves** 4

---

1½lb (680g) mixed **fresh mushrooms**, thinly sliced
1½ tablespoons **soy sauce**
¼ teaspoon freshly ground **black pepper**
1 tablespoon **butter**
4 large slices **artisan bread** or sourdough bread
1½ tablespoons **olive oil**
¼ teaspoon **coarse salt**
3 cloves **garlic**, minced
½ cup (120ml) **half-and-half** or light cream
3 tablespoons freshly grated **Parmesan cheese**

# Busy Day
# Parmesan Mushroom Toasts

Mushrooms are one of my favorite veggies, and their meaty texture and rich earthy flavor are so incredibly satisfying. This quick weeknight fix starts with a skillet of garlicky fried mushrooms finished with a little cream and Parmesan cheese. Serve it over a toasted slice of artisan bread brushed with olive oil for the perfect instant gratification meal.

1. Preheat the broiler to high heat.
2. In a medium bowl, toss the mushrooms with the soy sauce and pepper.
3. In a 12-inch (30cm) skillet over medium-high heat, melt the butter. Add the mushrooms and cook until the mushrooms release their liquid.
4. Increase the heat to high and continue to cook for 6 to 8 minutes, stirring occasionally, or until the liquid has evaporated and the mushrooms are cooked.
5. Meanwhile, brush each slice of bread on both sides with the olive oil, sprinkle with salt, and place on a baking sheet. Place the baking sheet 4 inches (10cm) under the broiler, broil for 2 minutes or until toasted, then flip and broil the opposite sides, about 2 minutes more.
6. Add the garlic to the mushrooms and cook until fragrant, about 1 minute. Stir in the half-and-half, and simmer uncovered over medium-high heat until it is slightly thickened, about 2 to 3 minutes. Remove from the heat and stir in the Parmesan cheese. Season with additional salt and pepper to taste.
7. Spoon the mushrooms over the toast and garnish as desired.

**TIP**
Any variety of fresh mushrooms can be used in this recipe. You can use mixed mushrooms, portobellos, cremini, or white mushrooms.

**FEELING FANCY?**
There are countless ways to dress up mushroom toast, so get creative! Try topping with microgreens, arugula, freshly chopped chives, or additional Parmesan cheese. If you have truffle oil, you can add a little drizzle along with the Parmesan cheese.

**SOMETHING ON THE SIDE**
Mushroom toast is perfect topped with a fried or poached egg with a runny yolk.
To poach an egg, bring 4 inches (10cm) of water to a gentle simmer in a small saucepan. Break an egg into a small bowl and slide the egg gently from the bowl into the simmering water. Cook until the white is set and the yolk is still slightly runny, about 4 minutes. Remove the poached egg with a slotted spoon and place it on the mushroom toast. Season with salt and pepper.

**Prep Time:** 15 minutes
**Total Time:** 15 minutes
**Serves** 4

2 tablespoons **soy sauce**
1 tablespoon **rice vinegar**
1½ teaspoons **toasted sesame oil**
3 cups (600g) **cooked brown rice**
1 cup (150g) thinly sliced **cucumber**
1 cup (65g) shredded **red cabbage**
1 cup (85g) **shelled edamame**
1 (12oz / 340g) can **chunk white tuna in water**, drained
1 large **avocado**, sliced
2 **green onions**, thinly sliced
1 tablespoon **sesame seeds**

**FOR THE SAUCE**
¼ cup (60ml) **mayonnaise**
1 teaspoon **sriracha**
1½ teaspoons **water**

> **Ingredient Swap**
> Replace the shredded cabbage with 1 cup (85g) **coleslaw mix**.

# Avocado Tuna Bowl
# with Sriracha Mayo

Perfect for meal prep or a quick weeknight fix, grain bowls are hearty, healthy, and vibrant. This bowl starts with cooked brown rice and canned tuna with a sesame-soy drizzle inspired by my favorite dumpling dip. Top it all off with a handful of fresh, crisp veggies for a great lunch or dinner. With the simplest of ingredients, this bowl is nourishing and nothing short of delicious.

1. In a small bowl, combine the soy sauce, rice vinegar, and sesame oil. Set aside.
2. **To make the sauce,** in a separate small bowl, combine the mayonnaise, sriracha, and water.
3. Divide the cooked rice among 4 bowls. Top with the cucumber, cabbage, and edamame.
4. Gently break the tuna apart and divide over the bowls. Spoon the soy sauce mixture over the tuna. Add the avocado.
5. Drizzle the bowl with the spicy mayonnaise sauce and top with the green onions and sesame seeds.

**SERVING SUGGESTIONS**
One of my favorite parts of a grain bowl is adding a variety of textures and flavors on top. Don't limit yourself to the suggested toppings; feel free to add your own shredded, spiralized, or julienned veggies, such as carrots or jicama.

**HEY! IT'S OKAY TO . . .**
Replace the rice with any kind of cooked grain. Instant brown rice or packets of precooked rice or quinoa are the perfect addition to these bowls!

---

1 tablespoon **olive oil**
1lb (454g) **large shrimp**, peeled
  and deveined
1½ teaspoons **lemon-pepper
  seasoning**
1 small clove **garlic**, minced
2 teaspoons **all-purpose flour**
¼ cup (60ml) **white wine**
¾ cup (180ml) **chicken broth**
1½ tablespoons freshly squeezed
  **lemon juice**
4 tablespoons cold **butter**
3 tablespoons drained **capers**
**Salt** and freshly ground
  **black pepper,** to taste
1 tablespoon chopped
  **fresh parsley,** to garnish

### Ingredient Swaps

- Replace the shrimp with 1 pound (454g) **boneless, skinless chicken breasts** or cutlets, ½ inch (1.5cm) thick. Season as directed in step 2, and cook in batches in the skillet for 5 to 7 minutes or until the chicken is cooked through to 165°F (74°C). Prepare the sauce as directed in the recipe.
- Wine can be replaced with additional **chicken broth**.

# Fast & Fancy
# Weeknight Shrimp Piccata

This quick weeknight dinner is a restaurant-worthy meal that's on your table in about 20 minutes—and it needs just one skillet. Juicy pan-seared shrimp are tossed in a superfast lemon white wine butter sauce with capers and parsley. It has fresh citrus vibes and a briny punch for weeknight elegance in minutes.

1. Heat the oil in a large 10-inch (25cm) skillet over medium-high heat.
2. Pat the shrimp dry with a paper towel. In a medium bowl, gently toss the shrimp with the lemon-pepper seasoning and garlic. Sprinkle the flour over the shrimp and gently toss to combine.
3. Add half of the shrimp to the skillet and cook, stirring constantly, for 2 to 3 minutes or until the shrimp is pink and almost cooked through. Transfer the shrimp to a bowl and repeat with the remaining shrimp. Set aside.
4. Add the wine to the skillet and simmer for 2 minutes. Whisk in the broth and lemon juice, and simmer for an additional 5 to 6 minutes or until the liquid is reduced by half.
5. Reduce the heat to low and whisk in the cold butter, one tablespoon at a time, whisking continuously.
6. Stir in the capers and simmer for 2 minutes or until the liquid has thickened. Stir in the shrimp with juices and cook just until heated through, about 1 minute more. Taste and season with salt and pepper.
7. Garnish with parsley and serve over pasta, if desired.

---

 **SERVING SUGGESTIONS**
This shrimp is perfect served over pasta or with a thick slice of crusty bread and a fresh salad. If serving this with pasta, the sauce can be doubled.

 **TIPS**
- The tails look beautiful if serving to guests, but feel free to remove them before cooking if you'd prefer.
- For a touch of heat, add ¼ teaspoon red pepper flakes with the lemon juice in step 4.

 **SOMETHING ON THE SIDE**
This dish pairs well with roasted asparagus. Toss 1 pound (454g) asparagus spears with ½ tablespoon olive oil, and season with salt and pepper. Roast in the oven at 425°F (220°C) for 7 to 12 minutes, or cook in the air fryer for 6 to 8 minutes or just until tender-crisp.

**Prep Time:** 5 minutes
**Total Time:** 18 minutes
**Serves** 4

---

18oz (510g) **fresh cheese tortellini**
1 cup (240ml) **heavy whipping cream**
1 cup (240ml) **chicken broth**
½ teaspoon **garlic powder**
½ cup (50g) grated **Parmesan cheese**, divided
Pinch of **nutmeg**
**Salt** and freshly ground **black pepper,** to taste

**Ingredient Swaps**

- If using **frozen tortellini,** add an extra ¼ cup (60ml) broth and cook for 7 to 8 minutes.
- Cheese tortellini can be replaced with **another variety of tortellini,** such as spinach or mushroom.

# Six-Ingredient, One-Pot
# Tortellini Alfredo

With one pot, six ingredients, and no strainer required, this meal is on the table in less than 20 minutes from start to finish. You won't believe that a from-scratch Alfredo sauce can come together this quickly and pack so much flavor into every bite. It's extra versatile, so peek in the fridge and add some steamed broccoli, peas, spinach, or leftover cooked chicken.

1. In a medium saucepan, combine the tortellini, cream, broth, and garlic powder.
2. Bring to a boil over medium-high heat, reduce the heat to a simmer, and cover. Cook for 4 to 5 minutes, stirring occasionally.
3. Once the tortellini is cooked through, remove it from the heat and stir in ¼ cup (25g) Parmesan cheese and nutmeg. Season with salt and pepper to taste, and let it rest uncovered for 3 minutes to allow the sauce to thicken.
4. Top with the remaining ¼ cup (25g) Parmesan cheese.

---

 **SERVING SUGGESTIONS**
We love this dish as a meatless meal with salad and bread. It's also great topped with grilled chicken breast or shrimp.

 **TIPS**
- Brands of tortellini can vary slightly; add more water (and cooking time) if needed.
- To get a pinch of nutmeg, use your index finger and thumb to squeeze a little bit out of the spice jar.
- The sauce will thicken once the cheese is added.

 **FEELING FANCY?**
Take this simple supper to the next level with the addition of a drizzle of truffle oil. While truffle oil comes with a hefty price tag in restaurants, a small bottle online is relatively inexpensive, and since a little goes a very long way, it can flavor countless dishes from Garlicky Mashed Potatoes (page 256) to popcorn.

# Skillet
## *Suppers*

**48**   Maple Sesame Salmon Bites with Broccoli & Peppers

**51**   Seared Pork Chops & Creamy Spinach Gnocchi

**52**   Crispy Rosemary Chicken Thighs with Root Veggies

**55**   Cheesy Beef & Salsa Burrito Supreme

**56**   Easy Fried Rice

**59**   Herbed Ground Beef & Rice Stroganoff Skillet

**60**   Crispy Chicken & Potato Patties with Creamy Corn

**63**   Cabbage Roll Skillet with Garlic Butter Dill Rice

**64**   Beef & Asparagus Roll-Ups with Tarragon Sauce

**67**   30-Minute Creamy Dijon Chicken

**68**   Moroccan-Spiced Chicken Couscous Bowls

**Prep Time:** 10 minutes
**Total Time:** 25 minutes
**Serves** 4

1lb (454g) **skinless salmon fillets**
¾ teaspoon **salt**, divided
¼ teaspoons freshly ground
   **black pepper**
2 tablespoons **soy sauce**
2 tablespoons **maple syrup**
1½ teaspoons minced
   **fresh ginger**
1½ teaspoons **toasted sesame oil**
4 cups (300g) **broccoli florets**
1 **red bell pepper**, cut into 1-inch
   (2.5cm) pieces
2 tablespoons **vegetable oil**,
   divided
2 cloves **garlic**, minced
1 tablespoon **white sesame seeds**
1 teaspoon **black sesame seeds**
3 cups (420g) **cooked rice**

**FOR THE DRIZZLE**
¼ cup (56g) **mayonnaise**
1½ teaspoons **water**
1 teaspoon **sriracha**
¼ teaspoon **sesame oil**

# Maple Sesame Salmon Bites
## with Broccoli & Peppers

This recipe has been crowned the "best salmon I've ever had" by our fisherman friend! The salmon is deliciously sweet with a candied sesame crust and tons of flavor in every bite. It's served bowl style over rice with fresh garlicky veggies and a spicy mayo drizzle. Feel free to dress it up with your favorite fresh crisp toppings for an easy, feel-good favorite.

1. **To make the drizzle,** in a small bowl, combine the mayonnaise, water, sriracha, and sesame oil. Refrigerate until ready to serve.
2. Cut the salmon into 1-inch (2.5cm) pieces and season with ½ teaspoon salt and ¼ teaspoon pepper. In a medium bowl, gently toss the salmon with the soy sauce, maple syrup, ginger, and sesame oil. Let marinate for 10 to 15 minutes.
3. Meanwhile, in a medium bowl, combine the broccoli, bell pepper, 1½ teaspoons vegetable oil, garlic, and the remaining ¼ teaspoon salt.
4. Heat 1½ teaspoons vegetable oil in a 12-inch (30cm) nonstick skillet over medium-high heat. Once hot, add the broccoli and bell pepper, along with 1 tablespoon water. Cook, stirring occasionally, until tender-crisp, about 4 minutes. Remove the vegetables from the pan and set aside, lightly covered to keep warm.
5. Gently drain the salmon, and discard the marinade. Add the white and black sesame seeds to the salmon and gently toss to combine.
6. In the same skillet, heat the remaining 1 tablespoon vegetable oil over medium-high heat. Once hot, add the salmon pieces in a single layer. Cook for 2 minutes or until golden brown. Use tongs to turn the salmon pieces and cook for an additional 2 to 3 minutes or until the salmon is almost cooked through.
7. Serve the salmon and vegetables over rice with a drizzle of the sauce. Garnish as desired.

**TO PREPARE IN AN AIR FRYER**
1. Prepare the salmon and vegetables as directed in the recipe.
2. Preheat the air fryer to 400°F (200°C) and add the broccoli and bell pepper to the air-fryer basket. Cook for 5 to 7 minutes or until tender-crisp, shaking the basket after 4 minutes.
3. Remove from the basket and transfer to a bowl; cover to keep warm.
4. Add the salmon to the air-fryer basket in a single layer and cook for 3 to 5 minutes or just until the salmon is almost cooked through.

**SERVING SUGGESTIONS**
We love to pile on fresh garnishes and toppings like sliced cucumber, green onions, cilantro, radishes, or bean sprouts.

**TIP**
The salmon cooks very quickly and will continue to cook once removed from the skillet or air fryer, so be sure not to overcook.

10oz (284g) **fresh spinach,** chopped

4 boneless **pork loin chops,** cut ¾ inch (2cm) thick

1 teaspoon **Italian seasoning** (for homemade, see page 18)

¾ teaspoon **garlic powder**

¾ teaspoon **salt**

½ teaspoon freshly ground **black pepper,** divided

1 tablespoon **olive oil**

2 tablespoons **butter**

1 small **yellow onion,** finely diced

6oz (170g) **cream cheese**

1½ cups (360ml) **reduced-sodium chicken broth**

3 tablespoons grated **Parmesan cheese,** divided

1 (17.6oz / 499g) package **shelf-stable gnocchi**

---

### Ingredient Swaps

- Replace fresh spinach with 5 ounces (142g) **frozen chopped spinach,** thawed and squeezed dry.
- Replace the pork with 1 pound (454g) **chicken cutlets,** cut ¼ inch (0.6cm) thick, and cook for 3 minutes per side.
- Replace gnocchi with 12 ounces (340g) **medium-size pasta,** such as penne. Cook according to package directions and drain well before adding to the skillet.

# Seared Pork Chops & Creamy Spinach Gnocchi

This saucy skillet turns one of my most-loved side dishes—creamed spinach—into a quick and flavorful sauce paired with pan-seared pork chops and tender gnocchi. I love how versatile this meal is; it's equally delicious with pork or chicken, great with fresh or frozen spinach, and you can even substitute your favorite pasta for gnocchi.

1. Bring a large pot of salted water to a boil. Cover and reduce the heat to low.
2. Heat a 12-inch (30cm) nonstick skillet over medium heat. Add the chopped spinach and cook for 2 to 3 minutes or until wilted. Transfer the spinach to a bowl to cool.
3. Pat the pork chops dry with a paper towel, and if the pork chops have a fat cap, cut 2 or 3 diagonal slits in the fat. Season with the Italian seasoning, garlic powder, salt, and ¼ teaspoon pepper.
4. Add the oil to the skillet and increase the heat to medium-high. Place the pork chops in the skillet and cook for 3 to 4 minutes per side or until they reach an internal temperature of 140°F (60°C). Transfer them to a plate, and loosely cover it with foil to keep them warm.
5. Reduce the heat to medium and add the butter and onion to the skillet. Cook just until the onion is tender, about 3 to 4 minutes.
6. Add the cream cheese to the onion and whisk until melted. Gradually add the broth, whisking the sauce until smooth after each addition.
7. Squeeze the spinach to remove excess moisture, stir it into the sauce along with 2 tablespoons Parmesan cheese and the remaining ¼ teaspoon pepper, and simmer for 3 minutes.
8. Meanwhile, bring the pot of salted water back to a boil over high heat. Add the gnocchi and cook according to package directions, about 3 to 4 minutes or just until they float. Drain well.
9. Stir the gnocchi into the spinach sauce. Add the pork chops and simmer for 2 minutes more or until the pork is heated through. Remove from the heat and rest for 3 to 5 minutes to thicken the sauce.
10. Garnish with the remaining 1 tablespoon Parmesan cheese. Serve immediately.

**TIPS**

- If using thinner or fast-fry pork chops (¼in / 0.6cm thick), reduce the cooking time to 2 minutes per side.
- If reheating leftovers, add a little bit of water or milk to the gnocchi if needed.

2 cups (235g) cubed **butternut squash** or sweet potatoes
2 medium **parsnips**, cut into 1 × ½-inch (2.5 × 1.5cm) pieces
2 medium **carrots**, cut into 1 × ½-inch (2.5 × 1.5cm) pieces
1½ tablespoons **vegetable oil**, divided
1¾ teaspoons **salt**, divided
2 cloves **garlic**, minced
1 teaspoon **lemon zest**
6 **bone-in, skin-on chicken thighs,** about 5oz (140g) each
¼ teaspoon freshly ground **black pepper**
1 teaspoon **dried rosemary**
½ cup (120ml) **chicken broth**
⅓ cup (80ml) **dry white wine**
1 tablespoon freshly squeezed **lemon juice**
2–3 tablespoons cold **butter**

### Ingredient Swaps
- Replace the vegetables with 6 cups (900g) **baby potatoes, chopped red potatoes,** or **other root veggies.**
- **Split chicken breasts** with bone in and skin on can be used in place of chicken thighs. Cut the breasts in half, through the bone, before cooking.
- Replace the wine with **apple juice** or additional **chicken broth.**

# Crispy Rosemary Chicken Thighs with Root Veggies

You know those kinds of meals that look fancy, like they could be served in a 5-star restaurant, but they're actually easy to whip up? This is that kind of meal. Juicy rosemary chicken thighs with crispy, crunchy skin and a rustic blend of root vegetables are cooked in a simple white wine sauce. With cozy fall vibes, this recipe comes together quickly in just one pan, and cleanup is a snap.

1. Preheat the oven to 425°F (220°C).
2. Toss the butternut squash, parsnips, and carrots with 1 tablespoon oil, ½ teaspoon salt, garlic, and lemon zest. Set aside.
3. Season the chicken thighs with ¾ teaspoon salt and ¼ teaspoon pepper. Sprinkle the rosemary on the skin.
4. In a 12-inch (30cm) oven-safe skillet, heat the remaining ½ tablespoon oil over medium-high heat. Add the chicken, skin side down, and brown without moving the chicken for 3 to 4 minutes. Remove the chicken from the pan and set aside.
5. Remove the skillet from the heat and add the broth, white wine, and lemon juice all at once. Place it back on the heat, bring to a boil, and let simmer for 2 minutes.
6. Place the chicken, skin side up, in the skillet. Arrange the vegetables around the chicken, ensuring the chicken isn't covered.
7. Place the skillet in the preheated oven, and bake uncovered for 22 to 26 minutes or until the chicken is cooked through and reaches an internal temperature of 165°F (74°C).
8. Transfer the chicken and vegetables to a serving platter.
9. Place the skillet on the stovetop and bring the juices to a simmer over medium-high heat. *Keep in mind that the handle is hot from the oven!* Cook until the sauce has reduced to ½ cup (120ml), about 2 to 3 minutes.
10. Reduce the heat to medium and whisk in the cold butter a little bit at a time until the sauce is thickened and creamy. Taste and season with additional salt and pepper, if desired.

**SERVING SUGGESTIONS**
This dinner is a complete meal by itself. We love to serve it with a fresh garden salad and some crusty bread for sopping up any extra sauce.

**TIP**
The pan sauce in this recipe is ideal for serving on the side for dipping; drizzling it directly over the chicken will cause the skin to lose its crispiness.

**LOVE YOUR LEFTOVERS**
Leftovers from this dish make a great cold chicken salad. Remove the chicken from the bones and discard the skin. Chop the chicken and any leftover vegetables. For each cup of chopped chicken and vegetables, add ¼ cup (35g) finely chopped celery, 2 tablespoons mayonnaise, 2 tablespoons sour cream, and 2 teaspoons freshly squeezed lemon juice. Enjoy the salad on its own or over mixed greens.

## FOR THE FILLING

8oz (227g) **lean ground beef**

½ medium **yellow onion**, diced

2–2⅓ cups (480–560ml) **chicken broth**, as needed

1 (15.25oz / 432g) can **black beans**, drained and rinsed

1 **red bell pepper**, diced

⅔ cup (160ml) **salsa**, any flavor

½ cup (99g) uncooked **long-grain white rice**

2 tablespoons **taco seasoning** (for homemade, see page 18)

½ cup (57g) shredded **sharp cheddar cheese**

¼ cup (76g) **sour cream**

## FOR THE BURRITOS

6 (10in / 25cm) **flour tortillas**

1 large **tomato**, diced

½ cup (113g) **sour cream**

¾ cup (180g) **guacamole** (optional)

**Additional toppings** (optional)

# Cheesy Beef & Salsa
# **Burrito Supreme**

Easy and oh-so-cheesy, this one-pan wonder checks all the boxes: it's quick to prepare, perfect to make ahead, and cleanup is a breeze. Seasoned ground beef, rice, and beans come together to create a filling so good, it's hard to resist sneaking bites right from the pan. Wrap it in warm tortillas or spoon it into bowls and pile it high with toppings. These burritos can be wrapped ahead of time and reheated just before serving.

1. **To make the filling,** heat a large 12-inch (30cm) nonstick skillet over medium-high heat. Add the beef and onion and cook, breaking up the meat with a spoon, for 5 to 6 minutes or until no pink remains. Drain any fat.
2. Stir in 2 cups (480ml) broth along with the beans, bell pepper, salsa, rice, and taco seasoning.
3. Bring to a boil over medium-high heat, reduce the heat to a gentle simmer, and cover. Simmer for 22 to 25 minutes or until the rice is tender, stirring occasionally and adding more broth as needed to keep it slightly saucy.
4. Remove from the heat and stir in the cheddar cheese and sour cream. Cover and let rest for 5 minutes. Season with salt to taste.
5. **To make the burritos,** place the flour tortillas on a plate and top with a damp paper towel. Cover with plastic wrap and microwave for 20 to 30 seconds or until tortillas are warm.
6. Add ¾ cup (175g) burrito filling to each tortilla. Top with tomato, sour cream, guacamole (if using), and additional toppings as desired. Fold in the sides of the burrito and then roll top to bottom. Serve warm.

 **SERVING SUGGESTIONS**

Skip the rolling and enjoy the filling in a burrito bowl. Whether you're serving it burrito style or enjoying it as a bowl, this is a great recipe for customizing. Set out corn chips, extra diced tomatoes, chopped fresh cilantro, diced avocado, or sliced jalapeños, and let everyone create their own masterpiece!

 **FEELING FANCY?**

The burritos can be crisped on the outside. Once the burritos are filled, brush the outside with a little bit of vegetable oil and place them in a nonstick skillet, seam side down, over medium heat. Crisp the burritos for 2 to 3 minutes per side or until browned and crisp. Filled burritos can also be crisped in the air fryer at 370°F (190°C) for about 4 to 5 minutes.

 **MAKE AHEAD**

These burritos can be made ahead of time (omit the sour cream and guacamole, if using) and frozen. Wrap the burritos tightly in plastic wrap and freeze for up to 3 months. To heat, remove the plastic wrap and wrap the burrito in a damp paper towel. Heat in the microwave from frozen for about 1 minute 45 seconds per side or until heated through.

**Prep Time:** 10 minutes
**Total Time:** 20 minutes
**Serves** 4

---

2 tablespoons **vegetable oil**, divided

3 **eggs**, beaten

¼ teaspoon **salt**

2 cloves **garlic**, minced

2 teaspoons grated **fresh ginger**

4 **green onions**, thinly sliced, white and green parts separated

2 cups (288g) **frozen mixed vegetables**

4 cups (800g) cold **cooked white rice**

1 cup (125g) finely chopped **cooked chicken**, pork, or shrimp

3 to 4 tablespoons **soy sauce**

1 teaspoon **toasted sesame oil**

**Sesame seeds** (optional), to garnish

---

### Ingredient Swap

To use **fresh vegetables**, add 1½ cups (216g) finely chopped vegetables to the skillet before adding the garlic and ginger. Cook for 4 to 6 minutes or until tender.

# Easy **Fried Rice**

Fried rice is my daughter Kailey's favorite dish ever, and I love it because it's the perfect way to transform little bits of leftovers into a complete meal. In this recipe, rice is pan-fried with garlic, ginger, and egg. Add any variety of chopped vegetables, along with cooked chicken, pork, or shrimp. Not only is this dish versatile, it's on the table in about 20 minutes.

1. Heat a 12-inch (30cm) nonstick skillet over medium heat. Add 1 teaspoon vegetable oil, eggs, and salt and cook, breaking up the eggs into small pieces, about 3 minutes. Transfer the eggs to a bowl.
2. Add 2 teaspoons vegetable oil to the skillet and stir in the garlic, ginger, and the white part of the sliced green onion. Cook until fragrant, about 1 minute.
3. Stir in the mixed vegetables and cook for 2 to 3 minutes or until heated.
4. Increase the heat to medium-high and add the remaining 1 tablespoon vegetable oil and the cooked rice. Cook, stirring occasionally, until the rice is slightly crisped and starting to brown.
5. Add the cooked eggs, along with the chicken, soy sauce, sesame oil, and half of the green part of the sliced green onion. Stir well to coat.
6. Garnish with the remaining green onion and sesame seeds, if desired.

---

 **SERVING SUGGESTIONS**
This recipe makes four main-dish servings or eight side-dish servings. It's perfect reheated for lunches too!

 **TIP**
Day-old rice is best for fried rice as it's cooled and slightly dried. Using freshly cooked, warm rice can result in mushy, clumpy fried rice. If you don't have day-old rice, cooked and cooled rice can be used. Cook the rice as directed and spread it on a sheet pan. Let it cool slightly, then place it in the freezer for at least 25 minutes.

 **VARIATIONS**
Any leftover vegetables or meats can be added to this recipe. Leftover vegetables can be added in place of frozen mixed vegetables. If using a meat that contains a lot of salt (like bacon or ham), reduce the soy sauce slightly.

**Prep Time:** 10 minutes
**Total Time:** 1 hour
**Serves** 4

12oz (340g) **lean ground beef**

½ medium **yellow onion**, diced

4 cloves **garlic**, minced

6oz (170g) **cremini** or **white mushrooms**, sliced

3 cups (720ml) **beef broth**, plus more as needed

¾ cup (150g) uncooked **long-grain white rice**

2 **bay leaves**

1½ tablespoons **Worcestershire sauce**

¾ teaspoon **dried rosemary**

¾ teaspoon **dried thyme leaves**

½ cup (76g) **sour cream**

½ teaspoon **seasoned salt**

½ teaspoon freshly ground **black pepper**

2 tablespoons chopped **fresh parsley**, to garnish

2 tablespoons **crispy fried onions**, for garnish

# Herbed Ground Beef & Rice
# **Stroganoff Skillet**

This dish adds homey casserole vibes to a simple stovetop meal, and my family absolutely raves about it. Seasoned ground beef, onions, and garlicky mushrooms are cooked with herbs. It's all smothered in a creamy stroganoff sauce and topped off with crispy fried onions for serving. Best of all, you can skip the mountain of dishes because it all cooks in just one skillet.

1. Heat a 12-inch (30cm) skillet over medium-high heat. Add the beef and onion and cook, breaking up the meat with a spoon, for 5 to 6 minutes or until no pink remains. Drain any fat.
2. Stir in the garlic and mushrooms and cook for 2 to 3 minutes or until the mushrooms start to soften.
3. Add the broth, rice, bay leaves, Worcestershire sauce, rosemary, and thyme.
4. Bring to a boil over medium-high heat, reduce the heat to a gentle simmer, and cover. Simmer, stirring occasionally, for 22 to 25 minutes or until the rice is tender. Add more broth as needed to keep it slightly saucy.
5. Remove the skillet from the heat. Remove and discard the bay leaves. Stir in the sour cream, seasoned salt, and pepper. Cover and let rest for 5 minutes. Garnish with the parsley and crispy fried onions.

**SERVING SUGGESTIONS**

Serve this dish with something fresh and green, like a handful of green peas, some buttery sautéed broccolini, or spinach.

**Prep Time:** 20 minutes
**Total Time:** 45 minutes
**Serves** 4

---

### FOR THE PATTIES

3 cups (255g) **frozen shredded hash brown potatoes**, thawed

2 cups (300g) chopped **cooked chicken**

2 **eggs**

½ cup (57g) shredded **cheddar cheese**

¼ cup (25g) shredded **Parmesan cheese**

¼ cup (30g) **all-purpose flour**

1 **green onion**, finely chopped

1 teaspoon **garlic powder**

½ teaspoon **seasoned salt**

½ teaspoon freshly ground **black pepper**

1 tablespoon **butter**

### FOR THE CORN

3 cups (432g) **frozen corn kernels**, thawed and divided

1 cup (240ml) **whole milk**

2 teaspoons **cornstarch**

2 teaspoons **granulated sugar**

¾ teaspoon **salt**

½ teaspoon freshly ground **black pepper**

½ cup (120ml) **heavy whipping cream**

1 tablespoon **butter**

---

### Ingredient Swap

Replace the hash brown potatoes with 1 pound (454g) **russet potatoes.** Peel and quarter the potatoes. Boil for 9 to 10 minutes or until almost cooked but still slightly firm. Cool and shred the potatoes on the large side of a box grater. Add an additional ½ teaspoon seasoned salt to the mixture.

# Crispy Chicken & Potato Patties
## with Creamy Corn

Satisfying and incredibly comforting, these chicken potato patties are crispy on the outside and cheesy-delicious inside. Prep them quickly with frozen hash browns, or use baking potatoes to make them from scratch. They're versatile too—add chopped fresh herbs, leftover ham, or bacon. Paired with a side of quick and creamy corn, this is an easy meal you'll make time and again.

1. **To make the patties,** to a medium bowl, add the hash browns and use your hands to gently break them up a little bit. Add the chicken, eggs, cheddar cheese, Parmesan cheese, flour, green onion, garlic powder, seasoned salt, and pepper.

2. Mix well and form into eight 4-inch (10cm) patties, each ½ inch (1.5cm) thick.

3. Heat a 12-inch (30cm) skillet over medium-high heat. Melt 1 tablespoon butter and add the chicken patties. Cook for 3 to 4 minutes per side or until cooked through. Transfer to a plate, and cover lightly with foil to keep warm.

4. **To make the corn,** in a blender or with a hand blender, combine 1 cup (144g) corn, milk, cornstarch, sugar, salt, and pepper. Pulse until smooth.

5. Pour the blended mixture into the skillet used to cook the patties and add the remaining 2 cups (288g) corn and the cream.

6. Bring to a boil, while stirring, over medium-high heat; reduce to a simmer, and let cook, stirring occasionally, for 4 minutes or until thickened.

7. Whisk in 1 tablespoon butter and season with additional salt and pepper to taste.

### TO PREPARE IN AN AIR FRYER

The chicken patties can be cooked in an air fryer. Preheat the air fryer to 370°F (190°C) and cook the patties, 4 at a time, for 6 minutes. Turn the patties over and cook for an additional 4 to 6 minutes or until crisp and cooked through.

---

**SERVING SUGGESTIONS**

This recipe is a complete meal on its own. I love a dollop of herby sour cream with almost any potato dish. Mix ½ cup (120ml) sour cream with 1 to 2 tablespoons chopped fresh herbs, like chives, parsley, dill, or basil.

**TIP**

If using a smaller skillet, cook the patties in batches.

## FOR THE RICE

2 tablespoons **butter**
1 clove **garlic**, minced
1 cup (198g) uncooked **long-grain white rice**
2 cups (480ml) **chicken broth**
1 teaspoon **dried dill**
¼ teaspoon **salt**

## FOR THE SKILLET

½lb (227g) **lean ground beef**
½lb (227g) **lean ground pork**
1 small **yellow onion**, finely diced
1 clove **garlic**, minced
1 (28oz / 794g) can **whole tomatoes**, with juices
6 cups (546g) **green cabbage**, cut into 1½ × ½-inch (4 × 1.5cm) strips
1 cup (240ml) **tomato sauce**
½ cup (120ml) **chicken broth**
1 teaspoon **paprika**
½ teaspoon **dried thyme leaves**
¼ teaspoon **salt**, plus more to taste
⅛ teaspoon freshly ground **black pepper**, plus more to taste
3 tablespoons chopped **fresh parsley**

### Ingredient Swaps

- My grandma always used a combination of beef and pork in her cabbage rolls; if you have just one or the other, that's okay!
- I find whole tomatoes thicken slightly better than other varieties, but if you have **canned diced tomatoes,** they will work in this recipe too.

# Cabbage Roll Skillet
## with Garlic Butter Dill Rice

Cabbage rolls were a staple in my Grandma Mary's kitchen, lovingly rolled, smothered in tomato sauce, and slow baked in the oven. I've taken the flavors from Grandma's cabbage rolls and turned them into a delicious weeknight meal with tender cabbage and a blend of beef and pork simmered in a savory, seasoned tomato sauce. Serve this over garlicky, buttery dill rice for a modern spin on a beloved family tradition.

1. **To make the rice,** in a medium saucepan over medium heat, melt the butter. Add the garlic and cook just until fragrant, about 1 minute. Add the rice and stir to coat.
2. Stir in the broth, dill, and ¼ teaspoon salt. Cover and bring to a boil; reduce the heat to medium-low, and let the rice simmer for 13 to 15 minutes or until the liquid is absorbed. Remove from the heat and let rest, covered, for 5 to 10 minutes.
3. Meanwhile, to make the skillet, heat a large 12-inch (30cm) nonstick skillet over medium-high heat. Add the beef, pork, and onion, and cook, breaking up the meat with a spoon, for 5 to 6 minutes or until no pink remains. Drain any fat.
4. Stir in the garlic and cook for 1 minute. Add the whole tomatoes with juices to the skillet, breaking up the tomatoes with your hands as you add them.
5. Stir in the cabbage, tomato sauce, broth, paprika, thyme, ¼ teaspoon salt, and ⅛ teaspoon pepper.
6. Bring to a simmer, cover, and cook for 15 to 17 minutes or until the cabbage is tender. Stir in the parsley and season with additional salt and pepper to taste.
7. Fluff the rice with a fork. Serve the cabbage mixture over rice.

**SERVING SUGGESTIONS**
This dish makes four hearty portions; serve it with garlic bread or even a loaf of crusty bread topped with a pat of cold butter, just like Grandma Mary would have.

**HEY! IT'S OKAY TO . . .**
Skip the chopping and replace the cabbage with 6 cups (546g) coleslaw mix. Coleslaw is finely cut, so simmer the tomato mixture on its own for about 10 minutes before adding the coleslaw. Add the coleslaw mixture and cook covered for 3 to 5 minutes or just until tender.

**LOVE YOUR LEFTOVERS**
Stretch leftovers even further by turning them into Cabbage Roll Soup! Add 1 to 2 cups (240–480ml) chicken or beef broth to a medium saucepan, along with a handful of chopped vegetables, like diced carrots and celery. Simmer until the vegetables are tender and then add any leftover rice and cabbage mixture. Simmer until everything is heated through, about 4 to 6 minutes.

# Beef & Asparagus Roll-Ups
## with Tarragon Sauce

**Prep Time:** 40 minutes
**Total Time:** 1 hour
**Serves** 4

2 tablespoons **olive oil**, divided
1 tablespoon **soy sauce**
1 tablespoon **balsamic vinegar**
1 teaspoon **brown sugar**
1 teaspoon **garlic powder**
1½lb (680g) **thin-cut sirloin steak**
   or top round steak, ¼ inch
   (0.6cm) thick
1lb (454g) **asparagus spears**,
   trimmed
1 tablespoon **butter**
½ **red bell pepper**, thinly sliced
¾ teaspoon **salt**
½ teaspoon freshly ground
   **black pepper**

**FOR THE SAUCE**
½ cup (120ml) **chicken broth**
½ cup (120ml) **heavy whipping
   cream**
2 teaspoons **Dijon mustard**
¾ teaspoon **dried tarragon**
1 tablespoon cold **butter**

---

**Ingredient Swaps**
- Tarragon has a unique flavor with a delicate anise note. You can use **dried basil** instead, if needed.
- Asparagus can be replaced with other thinly sliced vegetables, like **green beans** or **broccolini**. Be sure to cook and slightly cool the vegetables before rolling, as the roll-ups cook very quickly.

Add a touch of easy elegance to your weeknight menu with this delicious spin on a steak dinner. Thinly cut steak is marinated and wrapped around bundles of asparagus and bell pepper. The rolls cook quickly on the stovetop and are served with an effortless, but luxurious, tarragon sauce.

1. To make the marinade, in a medium glass bowl or large zipper-lock freezer bag, combine 1 tablespoon olive oil, soy sauce, balsamic vinegar, brown sugar, and garlic powder.
2. Using the textured side of a meat mallet, pound the steak to tenderize. Use the flat side of the mallet to pound to a thickness of ⅛ inch (0.3cm). Add the steak to the marinade and refrigerate for at least 20 minutes or up to 8 hours.
3. To prepare the roll-ups, heat a 12-inch (30cm) skillet over medium-high heat. Add the asparagus and 3 tablespoons water, and cook, stirring occasionally, until the water has evaporated, about 4 minutes. Add the butter and bell pepper and cook, stirring frequently, for 2 to 5 minutes more or until the asparagus is tender-crisp. Set the asparagus and bell pepper aside to cool.
4. Remove the steak from the marinade. On a cutting board, lay out the steak slices. Divide the asparagus and bell pepper among the steak slices, placing a small bundle of veggies at the end of each piece. Sprinkle the salt and pepper over the steak and veggies. Roll up each piece, jelly-roll style, and secure with a toothpick. You should have about 8 roll-ups.
5. Heat the skillet over medium-high heat and add the remaining 1 tablespoon olive oil. Once hot, add the steak rolls in two batches and cook for 1 to 2 minutes per side or until browned. Transfer the rolls to a plate and cover with foil to keep warm.
6. Wipe the skillet with a paper towel. **To make the sauce,** whisk in the chicken broth, cream, mustard, and tarragon. Let simmer over medium-high heat, whisking occasionally, for 6 to 7 minutes or until thickened. Whisk in 1 tablespoon cold butter and season with salt and pepper to taste.
7. Serve the sauce over the roll-ups.

---

**SERVING SUGGESTIONS**
This dish pairs perfectly with Simply Seasoned Garlic Rice (page 259) or our favorite Creamy Cheesy Crowd-Pleasin' Rice (page 259).

**TIPS**
- Even if the beef is thin enough, it should still be pounded with a meat mallet or rolling pin to tenderize. Each piece of beef should be about 4 inches (10cm) wide and 4 to 6 inches (10–15cm) long. Check your grocery store for thinly sliced beef or ask the butcher to slice it.
- Ensure you use a large 12-inch (30cm) skillet or the sauce will not thicken enough.

**Prep Time:** 10 Minutes
**Total Time:** 30 Minutes
**Serves** 4

4 boneless, skinless **chicken breasts**, about 6oz (170g) each

½ teaspoon **salt**

¼ teaspoon freshly ground **black pepper**

1 tablespoon **olive oil**

2 tablespoons **butter**

3 cloves **garlic**, minced

⅓ cup (80ml) **dry white wine**

⅓ cup (80ml) **heavy whipping cream**

¼ cup (60ml) **chicken broth**

1 teaspoon **soy sauce**

2 tablespoons **Dijon mustard**

⅛ teaspoon **dried thyme leaves** or 1 sprig fresh thyme

---

**Ingredient Swap**

White wine adds great flavor to this recipe, but you can substitute either **chicken** or **vegetable broth** if needed.

# 30-Minute
# Creamy Dijon Chicken

Since the day this recipe was first shared on Spend with Pennies, rave reviews have continued to pour in—and once you try it, you'll know why. Tender chicken breasts are smothered in an easy, creamy Dijon sauce so good you'll want to lick your plate. (You can—I won't judge!) The flavor is incredibly elevated yet it's so easy to make in just one skillet.

1. Layer the chicken breasts between two sheets of plastic wrap and use the flat side of a meat mallet or a rolling pin to pound to an even thickness of 1 inch (2.5cm). Season with salt and pepper.

2. In a 12-inch (30cm) skillet or braiser, heat the oil over medium-high heat. Add the chicken and cook for 5 to 6 minutes per side or until it's browned and has reached an internal temperature of 165°F (74°C). Remove the chicken from the pan and set aside, lightly covered with foil.

3. Add the butter and garlic to the pan. Cook just until fragrant, about 30 seconds.

4. Stir in the wine, making sure to scrape up any browned bits from the bottom of the pan. Simmer until the wine is reduced by half, about 3 minutes.

5. Whisk in the heavy cream, chicken broth, soy sauce, mustard, and thyme. Simmer for 2 to 4 minutes or until slightly thickened. Season with additional salt to taste.

6. Add the chicken along with any juices back to the pan and cook just until heated through, about 2 minutes.

**SERVING SUGGESTIONS**

Parmesan and fresh parsley are great optional garnishes for this recipe. The sauce is deliciously rich, so I love to add a fresh, simple vegetable on the side, like stovetop broccoli or asparagus (page 264). The sauce is perfect drizzled over Soul-Soothing Buttered Noodles (page 260) or rice for a complete meal.

**TIPS**

- Pound the chicken breasts to ensure they cook evenly. Covering them with plastic wrap prevents splattering.

- Use a large skillet to ensure the chicken browns evenly and the sauce reduces well.

- The sauce in this recipe is delicious; if you'd like extra sauce for serving, it can be doubled. You will need to increase the simmering time to 4 to 6 minutes.

½ cup (60g) **sliced almonds** or slivered almonds

1lb (454g) boneless, skinless **chicken breasts**, cut into ½-inch (1.5cm) cubes

1 tablespoon **olive oil**

1¼ cups (300ml) **chicken broth**

1 **carrot**, grated

1 cup (180g) uncooked **plain instant couscous**

½ cup (80g) **golden raisins**

¼ teaspoon **ground cinnamon**

2 tablespoons **butter**

¼ cup (14g) chopped **fresh flat-leaf parsley**

1 **English cucumber**, diced

¼ cup (14g) chopped **fresh mint leaves**

**FOR THE SPICE MIX**

1½ teaspoons **ground cumin**

1½ teaspoons **ground coriander**

1 teaspoon **salt**

¾ teaspoon **smoked paprika**

½ teaspoon **ground ginger**

½ teaspoon **ground cinnamon**

¼ teaspoon **turmeric powder**

½ teaspoon freshly ground **black pepper**

# Moroccan-Spiced Chicken
## Couscous Bowls

I can't tell you how much we love this beautifully fragrant dish; my daughter Ayla makes it for her family on repeat. Chicken is generously seasoned with a homemade Moroccan-inspired spice mix and cooked until deeply golden brown. It's served over a simple, nutty, herbed couscous and topped with fresh mint. Fresh herbs are imperative to the flavor of this dish, so be sure not to skip them!

1. Heat a 10-inch (25cm) nonstick skillet over medium heat. Add the almonds and cook, stirring frequently, until lightly toasted, about 4 to 5 minutes. Set aside.
2. **To make the spice mix,** in a medium bowl, combine the cumin, coriander, salt, smoked paprika, ginger, ½ teaspoon cinnamon, turmeric, and pepper. Add the chicken to the spice mix and toss to coat.
3. Heat the oil in the skillet and add the seasoned chicken. Cook, stirring occasionally, until no pink remains and the chicken is cooked through to 165°F (74°C). Transfer the chicken to a bowl and lightly cover with foil to keep warm.
4. Add the chicken broth and grated carrot to the skillet, scraping up any browned bits. Stir in the couscous, raisins, and ¼ teaspoon cinnamon, and bring to a boil. Cover, remove from the heat, and let rest for 5 minutes. Fluff the couscous with a fork and stir in the butter. Stir in the toasted almonds and parsley.
5. Divide the couscous among 4 bowls and top with the chicken. Top with diced cucumber and fresh mint.

**SERVING SUGGESTIONS**
This dish pairs well with roasted cauliflower or zucchini (page 262) and grilled flatbread. For a pop of freshness, add extra toppings like rolled carrot and cucumber ribbons and chopped olives.

**HEY! IT'S OKAY TO . . .**
Replace the spice mix with 2 tablespoons of your favorite Moroccan-inspired spice blend or 2 tablespoons *ras el hanout*, a beautiful Moroccan spice blend.

# Comforting Classics
## *with a Twist*

**72**     Chicken Pot Pie–Stuffed Shells with Herb Butter Crumbs

**75**     Hearty Ground Beef Stew with Rosemary Dumplings

**76**     My Mom's Hoisin Pork Tenderloin Sammies

**79**     Spicy Sausage Pimento Mac & Cheese

**80**     Lentil Shepherd's Pie

**83**     Flaky Broccoli Cheddar Chicken Pockets

**84**     Zesty Unstuffed-Shells Soup with Basil Ricotta

**87**     BLT Baked Chicken Burgers with Chipotle Mayo

**88**     Crispy Oven Chicken with Savory Cheddar Waffles

**91**     Must-Make Pizza Meatballs & Spaghetti

**Prep Time:** 1 hour
**Total Time:** 1 hour 30 minutes
**Serves** 4

1lb (454g) boneless, skinless
　**chicken breasts**
2½ cups (600ml) **chicken broth**
20 **jumbo pasta shells**
2½ cups (212g) **frozen mixed
　vegetables**, thawed

**FOR THE SAUCE**
½ cup (113g) **butter**
1 medium **yellow onion**,
　finely diced
3 cloves **garlic**, minced
½ cup (60g) **all-purpose flour**
2 teaspoons **poultry seasoning**
　(for homemade, see page 18)
½ teaspoon **dried thyme leaves**
1 cup (240ml) **half-and-half** or
　light cream
2 teaspoons **dried parsley**
¾ teaspoon **salt**
1 teaspoon freshly ground
　**black pepper**

**FOR THE TOPPING**
¼ cup (13g) **panko bread crumbs**
1 tablespoon **butter**, melted
1 teaspoon **dried parsley**
½ teaspoon **dried basil**

**Ingredient Swaps**
- Replace the chicken breasts and
  broth with 3 cups (300g) **cooked
  shredded chicken.**
- Skip the frozen vegetables and
  clean out your fridge! Chop 2 cups
  (200g) **fresh vegetables,** like
  carrots, celery, mushrooms, peas,
  green beans, or fresh corn. Cook
  just until tender and use in place
  of frozen veggies.

# Chicken Pot Pie Stuffed Shells
# with Herb Butter Crumbs

This comforting recipe has been a warm hug on some of our toughest days. Not only is it a favorite of my niece London and my nephew Bailey, it's loved by everyone I know. The homey goodness of my favorite five-star filling is tucked into pasta shells, smothered in a seasoned creamy pot pie sauce, and topped with herby bread crumbs. Pretty much perfection on a plate.

1. Preheat the oven to 375°F (190°C). Grease a 3-quart (2.8L) baking dish and set aside.
2. To a medium saucepan, add the chicken breasts and broth and bring to a simmer over medium heat. Reduce to medium-low, cover, and let the chicken breasts gently simmer for 15 to 20 minutes or until the chicken reaches an internal temperature of 165°F (74°C).
3. Once the chicken is cooked, remove it from the broth (reserve the broth for the sauce) and let cool for 5 minutes. Shred the chicken with two forks and set aside.
4. Meanwhile, bring a large pot of salted water to a boil, cook the shells al dente according to the package directions. Drain well and rinse under cold water to stop the pasta from cooking further.
5. **To make the sauce,** in a medium saucepan, add the butter, onion, and garlic. Cook over medium heat until the onion begins to soften, about 3 to 4 minutes. Sprinkle the flour, poultry seasoning, and thyme over the onions. Stir and cook for 1 minute more.
6. Gradually whisk in 2¼ cups (540ml) reserved chicken broth and add the half-and-half a little at a time, stirring until smooth after each addition. The mixture will seem very thick at first. Once smooth, bring it to a boil, and boil for 1 minute.
7. Turn off the heat and stir in the parsley, salt, and pepper. Set aside.
8. In a medium bowl, combine the shredded chicken, thawed vegetables and 1 cup (240ml) sauce.
9. Spread 2 cups (480ml) sauce on the bottom of the baking dish. Using a small spoon, fill each shell with 3 tablespoons chicken mixture, and place it in the prepared baking dish. Spoon the remaining sauce over the shells.
10. **To make the topping,** combine the panko, butter, parsley, and basil. Sprinkle the topping over the shells.
11. Bake uncovered for 20 to 25 minutes or until hot and the sauce is bubbling around the edges. Rest for 5 minutes before serving.

 **TIP**
I usually cook a few extra shells in case any break when cooking or filling them.

### HEY! IT'S OKAY TO . . .

Save some time and make a shortcut sauce!
Instead of making the sauce as directed, stir together
2 (10.5oz / 298g) cans cream of chicken soup, 1⅓ cups
(320ml) milk, ½ cup (113g) sour cream, and 1 teaspoon
poultry seasoning. Continue from step 8 as directed.

**Prep Time:** 15 minutes
**Total Time:** 1 hour
**Serves** 4

---

1lb (454g) **lean ground beef**

1 medium **yellow onion**, cut into
1-inch (2.5cm) pieces

3 tablespoons **all-purpose flour**

4 cups (960ml) **beef stock**

1lb (454g) **baby potatoes**, halved

1 large **carrot**, thickly sliced

2 ribs **celery**, thickly sliced

4oz (113g) **mushrooms**, sliced

2 tablespoons **tomato paste**

1 tablespoon **Worcestershire
sauce**

2 cloves **garlic**, minced

½ teaspoon **dried thyme leaves**

½ teaspoon freshly ground
**black pepper**

2 tablespoons **cornstarch**

2 tablespoons cold **water**

¾ cup (128g) **frozen peas**, thawed

**FOR THE DUMPLINGS**

⅔ cup (80g) **all-purpose flour**

1 ½ teaspoons **baking powder**

1 teaspoon **dried rosemary**,
crushed

½ teaspoon **salt**

2 tablespoons cold **butter**

⅓ cup (80ml) **milk**

---

### Ingredient Swaps

- Skip the chopping and use
2 cups (170g) **frozen vegetables**
in place of the carrot, celery, and
mushrooms. Frozen vegetables
don't need much time to cook, so
they should be stirred in just before
adding the dumplings to the pot in
step 5.
- **Beef broth** can be used in place of
beef stock, but the flavor isn't as
rich. If using beef broth, stir in half
a bouillon cube.

# Hearty Ground Beef Stew
## with Rosemary Dumplings

There's something about a warm, hearty beef stew that's both rustic and soul soothing; it's perfect in every way. This easy-to-make version has all the flavor of a classic beef stew but with a twist—no hours of simmering required. The rich, brothy gravy is loaded with ground beef and veggies and topped off with pillowy herbed dumplings, just like my mom used to make. So much goodness.

1. In a 4-quart (3.8L) Dutch oven or stockpot, cook the ground beef and onion over medium heat, breaking up the meat with a spoon, for 5 to 6 minutes until no pink remains. Do not drain the fat.
2. Stir in the flour and cook for 2 minutes. Add the stock, making sure to scrape up any brown bits at the bottom of the pot. Stir in the potatoes, carrot, celery, mushrooms, tomato paste, Worcestershire sauce, garlic, thyme, and pepper.
3. Bring to a boil over medium-high heat. Once boiling, reduce the heat to medium-low, cover, and simmer for 12 minutes or until the vegetables are almost cooked through.
4. While the vegetables simmer, **make the dumplings.** In a medium bowl, combine the flour, baking powder, rosemary, and salt. With a fork, mix in the cold butter until crumbly. Stir in the milk to form a dough.
5. Dip a tablespoon into the boiling stew and use the hot spoon to scoop spoonfuls of dough, enough to make 8 dumplings.
6. Drop the dough on top of the simmering stew and cover. Simmer for 7 to 9 minutes or until the dumplings are cooked through.
7. Remove the dumplings with a slotted spoon and place them in a bowl. Set aside.
8. In a small bowl, stir together the cornstarch and water to make a slurry. Gradually drizzle the slurry into the stew while whisking to thicken the mixture. You may not need all of the slurry to achieve your desired consistency. Stir in the peas. Season with additional salt and pepper to taste. Serve with the dumplings.

---

 **TIPS**

- Dumpling dough can be doubled and simmered in two batches. If doubling dumplings, increase the beef stock to 4⅔ cups (1.1L).
- Dumplings are done when a toothpick inserted into the center comes out clean.
- For a darker gravy, add about 1 tablespoon browning sauce, such as Kitchen Bouquet, along with the cornstarch.

 **MAKE AHEAD**

This stew can be made up to 4 days ahead of time and reheated. To freeze, cool the stew completely and store in a zipper-lock freezer bag or an airtight freezerproof container for up to 4 months. Dumplings should be frozen separately. Thaw in the refrigerator overnight and heat on the stove or in the microwave until heated through.

**Prep Time:** 20 minutes
**Total Time:** 4 hours 40 minutes
**Serves** 6

---

½ cup (120ml) **hoisin sauce**
2 tablespoons **rice vinegar**
2 tablespoons **soy sauce**
1 teaspoon **toasted sesame oil**
1 teaspoon **garlic powder**
1½ teaspoons **ground ginger**
½ teaspoon **red pepper flakes**
2 **pork tenderloins**, about
 1lb (454g) each

**FOR SERVING**

6 fresh, **crusty rolls**, 6–7 inches
 (15–18cm) long
¼ cup (60ml) spicy **mayonnaise**
 (optional)
1 **English cucumber**, cut into
 4-inch (10cm) matchsticks
¼ cup (14g) **fresh cilantro** leaves
3 **green onions**, julienned
½ cup (120ml) **hoisin sauce**

---

### Ingredient Swap

Replace the pork tenderloin with
1½ pounds (680g) **boneless, skinless
chicken thighs.** Marinate the thighs
as directed. Grill over medium-high
heat, 400°F (200°C), for 4 minutes
per side. Chicken thighs can also be
baked at 425°F (220°C) for 15 minutes.
Rest for 5 minutes and thinly slice.

# My Mom's Hoisin
# **Pork Tenderloin Sammies**

My entire family is obsessed with these sandwiches, they're one of my mom
and dad's specialties. Hoisin-marinated pork tenderloin is grilled to juicy
perfection and then very thinly sliced. It's piled high on fresh crusty rolls with
an extra drizzle of hoisin sauce, cucumbers, cilantro, and thinly sliced green
onions. This recipe is great with chicken thighs too!

1. In a medium bowl or zipper-lock freezer bag, combine the hoisin sauce, rice
 vinegar, soy sauce, sesame oil, garlic powder, ginger, and red pepper flakes.
2. Trim the silverskin and fat off the pork tenderloins. (See page 145, Bacon-
 Wrapped Pork Tenderloin, for instructions.) Add the trimmed tenderloins to
 the marinade. Turn to coat them, and place in the fridge to marinate for at
 least 4 hours or overnight.
3. Remove the pork from the fridge 20 minutes before grilling. Remove the
 pork from the marinade and let the excess drip off. Discard the marinade.
4. Preheat a gas grill to medium-high heat, 400°F (200°C). Place the pork on
 the grill and sear each side for 2 to 3 minutes. Turn one burner to low heat,
 leaving the other burners on medium-high, and cook the pork over the
 burner on low heat, frequently turning, for 18 to 20 minutes or until the
 pork reaches 140°F (60°C). (Pork will continue to cook as it rests.)
5. Transfer the pork to a serving plate, lightly cover with foil, and let rest for
 5 minutes or until the internal temperature reaches 145°F (63°C).
6. Slice the pork as thinly as possible and drizzle the sliced pork with any juices
 from the plate.
7. **To serve,** spread each crusty roll with the mayonnaise, if using, and fill the
 rolls with sliced pork, cucumber, cilantro, green onions, and a drizzle of
 hoisin sauce.

**TO PREPARE IN THE OVEN**

1. Preheat the oven to 450°F (230°C). Line a rimmed baking sheet with
 nonstick foil or foil sprayed with cooking spray.
2. Place the pork on the prepared baking sheet and roast for 16 to 18 minutes
 or until the pork reaches 140°F (60°C). Rest as directed.

**TO PREPARE IN AN AIR FRYER**

1. Preheat the air fryer to 400°F (200°C).
2. Place the pork in the air-fryer basket and roast for 10 minutes. Turn the pork
 over and roast for an additional 6 to 8 minutes or until the pork reaches
 140°F (60°C). Rest as directed.

---

**TIP**
If you have an electric carving
knife, it's perfect to make thin
slices of pork for these sandwiches.

**SERVING SUGGESTIONS**
We serve these sandwiches with
a fresh side salad and some
sweet potato fries or oven fries.

## Prep Time: 35 minutes
**Total Time:** 1 hour 5 minutes
**Serves** 6

---

12oz (340g) **cavatappi**

5 tablespoons **butter**, divided

14oz (397g) **smoked sausage**,
  sliced into ½-inch (1.5cm) half
  moons

1 small **yellow onion**, finely diced

1½ teaspoons **red pepper flakes**

⅓ cup (40g) **all-purpose flour**

1 (12oz / 354ml) can **evaporated
  milk**

1¾ cups (420ml) **chicken broth**

1 tablespoon **Cajun seasoning**
  (for homemade, see page 18)

¼ teaspoon **salt**

¼ teaspoon freshly ground
  **black pepper**

3 cups (339g) freshly grated **sharp
  cheddar cheese**, divided

½ cup (50g) freshly grated
  **Parmesan cheese**

1 (4oz / 113g) jar **pimentos**, lightly
  drained

# Spicy Sausage Pimento
## Mac & Cheese

Ever since I was little, mac and cheese has been one of my favorite meals. There's something incredibly nostalgic and comforting about a bowl of mac and cheese. This version kicks it up a notch with smoked sausage and curly cavatappi smothered in a rich cheese sauce. The edges are crispy and crunchy, while the pasta itself is decadent and creamy goodness. This one is hard to resist.

1. Preheat the oven to 425°F (220°C) and grease a 9 × 13-inch (23 × 33cm) baking dish.

2. Bring a medium saucepan of salted water to a boil. Cook the cavatappi al dente according to the package directions. Drain, rinse under cold water, and set aside.

3. In a medium saucepan, melt 1 tablespoon butter over medium-high heat. Add the sausage and cook until browned, stirring occasionally. Remove the sausage with a slotted spoon and drain on a plate lined with paper towel.

4. Reduce the heat to medium-low and add the remaining 4 tablespoons butter, onion, and red pepper flakes. Cook until tender, about 4 to 5 minutes.

5. Increase the heat to medium. Stir in the flour and cook for 1 minute.

6. Gradually add the milk and broth, whisking until smooth after each addition. Stir in the Cajun seasoning, salt, and pepper. Bring the mixture to a boil, whisking continuously, and boil for 1 minute.

7. Remove the saucepan from the heat and whisk in 2½ cups (283g) cheddar cheese and the Parmesan cheese. Gently fold in the drained pimentos. Taste and add additional salt if needed.

8. Combine the cavatappi, sausage, and sauce and transfer to the prepared baking dish. Sprinkle the remaining ½ cup (57g) cheddar cheese over the top.

9. Bake for 18 to 20 minutes or until bubbly. Rest 10 minutes before serving.

---

 **TIPS**
- Any variety of smoked sausage will work well in this recipe, including kielbasa or smoked turkey sausage.
- Cajun seasoning can vary by brand in both the level of heat and salt. This recipe is lightly salted, so adjust the salt based on your Cajun seasoning. Once the cheese sauce is prepared, taste it, and stir in additional salt if needed.

 **MAKE AHEAD**
Prepare the pasta as directed and transfer to a 9 × 13-inch (23 × 33cm) baking dish, cover with foil, and refrigerate for up to 3 days. Remove the casserole from the fridge 30 minutes before baking. Bake, covered, at 400°F (200°C) for 20 minutes. Remove the foil and bake for an additional 5 to 10 minutes or until heated through. Broil for 1 minute to brown the top, if desired.

# Lentil Shepherd's Pie

**Prep Time:** 60 minutes
**Total Time:** 1 hour 20 minutes
**Serves** 6

1 cup (200g) **brown or green dried lentils**

3¾ cups (900ml) **beef broth**

2lb (907g) **russet potatoes** or Yukon Gold potatoes, peeled and cut into 2-inch (5cm) chunks

5 tablespoons **butter**, divided

4oz (113g) **cremini mushrooms**, finely diced

½ medium **yellow onion**, chopped

1½ teaspoons **all-purpose flour**

¼ teaspoon **dried thyme leaves**

3 tablespoons **red wine**

3 tablespoons **tomato paste**

2 teaspoons **Worcestershire sauce**

1 teaspoon **salt**, divided

½ teaspoon freshly ground **black pepper**, divided

2 cups (385g) **frozen mixed vegetables**, thawed

1 tablespoon **dried parsley**

¾ cup (180ml) **half-and-half** or light cream, warmed

---

### Ingredient Swaps

- Wine can be replaced with additional **broth,** if desired.
- **To make this meal vegetarian,** replace the beef broth with mushroom broth and ensure you use vegetarian Worcestershire sauce.

This is the recipe that made me love lentils! While a traditional shepherd's pie is made with lamb, I created this version from pantry ingredients during the pandemic when groceries were scarce, and now it's a family favorite. With a rich and hearty sauce, this homey twist is just as cozy as the original—even the meat-eaters in your family will ask for seconds.

1. Preheat the oven to 400°F (200°C).
2. In a medium saucepan over medium-high heat, combine the lentils and broth and bring to a boil. Reduce the heat to a simmer, cover, and cook for 20 to 25 minutes or until the lentils are tender.
3. Meanwhile, add the potatoes to a large pot of cold salted water. Place over high heat and bring to a boil. Once boiling, reduce the temperature to medium-high and boil the potatoes uncovered for 15 to 20 minutes or until they are fork-tender. Drain well and let the potatoes rest in the strainer for 5 minutes.
4. In a 10-inch (25cm) ovenproof skillet, melt 1 tablespoon butter over medium heat. (If you don't have an overproof skillet, use a 2½-quart [2.4L] Dutch oven.) Add the mushrooms and onion and cook for 3 to 4 minutes or until tender. Stir in the flour and thyme and cook for 1 minute more.
5. Add the cooked lentils with any liquid, along with the red wine, tomato paste, Worcestershire sauce, and ¼ teaspoon each salt and pepper. Simmer uncovered over medium-high heat for 7 to 10 minutes or until slightly thickened but still saucy. Stir in the thawed vegetables and parsley and cook for 1 minute more. Taste and season with additional salt and pepper, if desired.
6. Transfer the potatoes to a large bowl and mash with a potato masher. Add the remaining 4 tablespoons butter while mashing, and gradually add the warmed half-and-half as needed to reach a smooth and creamy consistency. Season with the remaining ¾ teaspoon salt and remaining ¼ teaspoon pepper or to taste.
7. Spoon the mashed potatoes over the lentil filling and bake in the preheated oven for 20 to 25 minutes or until the sauce is bubbling and the potatoes are browned.

---

**SERVING SUGGESTIONS**
Shepherd's pie is a full meal deal, but if you want to add some sides, it pairs well with steamed vegetables like peas or carrots or a fresh side salad.

**HEY! IT'S OKAY TO . . .**
- Replace the dried lentils with canned lentils. Drain and rinse 1 (15oz / 425g) can lentils. Add the lentils with 1⅓ cups (320ml) beef broth in place of the cooked lentils in step 5.
- Replace the homemade mashed potato topping with 4 cups (992g) of prepared mashed potatoes from the refrigerated section of your grocery store.

## VARIATION

For a meaty shepherd's pie, replace the lentils with 1 pound (454g) lean ground beef or lamb, increase the flour to 2 tablespoons, reduce the broth to 1⅓ cups (320ml) beef broth, and increase the salt and pepper to a ½ teaspoon each.

Brown the beef and onions in a 10-inch (25cm) ovenproof skillet, breaking up the meat with a spoon, and cooking for 5 to 6 minutes or until no pink remains. Drain any fat. Add the butter and mushrooms and cook for 3 to 4 minutes. Then continue from step 5 of the main recipe.

**Prep Time:** 30 minutes
**Total Time:** 1 hour 5 minutes
**Serves** 4

---

3 cups (175g) **fresh broccoli florets**, cut into ½-inch (1.5cm) pieces
⅔ cup (160ml**) whole milk**
⅓ cup (80ml) **chicken broth**
1 tablespoon **cornstarch**
1 teaspoon **dried parsley**
¼ teaspoon **onion powder**
¼ teaspoon **poultry seasoning** (for homemade, see page 18)
1½ cups (170g) shredded **sharp cheddar cheese**, divided
1 tablespoon grated **Parmesan cheese**
1½ cups (150g) shredded **cooked chicken**
¼ teaspoon **salt**
⅛ teaspoon freshly ground **black pepper**
1 (17.3oz / 490g) package frozen **puff pastry**, thawed in the refrigerator overnight
1 **egg**

> **Ingredient Swap**
> Replace the puff pastry with 2 (8oz / 226g) cans **refrigerated crescent rolls**. (This will make 16 crescent rolls.) Add 2 tablespoons of the prepared chicken mixture to the large end of each triangle and top with the remaining cheddar cheese. Roll the crescent roll, pinching the edges to seal. Bake at 375°F (190°C) for 10 to 12 minutes.

# Flaky Broccoli Cheddar
# **Chicken Pockets**

These puff pastry pockets have the same delicious flavors found in my favorite cheesy broccoli casserole. Tender broccoli florets and chicken smothered in a rich cheesy sauce make a filling so good I want to eat it by the spoonful. It's all tucked into a golden, flaky puff pastry pocket. Don't be intimidated by puff pastry; it's easy to work with, and best of all, it comes out looking super fancy with very little effort.

1. Preheat the oven to 400°F (200°C) and line a rimmed baking sheet with parchment paper.
2. Place the broccoli in a 10-inch (25cm) nonstick skillet and add 1 cup (240ml) water. Bring to a simmer over medium-high heat and cook uncovered for 2 to 3 minutes or just until the broccoli is tender-crisp. Drain well and set aside.
3. In a small bowl, whisk together the milk, chicken broth, cornstarch, parsley, onion powder, and poultry seasoning.
4. Pour the mixture into the skillet and bring to a boil over medium heat, whisking continuously until the mixture thickens. Boil for 1 minute more.
5. Reduce the heat to low and add 1 cup (113g) cheddar cheese and the Parmesan cheese, stirring until melted. Add the drained broccoli, shredded chicken, salt, and pepper, and stir to combine. Cool slightly before assembling.
6. On a lightly floured surface, roll each sheet of puff pastry into a 10 × 12-inch (25 × 30cm) rectangle. (There are 2 sheets.) Cut each sheet into 4 pieces of equal size. (You will have 8 pieces in total.)
7. Place 4 of the pieces onto the prepared baking sheet, leaving at least 1 inch (2.5cm) between each piece. To the center of each piece, add ¾ cup (180g) of the chicken mixture. Divide the remaining ½ cup (57g) cheddar cheese over the chicken mixture.
8. Beat the egg with 1 tablespoon water to make an egg wash. Brush the egg wash in a ½-inch (1.5cm) border around the outer edges of each piece of pastry, surrounding the filling.
9. Place a second piece of pastry on top of the filling and gently press the edges with a fork all the way around to seal the pocket. Lightly brush the top of each pocket with the egg wash. Use a small knife to cut two ½-inch (1.5cm) slits on the top of each pocket to allow steam to escape.
10. Bake for 21 to 23 minutes or until puffed and golden brown. Remove the pockets from the baking sheet and place on a cooling rack. Allow the pockets to cool for 10 minutes before serving.

---

 **TIPS**
- Frozen puff pastry can be found in almost any grocery store. It is very easy to work with and bakes golden brown with light, flaky layers.
- Store thawed puff pastry in the fridge; it's easiest to handle when it's cold.
- Seal any cracks in the puff pastry with a dab of water and gently press.

**Prep Time:** 10 minutes
**Total Time:** 55 minutes
**Serves** 6

## FOR THE HERBED RICOTTA
8oz (227g) **ricotta cheese**
1 teaspoon **dried parsley**
1 teaspoon **dried basil**
1 teaspoon **lemon zest**

## FOR THE SOUP
12oz (340g) **bulk Italian sausage**
1 large **yellow onion**, diced
1 **red bell pepper**, diced
2 cloves **garlic**, minced
1 (14.5oz / 411g) can **whole tomatoes**, with juices
3 cups (720ml) **reduced-sodium chicken broth**
1 cup (240ml) canned **crushed tomatoes**
1 teaspoon **Italian seasoning** (for homemade, see page 18)
½ teaspoon **salt**
½ teaspoon freshly ground **black pepper**
4oz (113g) **medium shell pasta**
1½ cups (60g) **fresh spinach**, chopped.

# Zesty Unstuffed-Shells Soup
## with Basil Ricotta

My husband and I used to visit a local Italian restaurant that had a pasta dish topped with fresh ricotta cheese. That's where I learned how incredible a scoop of fresh ricotta is when spooned over a bowl of hot pasta or soup. This soup has a zesty tomato broth filled with ground sausage and tender pasta shells. It's all topped off with—you guessed it—a big scoop of creamy basil ricotta. Absolute perfection in every way.

1. **To make the herbed ricotta,** in a small bowl, combine the ricotta cheese, parsley, basil, and lemon zest. Refrigerate until ready to serve.
2. **To make the soup,** heat a 4-quart (3.8L) Dutch oven over medium-high heat. Add the sausage and onion and cook, breaking up the meat with a spoon, for 5 to 6 minutes or until no pink remains. Drain any fat.
3. Stir in the bell pepper and garlic and cook until slightly softened, about 3 minutes.
4. Add the whole tomatoes with the juice, breaking up the tomatoes with your hands as you add them. Stir in the broth, crushed tomatoes, Italian seasoning, salt, and pepper. Bring to a boil, reduce the heat to a gentle simmer, cover, and cook for 10 minutes.
5. Meanwhile, bring a medium saucepan of salted water to a boil and cook the shells al dente according to the package directions, about 7 minutes.
6. Remove the soup from the heat and stir in the spinach. Allow the soup to rest for 3 minutes.
7. Divide the shells among 6 bowls. Ladle the soup on top of the shells and top each portion with about 2 tablespoons herbed ricotta cheese.

### SERVING SUGGESTIONS
Parmesan cheese and a sprinkle of fresh herbs like basil and parsley are the perfect finishing touch for this soup.

### TIP
To keep the pasta from getting mushy when storing leftovers, cook the pasta separately and add it to each bowl when serving. If you'd prefer to cook the pasta in the soup itself, add an additional 1 cup (240ml) water along with the broth. Stir in the pasta during the last 6 minutes of cooking time.

### FEELING FANCY?
- Dried herbs are delicious in the ricotta cheese mixture, but fresh basil and parsley take it to the next level. Replace the dried herbs with 1 tablespoon each of fresh chopped basil and parsley. Grab a basil plant at the grocery store next time you're there; it'll last longer, and basil is great on everything from pasta to sandwiches.
- You can make fresh ricotta cheese with just four ingredients. Easy peasy. You need just milk, cream, salt, and vinegar.

*Scan for my Homemade Ricotta Cheese recipe.*

### SERVING SUGGESTIONS

These burgers pair well with corn on the cob and a side of crispy french fries. Level up a batch of your favorite frozen fries by tossing them with a touch of olive oil, rosemary, and garlic powder before adding them to the oven.

**Prep Time:** 15 minutes
**Total Time:** 1 hour 5 minutes
**Serves** 4

---

12 slices **uncooked bacon**, divided
1lb (454g) **ground chicken**
3 tablespoons **seasoned bread crumbs**
2 teaspoons **Worcestershire sauce**
1 teaspoon **onion powder**
¾ teaspoon **smoked paprika**
½ teaspoon **salt**
½ teaspoon freshly ground **black pepper**

**FOR THE CHIPOTLE MAYO**
½ cup (112g) **mayonnaise**
¾ teaspoon **chipotle powder**

**FOR SERVING**
4 **brioche hamburger buns**
8 large pieces **leaf lettuce**
3 **Roma tomatoes**, thickly sliced

# BLT Baked Chicken Burgers
# with Chipotle Mayo

Say goodbye to boring chicken burgers; these are flavorful and juicy, and a double dose of bacon adds lots of smoky goodness. Tucked into buttery brioche buns, they're topped with thick tomato slices, fresh lettuce, crispy bacon, and a zippy chipotle mayo. Whether oven-baked, grilled, or air-fried, they deliver year-round deliciousness.

1. Finely chop 4 slices of bacon and place it in a medium bowl. Add the ground chicken, bread crumbs, Worcestershire sauce, onion powder, smoked paprika, salt, and pepper. Gently combine all ingredients.
2. Form the mixture into 4 patties, each 4 inches (10cm) in diameter and ½ inch (1.5cm) thick. Using your thumb, create a small indent in the middle of each patty. Transfer to a plate and refrigerate for 30 minutes.
3. Adjust one rack to the bottom of the oven and one rack to the center of the oven. Preheat the oven to 400°F (200°C) and line 2 large rimmed baking sheets with parchment paper.
4. **To make the chipotle mayo,** in a small bowl, whisk the mayonnaise and chipotle powder. Refrigerate until ready to serve.
5. Place the remaining 8 slices of bacon on one of the prepared baking sheets.
6. Place the chicken patties on the second baking sheet and place it on the middle rack in the oven. Place the baking sheet with the bacon on the bottom rack of the oven.
7. Bake the patties for 12 to 14 minutes or until they reach an internal temperature of 165°F (74°C).
8. Check the bacon for crispness after 10 minutes. Depending on the brand, bacon can take anywhere from 10 to 17 minutes to cook. Check it early and let it continue baking until crisp.
9. **To serve,** top each hamburger bun with 2 tablespoons chipotle mayonnaise, 3 slices tomato, 2 slices bacon, lettuce, and a chicken patty.

**TO PREPARE ON THE GRILL**
Preheat the grill to medium-high heat. Grill the chicken patties for 4 to 5 minutes per side or until cooked to an internal temperature of 165°F (74°C).

**TO PREPARE IN AN AIR FRYER**
Preheat an air fryer to 350°F (175°C). Place the chicken patties in a single layer in the air-fryer basket and cook for 5 to 6 minutes per side.

---

**HEY! IT'S OKAY TO . . .**
Replace the raw bacon with precooked bacon. Chop 4 slices of precooked bacon and add it to the chicken mixture as directed. Heat the remaining 8 slices of bacon as directed on the package for topping the sandwich.

**MAKE AHEAD**
These chicken patties can be prepared up to 48 hours in advance or prepared and frozen before cooking. If frozen, thaw in the fridge overnight before cooking.

**Prep Time:** 15 minutes
**Total Time:** 40 minutes
**Serves** 4

½ cup (120ml) **maple syrup**
1 tablespoon **sriracha**

**FOR THE CHICKEN**
2 **eggs**
⅔ cup (33g) **panko bread crumbs**
⅓ cup (37g) **seasoned bread
  crumbs**
1½ tablespoons **Cajun seasoning**
  (for homemade, see page 18)
½ cup (60g) **all-purpose flour**
1 teaspoon **salt**, divided
1lb (454g) boneless, skinless
  **chicken thighs**
½ teaspoon freshly ground
  **black pepper**
**Cooking spray**

**FOR THE WAFFLES**
2 cups (240g) **all-purpose flour**
1 tablespoon **baking powder**
¾ teaspoon **salt**
2 **large eggs**, yolks and whites
  separated
1⅔ cups (400ml) **milk**
5 tablespoons **butter**, melted
1 cup (113g) shredded **sharp
  cheddar cheese**
¼ cup (25g) shredded **Parmesan
  cheese**
3 **green onions**, thinly sliced
⅓ cup (37g) **bacon bits**

# Crispy Oven Chicken
## with Savory Cheddar Waffles

My mom has always made the best crispy oven chicken. It has all the flavor and crunch I crave without the mess and splatter of deep frying. In this recipe, my mom's crispy chicken is spiked with a hint of Cajun seasoning and served over the fluffiest cheesy waffles you've ever had. Finish it all off with a drizzle of spicy-sweet sriracha maple syrup for a delicious anytime kind of meal.

1. Preheat the oven to 375°F (190°C). Line a baking sheet with parchment paper and set aside.
2. Combine the maple syrup and sriracha; set aside for serving.
3. **To make the chicken,** beat the eggs in a shallow dish. On a plate, combine the panko bread crumbs, seasoned bread crumbs, and Cajun seasoning. In a separate shallow dish, combine the flour and ¼ teaspoon salt.
4. Layer the chicken thighs between two sheets of plastic wrap and use the flat side of a meat mallet to pound the thicker end of the thighs to an even thickness. Season with the remaining ¾ teaspoon salt and pepper.
5. Dip the chicken in the flour, then in the egg, and finally in the crumb mix, pressing the crumbs to adhere.
6. Place the chicken thighs on the prepared baking sheet and generously spray each side of the chicken with cooking spray. Bake for 20 minutes, turn the chicken over, and bake for an additional 15 to 20 minutes or until brown and crispy.
7. Meanwhile, **to make the waffles,** preheat a waffle iron according to the manufacturer's directions or to 400°F (200°C).
8. In a medium bowl, whisk together the flour, baking powder, and salt. In a small bowl, whisk the egg yolks, milk, and butter. Set aside.
9. In a stand mixer or using a hand mixer and a medium bowl, beat the egg whites on medium-high speed until stiff peaks form.
10. Add the egg yolk mixture to the dry ingredients and stir to combine; the batter should be lumpy. Gently fold in the egg whites, cheddar, Parmesan, green onions, and bacon bits.
11. Drop by large spoonfuls onto a greased waffle iron until most of the wells are covered. Close the lid and cook for about 4 to 5 minutes or until golden brown.
12. Serve the chicken and waffles with the sriracha maple syrup.

**TO PREPARE IN AN AIR FRYER**
Preheat the air fryer to 400°F (200°C). Spray each side of the chicken with cooking spray. Cook the chicken in batches for 9 to 12 minutes, turning the chicken over after 5 minutes.

**SERVING SUGGESTIONS**
This meal is the perfect blend of sweet and savory. It pairs well with a side of coleslaw for some added freshness.

**TIPS**
- Do not substitute chicken breasts in this recipe; they will dry out using this method.
- Be sure not to overmix the batter, it will appear slightly lumpy.

 **HEY! IT'S OKAY TO . . .**
Replace the homemade chicken with your favorite frozen breaded chicken strips. Bake them crispy according to package directions and drizzle them with the sriracha maple syrup!

 **VARIATION**
No waffle maker? No problem—turn the batter into pancakes! Prepare the waffle batter as directed and heat a lightly greased griddle or large skillet to medium heat. Use ⅔ cup (160ml) batter per pancake and cook until bubbles begin to pop on the edges, about 2 to 3 minutes. Flip and cook for 2 to 3 minutes more or until cooked through.

**Prep Time:** 20 minutes
**Total Time:** 1 hour
**Serves** 8

1½ cups (170g) shredded
  **mozzarella cheese**
¼ cup (30g) **pepperoni slices**
16oz (454g) **spaghetti**

**FOR THE MEATBALLS**
½ cup (60g) **pepperoni slices**,
  finely chopped
½ cup (70g) finely chopped **green
  bell pepper**
¼ cup (35g) finely diced
  **yellow onion**
1lb (454g) **lean ground beef**
1 **egg**
⅓ cup (39g) **seasoned bread
  crumbs**
2 tablespoons grated **Parmesan
  cheese**
1½ tablespoons **dried parsley**
1 teaspoon **dried oregano**
1 teaspoon **garlic powder**

**FOR THE SAUCE**
2 cups (480ml) **marinara sauce**
15oz (425ml) **pizza sauce**
1 (14.5 oz / 411g) can **petite-diced
  tomatoes**, drained
1 teaspoon **granulated sugar**
½ teaspoon **dried oregano**
¼ teaspoon **salt**
¼ teaspoon freshly ground
  **black pepper**

# Must-Make Pizza Meatballs
# & Spaghetti

You absolutely need these meatballs in your life; they're so flavor packed that literally everyone loves them. The inspiration for this dish came from Nicky, my assistant extraordinaire, and as the name says, it should be on your must-make list! All of the cozy goodness of classic spaghetti and meatballs meets the best-ever cheesy pepperoni pizza. It's all smothered in a zesty tomato sauce and baked under a layer of bubbly, golden-brown cheese with crispy pepperoni. Perfection.

1. Preheat the oven to 375°F (190°C).
2. **To make the meatballs,** heat a 10-inch (25cm) nonstick skillet over medium heat. Add the chopped pepperoni, green bell pepper, and onion. Cook until the onion is softened, about 3 to 4 minutes. Cool completely.
3. In a medium bowl, combine the beef, egg, bread crumbs, Parmesan cheese, parsley, oregano, garlic powder, and the cooled pepperoni mixture. Mix just until combined.
4. Roll the meat mixture into 32 meatballs, about ¾ inch (1.9cm) each.
5. Place the meatballs in a 9 × 13-inch (22 × 33cm) baking dish and bake uncovered for 18 minutes.
6. Meanwhile, **to make the sauce,** in a large bowl, combine the marinara sauce, pizza sauce, drained tomatoes, sugar, oregano, salt, and pepper.
7. After the meatballs have baked, spoon the sauce over the meatballs, and top with shredded mozzarella. Scatter ¼ cup (30g) pepperoni slices on top of the cheese. Bake uncovered for an additional 18 to 22 minutes or until the cheese is browned and bubbly.
8. Meanwhile, bring a large pot of salted water to a boil. Cook the spaghetti al dente in salted water per the package directions. Drain.
9. Serve the meatballs and sauce over the cooked spaghetti.

 **MAKE AHEAD**
The meatballs can be prepared ahead of time and refrigerated for 2 days. Bake refrigerated meatballs as directed.
Freeze uncooked meatballs on a baking sheet in until firm and then transfer them to a zipper-lock freezer bag or an airtight freezerproof container and freeze for up to 4 months.
To cook from frozen, follow the recipe as written, but bake the frozen meatballs for 25 minutes before adding the sauce and cheese on top.

 **LOVE YOUR LEFTOVERS**
I love these meatballs just as much tucked into rolls to make the ultimate Pizza Meatball Subs. Brush hoagie rolls with 1½ tablespoons butter and ⅛ teaspoon garlic powder. Place 6 inches (15cm) under the broiler and broil until lightly toasted, about 2 to 3 minutes. Heat the meatballs and sauce in the microwave or on the stovetop and add 4 to 5 meatballs to each toasted roll. Top with ¼ cup (28g) shredded mozzarella and broil for 2 minutes or until melted.

# Fresh &
## *Nourishing*

94    Steakhouse Surf 'n' Turf Salad

97    No-Roll Mini-Meatball Cabbage Soup

98    Flaky Fish Tacos with Lime Crema

101    Honey Dijon–Glazed Pork Tenderloin with Roasted Sweet Potatoes & Apples

102    Stuffed Spaghetti Squash with Zesty Turkey Sauce

105    Skillet Shrimp Fajitas with Corn Cucumber Salsa

106    Herb-Roasted Chicken Pasta Primavera

109    Hasselback Chicken Cordon Bleu with Skinny Dijon Sauce

110    Pan-Seared Cod with Fresh Mango Salsa

113    Cheesy Ratatouille Roll-Ups with Meat Sauce (or Not)

# Steakhouse **Surf 'n' Turf Salad**

**Prep Time:** 25 minutes
**Total Time:** 45 minutes
**Serves** 4

---

12oz (340g) **sirloin steak**, striploin
    steak, or ribeye steak
4 tablespoons **olive oil**, divided
1 tablespoon **Worcestershire
    sauce**
2 teaspoons **steak seasoning**
12oz (340g) **medium shrimp**,
    peeled and deveined
1 tablespoon **Cajun seasoning**
    (for homemade, see page 18)
4 cups (170g) chopped **kale**
4 cups (170g) chopped **romaine
    lettuce**
1 cup (65g) thinly sliced
    **red cabbage**
½ **English cucumber**, sliced
½ small **red onion**, thinly sliced
½ cup (60g) thinly sliced **radishes**
½ **baguette**
2 cloves **garlic**, minced
⅛ teaspoon **coarse salt**
¾ cup (180ml) **blue cheese
    dressing** or ranch dressing

If we go out for dinner, more often than not, we go to a steak house, and surf 'n' turf tops our list. This fresh, crisp salad packs in all the surf 'n' turf flavors we love. Skewers of juicy grilled steak and plump seasoned shrimp are served on top of greens with grilled garlic toast. Feeling fancy? Dress it with our lightened-up Homemade Blue Cheese Dressing for a fresh, herby flavor with a hint of tangy blue cheese or My All-Time Favorite Yogurt-Ranch Dressing (page 252).

1. Trim the steak and cut into 1-inch (2.5cm) cubes. Toss with 1 tablespoon olive oil, Worcestershire sauce, and steak seasoning. Set aside to marinate for 10 minutes.
2. Toss the shrimp with 1 tablespoon olive oil and season with the Cajun seasoning. Set aside.
3. To a large salad bowl, add the kale with a tiny drop of olive oil and massage the kale until it becomes tender and dark green in color. Add the romaine lettuce and cabbage, and toss to combine.
4. Top the salad mix with the cucumber, red onion, and radishes.
5. Thread the steak onto 4 skewers and the shrimp onto 4 skewers.
6. Cut the baguette in half lengthwise. Mix the remaining 2 tablespoons olive oil and minced garlic in a small bowl and brush it over the cut sides of the bread. Sprinkle the salt over top.
7. Preheat the grill to medium-high heat, 400°F (200°C). Add the bread, cut sides down, and grill for 2 to 3 minutes or until lightly toasted. Cut each piece of bread into 2 pieces and set aside.
8. Place the beef skewers on the grill and cook, turning frequently, for 8 to 10 minutes or until the steak reaches an internal temperature of 135°F (57°C) or to desired doneness. Add the shrimp skewers and cook for 2 to 3 minutes per side or until cooked through.
9. Divide the salad into 4 bowls and top each bowl with 1 skewer of beef and 1 skewer of shrimp. Drizzle with the dressing and serve with a piece of garlic bread.

---

**TIP**
If using bamboo skewers, soak them in water for at least 30 minutes to avoid burning.

**FEELING FANCY?**
For Homemade Blue Cheese Dressing, in a small food processor, combine ½ cup (120g) low-fat Greek yogurt, 3 tablespoons mayonnaise, 3 tablespoons blue cheese, 1 tablespoon lemon juice, and ½ teaspoon garlic powder. Pulse until smooth. Stir in 1 tablespoon finely crumbled blue cheese and season with salt and pepper to taste. Add milk 1 tablespoon at a time if needed to reach desired consistency.

**Prep Time:** 20 minutes
**Total Time:** 40 minutes
**Serves** 8

---

### FOR THE MEATBALLS

1lb (454g) **ground chicken**

¼ cup (28g) **bread crumbs**

¼ cup (25g) grated **Parmesan cheese**

1½ teaspoons **onion powder**

1 **large egg**

½ teaspoon **salt**

½ teaspoon freshly ground **black pepper**

### FOR THE SOUP

1 tablespoon **olive oil**

1 medium **yellow onion**, diced

8 cups (1920ml) **reduced-sodium chicken broth**

4 cups (364g) chopped **green cabbage,** ½-inch (1.5cm) pieces

2 large **carrots**, cut into ½-inch (1.5cm) pieces

2 ribs **celery**, cut into ½-inch (1.5cm) pieces

1 cup (240ml) **water**

½ cup (90g) **quinoa**, rinsed and drained

1 **bay leaf**

¾ teaspoon **dried dill**

¼ teaspoon freshly ground **black pepper**

---

**Ingredient Swaps**

- Replace the quinoa with 2 cups (280g) **cooked rice** (any variety). Add ¼ cup (35g) warm rice to each bowl when serving and ladle the soup over top.
- Replace the ground chicken with **ground beef** to make the meatballs.

# No-Roll Mini-Meatball
# **Cabbage Soup**

Healthy never tasted so good! This protein- and veggie-packed soup feels like a warm, cozy hug in a bowl. Bite-size chicken meatballs (no rolling required!) are cooked in a light and flavorful broth along with fresh vegetables and quinoa. It's hearty and delicious, and it reheats like a dream, making it a nourishing and cozy meal any time of day.

1. **To make the meatballs,** in a large bowl, gently mix the chicken, bread crumbs, Parmesan cheese, onion powder, egg, salt, and pepper. Set aside.
2. **To make the soup,** in a 4-quart (3.8L) Dutch oven or stock pot, heat the oil over medium heat. Stir in the diced onion and cook just until softened, about 3 minutes.
3. Add the broth, cabbage, carrots, celery, water, quinoa, bay leaf, dill, and pepper. Bring to a boil over medium-high heat.
4. Using a small spoon or small cookie scoop, scoop ¾-inch (1.9cm) spoonfuls of the meat mixture and drop them into the simmering soup.
5. Reduce the heat to medium. Simmer uncovered for 16 to 18 minutes or until the quinoa is tender and the meatballs reach an internal temperature of 165°F (74°C).
6. Remove the bay leaf and discard. Season with additional salt, if desired.

---

 **HEY! IT'S OKAY TO . . .**
Skip the homemade meatballs and swap them out with your favorite fully cooked frozen meatballs. Simply add 1 pound (454g) frozen meatballs of your choice to the soup and simmer as directed in the recipe.

 **MAKE AHEAD**
I love quinoa in this soup, not only because it adds extra protein, but also because it freezes beautifully. Prepare the soup as directed and cool. Ladle single-sized portions into zipper-lock freezer bags or small airtight freezerproof containers and freeze for up to 4 months. Thaw in the fridge overnight and heat on the stove or in the microwave until heated through. Add additional water or broth if needed.

**Prep Time:** 10 minutes
**Total Time:** 20 minutes
**Serves** 4

---

**FOR THE FISH**

1 tablespoon **olive oil**

2 tablespoons **taco seasoning**
(for homemade, see page 18)

1lb (454g) **cod fillets** or tilapia
fillets

**FOR THE LIME CREMA**

½ cup (113g) **sour cream**

1 tablespoon freshly squeezed
**lime juice**

1½ tablespoons finely minced
**fresh cilantro**

½ teaspoon **garlic powder**

Pinch of **salt**

**FOR SERVING**

8 (6in / 15cm) **corn tortillas** or
flour tortillas

1 cup (91g) shredded **green
cabbage** or coleslaw mix

1 **avocado**, sliced

**Lime** wedges

# Flaky Fish Tacos
# with Lime Crema

Taco night just got an upgrade! These fish tacos are absolutely craveable and are on the table in about 20 minutes, start to finish. Fish fillets are rubbed with a zesty seasoning blend, baked until tender and flaky, and tucked into warm tortillas. Pile on the toppings with a drizzle of crema for a healthy and fresh meal so good your family will request it on repeat.

1. Preheat the oven to 400°F (200°C). Line a baking sheet with parchment paper.
2. **To make the lime crema,** in a small bowl, combine the sour cream, lime juice, cilantro, garlic powder, and salt. Refrigerate until ready to serve.
3. **To make the fish,** in a medium bowl, combine the olive oil and taco seasoning. Pat the fish fillets dry with a paper towel and add them to the bowl. Gently toss to coat.
4. Place the fish on the prepared baking sheet and bake for 9 to 12 minutes or until the fish is flaky and reaches an internal temperature of 145°F (63°C).
5. Meanwhile, heat the tortillas according to package directions.
6. **To serve,** break the fish into large chunks and divide it among the tortillas. Top with the cabbage, avocado, and lime crema.

**TO PREPARE IN AN AIR FRYER**

Preheat the air fryer to 400°F (200°C). Season the fish as directed and place it in a single layer in the air-fryer basket. Cook for 6 to 11 minutes or until the fillets reach an internal temperature of 145°F (63°C).

---

 **SERVING SUGGESTIONS**

Set up a taco bar with toppings and let everyone create their own masterpiece. Try sliced jalapeños, pickled red onions, sliced radishes, or Mango Salsa (page 110).

 **LOVE YOUR LEFTOVERS**

Turn leftovers into a fish taco bowl! Fill a bowl with cooked rice and leftover fish, and top it all off with your favorite toppings and, of course, a generous drizzle of lime crema.

**Prep Time:** 20 minutes
**Total Time:** 45 minutes
**Serves** 4

---

Cooking spray
1lb (454g) **sweet potatoes**, peeled
    and cut into ¾-inch (1.9cm)
    pieces
3 medium **Gala apples**, peeled,
    cored, and cut into ¾-inch
    (1.9cm) pieces
2 tablespoons **vegetable oil**,
    divided
1 tablespoon **brown sugar**
1 teaspoon **salt**, divided
½ teaspoon freshly ground
    **black pepper**, divided
½ teaspoon **ground cinnamon**
2 tablespoons **water**
1¼lb (567g) **pork tenderloin**
4 cloves **garlic**, minced

**FOR THE GLAZE**
½ cup (168g) **honey**
3 tablespoons **Dijon mustard**
1 tablespoon **yellow mustard**
1 tablespoon freshly squeezed
    **lemon juice**
½ teaspoon **dried thyme leaves**

*Scan for instructions to
prepare in an air fryer.*

# Honey Dijon–Glazed Pork Tenderloin with Roasted Sweet Potatoes & Apples

I absolutely love cooking pork tenderloin because it's one of those dishes that looks and tastes impressive, but in reality, it's super easy to prepare. A tender and extra juicy glazed pork tenderloin roasts alongside cinnamon-kissed sweet potatoes and apples. Both sweet and savory, this is the perfect belly-warming good-for-you kind of meal. Don't skip the homemade glaze; it takes just a few minutes of prep, and it's so delicious, you'll practically want to drink it.

1. Preheat the oven to 425°F (220°C). Line a 13 × 18-inch (33 × 46cm) rimmed baking sheet with foil, and spray with cooking spray.
2. In a medium bowl, combine the sweet potatoes, apples, 1 tablespoon oil, brown sugar, ½ teaspoon salt, ¼ teaspoon pepper, and cinnamon. Toss to coat the sweet potatoes and apples, then spread them on one half of the prepared baking sheet. Sprinkle with the water.
3. **To make the glaze,** in a small bowl, combine the honey, Dijon mustard, yellow mustard, lemon juice, and thyme. Set aside.
4. Remove any silverskin from the pork and pat dry with a paper towel. Season the pork with the remaining ½ teaspoon salt and ¼ teaspoon pepper.
5. In a 12-inch (30cm) nonstick skillet, heat the remaining 1 tablespoon oil over medium-high heat. Add the pork to the skillet and brown for 2 minutes per side. Transfer the pork to a plate and set aside.
6. To the same skillet, add the garlic and cook just until fragrant, about 30 seconds. Whisk in the glaze mixture and bring to a boil over medium-high heat. Boil, whisking occasionally, for 4 minutes or until thickened.
7. Reserve ⅓ cup (87g) of the glaze for serving. Brush both sides of the pork with the remaining glaze.
8. Place the pork on the other half of the pan with the sweet potatoes and apples. Roast for 18 to 22 minutes or until or until the pork reaches an internal temperature of 140°F (60°C). (It will continue to cook as it rests.)
9. Remove the pork from the baking sheet and place it on a plate to rest for 5 to 7 minutes. Place the sweet potatoes and apples back in the oven while the pork is resting and roast for an additional 5 minutes or until tender.
10. Slice the pork into ½-inch (1.5cm) slices and serve with the reserved glaze and the apples and sweet potatoes.

---

 **TIPS**

• Pork tenderloin has a shiny membrane called *silverskin* that should be removed since it can be tough. Place a small sharp knife under the silverskin and slide it along the skin to remove it. If your pork tenderloin has any fatty bits, they can be removed as well.

• I love Gala apples for their balance of sweetness and texture, but any firm baking apple can be used.

• The secret to the juiciest pork tenderloin is to avoid overcooking it. This cut of meat is very lean, and it will become dry if overcooked. Use an instant-read thermometer and cook the pork to an internal temperature of 140°F (60°C). Once cooked, remove the pork from the pan and rest for at least 5 minutes to reach an internal temperature of 145°F (63°C). Pork tenderloin should be a little bit pink when sliced.

# Stuffed Spaghetti Squash
## with Zesty Turkey Sauce

**Prep Time:** 25 minutes
**Total Time:** 1 hour 5 minutes
**Serves** 4

3lb (1.4kg) **spaghetti squash**
1½ teaspoons **olive oil**
½ teaspoon **salt**
¼ teaspoon freshly ground **black pepper**
2 tablespoons **grated Parmesan cheese**
2 teaspoons **butter**
½ cup (57g) shredded **mozzarella cheese**

**FOR THE SAUCE**
1½ teaspoons **olive oil**
½lb (227g) **ground turkey**
¼ cup (30g) finely diced **yellow onion**
½ **red bell pepper**, chopped
1 **carrot**, shredded
2 ribs **celery**, finely diced
2 cloves **garlic**, minced
1½ teaspoons **Italian seasoning** (for homemade, see page 18)
1 (28oz / 794g) can **crushed tomatoes**
3 tablespoons **tomato paste**
½ teaspoon **granulated sugar**
¼ teaspoon **salt**
¼ teaspoon freshly ground **black pepper**
¼ cup (14g) chopped **fresh Italian parsley**

I absolutely love this meal because it's feel-good freshness that not only tastes great, it reheats like a dream. The zesty meat sauce is chock-full of veggies and has so much flavor, you'll be making it on repeat. Add in whatever veggies you have on hand (mushrooms and zucchini are great additions) and simmer until thick. Pile it high over stuffed spaghetti squash (or even pasta) and top with a sprinkle of cheese and a little fresh parsley for a healthy meal the whole family will love.

1. Preheat the oven to 400°F (200°C). Cut the spaghetti squash in half lengthwise. Use a large spoon to scrape out the seeds and discard them.
2. Brush the cut sides with olive oil and season with salt and pepper.
3. Place the squash halves cut sides down on a rimmed baking sheet. Bake for 30 to 40 minutes or until tender when poked with a fork. Once tender, remove the squash from the baking sheet to cool slightly.
4. Meanwhile, **to make the sauce,** in a 3-quart (2.8L) saucepan, heat the oil over medium-high heat. Add the turkey and onion and cook, breaking up the meat with a spoon, for 5 to 6 minutes or until no pink remains. Add the bell pepper, carrot, celery, garlic, and Italian seasoning, and cook for 3 minutes or until the bell pepper begins to soften.
5. Stir in the crushed tomatoes, tomato paste, sugar, salt, and pepper. Bring to a boil, reduce the heat to medium-low, and simmer uncovered, stirring occasionally, for 15 to 20 minutes or until thickened. Stir in the parsley.
6. Use a fork to scrape the strands of spaghetti squash and place them in a medium bowl. Stir in the Parmesan cheese and butter, and season with additional salt and pepper, if desired. Fill the squash shells with the seasoned squash.
7. Divide the sauce over the two squash halves and top with the mozzarella.
8. Bake for 7 to 9 minutes or until the cheese is melted.

**Scan for Air Fryer Spaghetti Squash.**

### TO PREPARE IN AN AIR FRYER
Scan QR code and cook spaghetti squash in air fryer. Prepare sauce and stuff squash as directed in main recipe. Once stuffed, return the squash to the air fryer and cook for 7 to 8 minutes at 370°F (190°C) to heat through.

 **TIPS**
- To make the squash easier to cut, poke it a few times with a fork and microwave on high for 3 to 4 minutes. Cool for a few minutes before cutting in half.
- Once the squash is baked, be sure to turn it over to allow the steam to release. If you leave it cut side down on the pan, it will continue to steam and can overcook.

 **HEY! IT'S OKAY TO . . .**
Take a shortcut and make a quick sauce! In a 10-inch (25cm) skillet, brown 1 pound (454g) ground turkey with 1 small onion, finely diced, and ½ teaspoon garlic powder. Break up the turkey with a spoon, and cook until no pink remains. Stir in 2¼ cups (540ml) jarred marinara sauce and simmer uncovered for 8 to 10 minutes, stirring occasionally, until thickened.

→

**MAKE AHEAD**

Double the sauce and freeze half for another meal. Cool completely, ladle into a zipper-lock freezer bag or an airtight freezerproof container, and freeze for up to 4 months. Thaw in the fridge overnight and reheat on the stovetop or in the microwave. The sauce can be served over pasta, vegetable noodles, or spaghetti squash.

**Prep Time:** 20 minutes
**Total Time:** 35 minutes
**Serves** 4

---

## FOR THE FAJITAS

1 **lime**, plus more lime wedges
 for serving

1lb (454g) **medium shrimp**,
 peeled and deveined

2 tablespoons **vegetable oil**,
 divided

2 teaspoons **chili powder**

½ teaspoon **garlic powder**

½ teaspoon **ground cumin**

½ teaspoon **seasoned salt**,
 divided

¼ teaspoon freshly ground
 **black pepper**

1 large **red onion**, sliced

1 **red bell pepper**, sliced

1 **green bell pepper**, sliced

8 (6in / 15cm) **flour tortillas**

## FOR THE SALSA

1 (15.25oz / 432g) can **corn**, drained

½ cup (70g) finely diced
 **cucumber**

2 tablespoons finely diced
 **red onion**

2 tablespoons finely chopped
 **fresh cilantro**

1 small **fresh jalapeño**, seeded
 and finely diced

¼ teaspoon **seasoned salt**

Juice of ½ **lime**

### Ingredient Swap

Replace the shrimp with ¾ pound
(340g) **boneless, skinless chicken
breasts** sliced into ½-inch (1.5cm)
strips. Cook the chicken in batches
for 4 to 5 minutes per batch or until
cooked through.

# Skillet Shrimp Fajitas
## with Corn Cucumber Salsa

Fajitas are always in our dinner rotation for a healthy meal that is totally
satisfying. I love the fresh flavor, versatility, and—best of all—how easy it is to
make! This version comes together quickly in just one pan and is served with a
quick and crunchy corn salsa. Tuck it into tortillas, serve it over salad, or turn it
into fajita bowls loaded with toppings—the possibilities are endless.

1. **To make the salsa,** in a medium bowl, combine the corn, cucumber, red
 onion, cilantro, jalapeño, and seasoned salt. Squeeze in the lime juice
 (about 1 tablespoon juice) and mix well. Refrigerate until ready to serve.

2. **To make the fajitas,** into a medium bowl, zest the lime (about 1 teaspoon
 lime zest). Cut the lime in half and squeeze the juice of one half (about
 1 tablespoon juice) into the bowl. (Reserve the other half for step 6.)
 Add the shrimp, 1 tablespoon oil, chili powder, garlic powder, cumin,
 ¼ teaspoon seasoned salt, and pepper, and toss to coat.

3. Heat a 10-inch (25cm) cast-iron skillet over medium-high heat and add
 2 teaspoons oil. Add the shrimp and cook for 3 to 4 minutes or just until
 pink and almost cooked through. Transfer the shrimp to a bowl and lightly
 cover with foil.

4. Add the remaining 1 teaspoon oil and the sliced red onion to the skillet.
 Cook for 2 minutes. Stir in the red and green bell peppers and the
 remaining ¼ teaspoon seasoned salt. Continue cooking for 4 to 5 minutes
 or just until the peppers are tender-crisp.

5. Add the shrimp along with any juices back to the skillet and cook for
 1 minute to heat through. Squeeze the remaining lime half over the skillet
 and season with additional salt to taste.

6. Heat the tortillas according to package directions. Fill the tortillas with
 the shrimp, onions, and peppers, and top with corn salsa. Serve with
 additional lime wedges.

---

 **SERVING SUGGESTIONS**

Warm flour or corn tortillas are
our favorite way to enjoy these
fajitas. We love to add guacamole,
sour cream or Mexican crema,
Cotija cheese, and shredded
cabbage or sliced radishes for
extra crunch.

 **FEELING FANCY?**

Replace the canned corn in
the salsa with 2 ears fresh
grilled corn. Shuck the corn,
lightly brush the kernels with
olive oil, and season with a little
bit of salt. Grill over medium-
high heat, turning the corn
occasionally, for 4 to 6 minutes
or until lightly charred. Cool and
use a sharp knife to cut the
kernels off the cob.

# Herb-Roasted Chicken
## Pasta Primavera

**Prep Time:** 10 minutes
**Total Time:** 45 minutes
**Serves** 4

---

2 boneless, skinless **chicken breasts**, about 6oz (170g) each

1½ tablespoons **olive oil**, divided

2 teaspoons **garlic-herb seasoning** (for homemade, see page 18)

8oz (227g) **penne**

1 medium **zucchini**, cut ½ inch (1.5cm) thick

1 **orange bell pepper**, sliced

1 cup (195g) **grape tomatoes**

4oz (113g) **asparagus spears**, cut into 1-inch (2.5cm) pieces

3 cloves **garlic**, minced

½ teaspoon **salt**

½ teaspoon freshly ground **black pepper**

3 tablespoons **light cream cheese**

1 tablespoon **butter**

⅔ cup (57g) **frozen peas**, thawed

⅓ cup (33g) shredded **Parmesan cheese**

2 teaspoons **lemon zest**

2 tablespoons chopped **fresh parsley** or basil leaves

---

### Ingredient Swap

Mix and match 6 cups (860g) of **any quick-cooking vegetables** in this recipe. Try small florets of broccoli, mushrooms, snap peas, summer squash, bok choy, or thinly sliced Brussels sprouts.

---

On those days when you're craving freshness but still want something to satisfy, this dish is exactly what you need! Oven-roasted chicken breasts, a medley of spring vegetables, and hearty penne are tossed in a light-and-fresh lemon cream sauce. Almost any veggie can be used, so peruse the farmers' market or the produce section and choose your own selection of goodness. This recipe is veggie-packed self-care at its finest; it's feel-good food through and through.

1. Preheat the oven to 400°F (200°C).
2. Rub the chicken breasts with ½ tablespoon olive oil and the garlic-herb seasoning. Place on a rimmed baking sheet and roast for 15 minutes.
3. Bring a medium saucepan of salted water to a boil, and cook the pasta according to the package directions. Reserve ½ cup (120ml) pasta water and drain the pasta but do not rinse it. Set aside.
4. Meanwhile, in a large bowl, combine the zucchini, bell pepper, tomatoes, asparagus, remaining 1 tablespoon olive oil, garlic, salt, and pepper, and mix well.
5. Add the vegetables to the baking sheet, arranging them in an even layer around the chicken, and roast for 8 to 12 minutes more or until the chicken reaches an internal temperature of 165°F (74°C). Transfer the chicken to a plate and cover lightly with foil.
6. Heat the broiler to high heat. Place the vegetables 4 inches (10cm) under the broiler and broil for 2 minutes. Remove from the oven and set aside.
7. In the same saucepan used for the pasta, combine the cream cheese, butter, and ¼ cup (60ml) reserved pasta water. Whisk over medium heat until smooth.
8. Add the vegetables with juices, pasta, peas, Parmesan cheese, and lemon zest. Stir to combine, adding some of the remaining pasta water if needed. Season with additional salt and pepper to taste.
9. Cut the chicken into ½-inch (1.5cm) slices and arrange on top of the pasta.
10. Garnish with parsley or basil leaves and additional Parmesan cheese to taste.

---

### TIP

Garlic-herb seasoning brands can vary in salt levels. If using a prepared seasoning mix, taste a little bit to see if it is salty. If not, add salt to the chicken (approximately ¼ teaspoon) if needed.

### VARIATION

This recipe is also delicious with shrimp in place of chicken. To prepare with shrimp, preheat the pan along with the oven before adding the vegetables. Season 12 ounces (340g) peeled and deveined medium shrimp with ½ tablespoon olive oil and 2 teaspoons garlic-herb seasoning. Add the shrimp to the baking sheet along with the vegetables and roast for 8 to 12 minutes or until the shrimp is cooked through. Remove the shrimp from the pan and broil the vegetables as directed in the recipe.

**Prep Time:** 25 minutes
**Total Time:** 45 minutes
**Serves** 4

2oz (57g) thinly sliced **ham**

3oz (85g) sliced **Swiss cheese**

4 boneless, skinless **chicken breasts**, about 6oz (170g) each

1 tablespoon **olive oil**

½ teaspoon **seasoned salt**

½ teaspoon **smoked paprika**

¼ teaspoon freshly ground **black pepper**

1 tablespoon grated **Parmesan cheese**

**FOR THE SAUCE**

2oz (57g) **light cream cheese**

½ cup (120ml) **chicken broth**

2 teaspoons **Dijon mustard**

½ teaspoon **cornstarch**

¼ teaspoon **garlic powder**

¼ teaspoon **onion powder**

# Hasselback Chicken Cordon Bleu
## with Skinny Dijon Sauce

Skip the heavy breading and deep-frying—this easy recipe packs all of the cheesy, smoky cordon bleu flavors you love into a lighter, oven-baked version. Tender chicken breasts are stuffed with bits of ham and Swiss cheese and baked until juicy. They're served with a Dijon sauce so good you'll want to slurp it up with a spoon. Feel free to double up on the sauce, it's delicious with veggies too!

1. Preheat the oven to 400°F (200°C).
2. Cut the ham and Swiss cheese into ½-inch (1.5cm) strips the approximate width of the chicken breasts.
3. Rub the chicken breasts with oil and season with seasoned salt, smoked paprika, and pepper. Place them on a cutting board and use a small knife to cut 6 to 7 slits across each breast, cutting ¾ of the way through. (Don't cut all the way through.) Tuck the ham and cheese strips evenly into each of the slits along the chicken breasts.
4. Sprinkle the Parmesan cheese over the chicken breasts and place them on a rimmed baking sheet. Bake for 18 to 22 minutes or until the chicken is cooked through and reaches an internal temperature of 165°F (74°C).
5. Meanwhile, **to make the sauce,** heat a small nonstick skillet over medium heat. Add the cream cheese and cook until melted and smooth.
6. In a small bowl, whisk the broth, mustard, cornstarch, garlic powder, and onion powder. Gradually add to the skillet, whisking continuously, and bring to a boil. Boil for 1 minute or until slightly thickened. Taste and season with salt, if desired.
7. Serve the sauce spooned over the chicken.

**TO PREPARE IN AN AIR FRYER**

Prepare the chicken as directed. Preheat the air fryer to 370°F (190°C). Cook the chicken breasts in a single layer for 11 to 14 minutes or until the chicken reaches an internal temperature of 165°F (74°C) while preparing the sauce.

**SERVING SUGGESTIONS**
Almost any green vegetable is a great side for cordon bleu. We love broccoli or asparagus.

**TIP**
You may have more slices of ham or cheese than slits in the chicken; continue tucking them into the breasts, doubling up if needed, until all of the ham and cheese is used.

**VARIATION**
Replace the ham and Swiss with smoked turkey breast and sliced brie or mozzarella.

**HEY! IT'S OKAY TO . . .**
Skip the cooked sauce and whip up a quick homemade dipping sauce instead. In a small bowl, whisk ¼ cup (60ml) plain Greek yogurt, 1 tablespoon Dijon mustard, and 1 tablespoon honey. Prepared honey mustard can also be used for dipping.

4 **cod fillets**, 1 inch (2.5cm) thick,
about 5oz (142g) each

1½ tablespoons **olive oil**, divided

**FOR THE SALSA**

1 **fresh mango**, finely diced

½ **red bell pepper**, finely diced

¼ cup finely diced **red onion**

1 **fresh jalapeño**, seeded and
finely diced

2 tablespoons chopped
**fresh cilantro**

1 tablespoon freshly squeezed
**lime juice** (about ½ lime)

**Salt**, to taste

**FOR THE RUB**

1 teaspoon **paprika**

1 teaspoon **smoked paprika**

½ teaspoon **ground cumin**

½ teaspoon **salt**

½ teaspoon **dried oregano**

½ teaspoon **garlic powder**

½ teaspoon **onion powder**

⅛ teaspoon **cayenne pepper**
(optional)

---

**Ingredient Swaps**

- Replace cod with any type of white
  fish such as **halibut** or **tilapia**.
- Substitute fresh mango with
  1½ cups (210g) thawed **frozen
  mango** or **peaches**.

# Pan-Seared Cod
# with Fresh Mango Salsa

Light and healthy, this meal brings a fresh tropical flavor to the dinner table in minutes. Seasoned with a flavor-packed homemade rub, the cod cooks up perfectly flaky in about 10 minutes. This mango salsa has been a family favorite for about 25 years, and it's totally addictive, so feel free to double up. It's great over chicken or fish, but it's also a perfect dipper for tortilla chips!

1. **To make the salsa,** in a medium bowl, combine the mango, bell pepper, red onion, jalapeño, cilantro, and lime juice. Season with salt to taste and set aside.

2. **To make the rub,** in a small bowl, combine the paprika, smoked paprika, cumin, salt, oregano, garlic powder, onion powder, and cayenne pepper, if using.

3. Pat the cod fillets dry with a paper towel. Drizzle 1 tablespoon oil over the cod and rub both sides with the seasoning rub.

4. Heat the remaining ½ tablespoon oil in a 12-inch (30cm) nonstick skillet over medium heat. Add the cod and cook uncovered for 3 to 4 minutes per side or just until the fish flakes easily. Immediately remove the cod from the skillet.

5. Serve with mango salsa.

**TO PREPARE IN THE OVEN**

Preheat the oven to 400°F (200°C). Place the seasoned cod on a rimmed baking sheet and bake for 8 to 12 minutes or just until cooked through and the fish flakes easily. (Do not overcook.) Immediately remove the fish from the baking sheet and set aside to rest for 5 minutes.

---

 **SERVING SUGGESTIONS**

This fish is also great served as fish tacos, tucked into corn tortillas and served with shredded cabbage.

 **TIPS**

- Thinner ½-inch (1.5cm) fillets will need 2 to 3 minutes per side to cook.
- The salsa can be made 24 hours in advance.
- Paprika and smoked paprika have very different flavor profiles. Paprika is slightly sweet while smoked paprika has a very distinct smoky flavor and aroma. This recipe uses a combination of the two for a perfect rub.

**FOR THE FILLING**
15oz (425g) **ricotta cheese**
¼ cup (25g) shredded **Parmesan cheese**
2 tablespoons chopped **fresh parsley**
1 teaspoon **lemon zest**

**FOR THE ROLL-UPS**
2 small **eggplants**, about 1¼lb (567g) total
3 medium **zucchini**, about 2½lb (1.1kg) total
3 tablespoons **olive oil**, divided
6 **Roma tomatoes**
1 teaspoon **salt**
½ teaspoon freshly ground **black pepper**
1 teaspoon **dried oregano**

**FOR THE SAUCE**
12oz (340g) **ground turkey sausage** (optional)
2 cloves **garlic**, minced
1 (15oz / 425g) can **crushed tomatoes**
½ cup (113g) **tomato sauce**
2 teaspoons **Italian seasoning** (for homemade, see page 18)
1 teaspoon **granulated sugar**

**FOR SERVING**
2 tablespoons each chopped **fresh basil and parsley**

# Cheesy Ratatouille Roll-Ups
## with Meat Sauce (or Not)

These roll-ups are the perfect union of my favorite layered ratatouille recipe and involtini, a rolled eggplant dish that I learned to make in Italy. Packed with fresh, flavorful ingredients, thin slices of eggplant, zucchini, and tomato are wrapped around a bright ricotta filling. Bake it in tomato sauce for a light meal or add some turkey sausage for a heartier favorite. As pretty as it is delicious, it's truly the best of both worlds.

1. Preheat the oven to 400°F (200°C). Grease a 9 × 13-inch (23 × 33cm) baking dish and set aside.
2. **To make the filling,** in a medium bowl, combine the ricotta cheese, Parmesan cheese, parsley, and lemon zest.
3. **To make the roll-ups,** using a mandoline slicer or a sharp knife, slice the eggplant and zucchini lengthwise into long strips about ¼ inch (0.6cm) thick; you should have about 14 to 16 slices of each vegetable. Arrange the slices in a single layer on large rimmed baking sheets; you may need two sheets. Brush with 2 tablespoons olive oil and season with salt and pepper. Roast for 15 to 20 minutes or until the vegetables are softened enough to roll. Remove from the oven and cool. Slice the tomatoes into ¼-inch (0.6cm) slices.
4. Meanwhile, **to make the sauce,** heat a 10-inch (25cm) skillet over medium-high heat. Add the sausage (if using) and garlic and cook, breaking up the meat with a spoon, for 5 to 6 minutes or until no pink remains. Drain any fat. (If omitting the sausage, sauté the garlic in an additional 1 tablespoon olive oil for 2 to 3 minutes.)
5. Stir in the crushed tomatoes, tomato sauce, Italian seasoning, and sugar, and simmer for 5 minutes or until the sauce has thickened. Transfer the sauce to the prepared baking dish.
6. To assemble each roll-up, stack 1 slice of zucchini, 1 slice of eggplant, 3 slices of tomato, and a sprinkle of oregano. Add 1½ tablespoons of the ricotta mixture at one end of the stack and roll jelly-roll style.
7. Place the rolls upright in the baking dish on top of the sauce and drizzle with the remaining 1 tablespoon olive oil.
8. Cover with foil and bake for 30 minutes. Uncover and bake for an additional 15 to 20 minutes or until the rolls are tender.
9. Let rest 5 to 10 minutes to thicken the sauce. **To serve,** sprinkle with the fresh basil and parsley and serve warm.

 **SERVING SUGGESTIONS**
This recipe makes 8 lighter servings or 6 heartier servings. It's nice and saucy, so to stretch the meal further, spoon the sauce over pasta and add some Garlic Herb Bread (page 255).

 **TIPS**
- The eggplant and zucchini are partially cooked in step 3 so they don't break as they're rolled. While the vegetables are roasting, the sauce and filling can be prepared.
- To prepare this as a vegetarian dish, skip the turkey sausage.

 **MAKE AHEAD**
Cheesy Ratatouille Roll-Ups can be prepared up to 24 hours in advance and refrigerated. Remove from the fridge 30 minutes before cooking and bake as directed.

# Cozy Pasta
## *Favorites*

**116**   Gonna-Want-Seconds Cheesesteak Pasta

**119**   Weeknight Spinach, Artichoke & Sundried Tomato Rigatoni

**120**   My All-Time Favorite Mac & Cheese

**123**   Lemon-Pesto Shrimp Pasta with Pepper Parm Crumbs

**124**   One-Pan Sausage & Penne in Creamy Rose Sauce

**127**   Kailey's Roasted Balsamic Cherry Tomato Pasta

**128**   Fast! Homemade Alfredo Sauce

**131**   Spicy-as-You-Like-It Shrimp Peanut Noodles

**132**   Roasted Red Pepper Pasta with Crispy Parmesan Chicken

**135**   All-Purpose Meaty Pasta Sauce

**Prep Time:** 15 minutes
**Total Time:** 55 minutes
**Serves** 6

---

1lb (454g) **strip loin** or sirloin steak

2 **green bell peppers**

1 large **yellow onion**

8oz (227g) **cremini mushrooms**

2 teaspoons **steak seasoning**, divided

1lb (454g) **fettuccine** or another long pasta

1 tablespoon **vegetable oil**

¼ cup (57g) **butter**

¼ cup (30g) **all-purpose flour**

2½ cups (600ml) **beef stock**

⅓ cup (80ml) **half-and-half** or light cream

2 tablespoons **Worcestershire sauce**

1 **beef bouillon cube**

½ teaspoon freshly ground **black pepper**

1 cup (113g) freshly grated **provolone cheese**, plus more to serve

---

**Ingredient Swap**

This pasta dish is equally delicious with 1 pound (454g) **lean ground beef** in place of the steak. Brown the ground beef over medium-high heat with 1½ teaspoons steak seasoning, breaking up the meat with a spoon and cooking until no pink remains. Drain any fat.

# Gonna-Want-Seconds
# Cheesesteak Pasta

I love a good cheesesteak sandwich with thinly cut steak, onions, and of course, lots of melty cheese—all of which appear in this pasta recipe. I've beefed it up with sliced mushrooms and green peppers and smothered it all in a delicious sauce that's both light and rich. This cozy, carby dinner might be my newest favorite weeknight pasta and trust me, you're gonna want seconds!

1. Place the steak in the freezer for about 15 minutes before slicing, or if the steak is frozen, thaw only part way.
2. Meanwhile, thinly slice the bell peppers and onion. Slice the mushrooms ¼ inch (0.6cm) thick. Set the vegetables aside.
3. Slice the steak as thinly as possible and toss with 1½ teaspoons steak seasoning.
4. In a large pot of boiling salted water, cook the fettucine al dente according to package directions. Reserve ½ cup (120ml) pasta water and drain well. Set aside.
5. In a 12-inch (30cm) skillet, heat the oil over medium-high heat until shimmering. Add the steak and cook in two batches until just browned, about 2 minutes per batch. Transfer to a medium bowl.
6. To the same skillet, add the onion, bell peppers, mushrooms, and remaining ½ teaspoon steak seasoning, and cook over medium-high heat for 8 to 10 minutes or until tender. Transfer the cooked vegetables to the bowl with the steak.
7. Return the skillet to the stovetop over medium heat, add the butter and flour, and cook for 1 minute. Gradually whisk in the beef stock, stirring after each addition until smooth. Add the half-and-half, Worcestershire sauce, bouillon cube, and pepper. Simmer for 3 to 4 minutes or until thickened. Remove from the heat and whisk in the provolone cheese until smooth.
8. Add the pasta, bell pepper mixture, and steak with juices, and toss to coat with the sauce, adding pasta water as needed to keep the mixture smooth.
9. Serve topped with additional shredded provolone, if desired.

---

 **SERVING SUGGESTIONS**

This recipe makes 6 generous portions. If you'd like to stretch it a little further, it can serve 8 with a side of garlic bread and a fresh, crisp salad.

**Prep Time:** 10 minutes
**Total Time:** 30 minutes
**Serves** 4

8oz (227g) **rigatoni**
14oz (397g) **water-packed artichoke hearts**, drained
1 tablespoon **unsalted butter**
2 cloves **garlic**, minced
1 teaspoon **dried basil**
¼ teaspoon **red pepper flakes**
4oz (113g) **cream cheese**
½ cup (120ml) **vegetable broth** or chicken broth
5oz (142g) **fresh spinach**, coarsely chopped
½ cup (60g) **oil-packed sundried tomatoes**, lightly drained and sliced
¾ cup (75g) freshly grated **Parmesan cheese**
¼ teaspoon **salt**, plus more to taste
¼ teaspoon freshly ground **black pepper**, plus more to taste

# Weeknight **Spinach, Artichoke & Sundried Tomato Rigatoni**

At the end of a long day, when you're craving something delicious but don't have the time (or energy!) to make a big fuss, enter this weeknight wonder. It's oh-so-creamy with no heavy cream required, and best of all, it comes together so fast. Jam-packed with spinach, artichokes, and sundried tomatoes, it's on the table in about 30 minutes. This is a meatless, full-meal deal, but you can stretch it even further by adding your favorite protein.

1. Bring a large pot of salted water to a boil. Add the rigatoni and cook al dente according to package directions.
2. While the pasta is cooking, chop the artichoke hearts into quarters if they are whole.
3. In a 10-inch (25cm) nonstick skillet, melt the butter over medium heat. Add the garlic, basil, and red pepper flakes. Cook just until fragrant, about 1 minute.
4. Add the cream cheese to the pan and whisk until melted and smooth. Gradually whisk in the broth until smooth.
5. Stir in the spinach, lightly drained sundried tomatoes, and artichokes. Cook until the spinach is wilted, about 2 to 3 minutes. Add the Parmesan cheese, salt, and pepper, and stir until smooth.
6. Stir in the cooked rigatoni and add pasta water 1 tablespoon at a time to reach the desired consistency.
7. Reduce the heat to low and cook until heated through, about 2 minutes. Season with additional salt and pepper to taste.

### SERVING SUGGESTIONS

- This pasta pairs well with a fresh salad and some crusty bread. Garnish with fresh basil and additional Parmesan cheese if you'd like.
- This recipe makes a light entrée for four. For heartier appetites, add a protein like grilled shrimp, pan-seared salmon fillets, or roasted chicken.

### TIP

This recipe uses canned artichokes, which are most often water-packed with a little bit of salt. Artichoke hearts are also sold in glass jars, marinated in oil, vinegar, and seasonings. I prefer the lighter flavor of canned artichokes in this recipe, but either variety can be used. Regardless of which type you use, be sure to drain them well, and if they're whole, chop them into quarters.

### SOMETHING ON THE SIDE

To add some extra protein, serve this pasta with some quick Garlic Butter Chicken Bites.

1. Cut 1 pound (454g) boneless, skinless chicken breasts into ¾-inch (1.9cm) cubes and season with ¼ teaspoon each salt and black pepper.
2. In a medium skillet, heat 2 teaspoons olive oil over medium-high heat and add the chicken. Cook for 3 minutes without stirring, then stir and continue cooking until the chicken is cooked through, about 3 minutes more.
3. Move the chicken to one side of the pan and add 2 tablespoons butter; 2 cloves garlic, minced; and 1 teaspoon dried parsley. Cook just until the garlic is fragrant. Stir the garlic butter into the chicken and spoon over the pasta.

**Prep Time:** 25 minutes
**Total Time:** 50 minutes
**Serves** 6

12oz (340g) **elbow macaroni**
¼ cup (57g) **butter**
¼ cup (30g) **all-purpose flour**
1½ cups (360ml) **milk**
1 cup (240ml) **half-and-half** or light cream
½ teaspoon **mustard powder**
1 teaspoon **onion powder**
½ teaspoon **salt**
¼ teaspoon freshly ground **black pepper**
4 cups (454g) freshly grated **sharp cheddar cheese**, divided
½ cup (50g) freshly grated **Parmesan cheese**

# My All-Time Favorite
# Mac & Cheese

Mac and cheese is definitely my love language, and I can assure you, this version is absolutely the best! A good mac and cheese needs to be super creamy and cheesy, so when I created this recipe, I was very generous with the sauce-to-pasta ratio. The result is the most luscious pasta smothered in heaps of a rich, homemade cheese sauce with a bubbly cheesy crust. There's good reason this recipe gets rave reviews from everyone who tries it.

1. Preheat the oven to 425°F (220°C). Grease a 9 × 13-inch (22 × 33cm) baking dish and set aside.
2. In a large pot of boiling salted water, cook the macaroni al dente according to the package directions. Rinse under cold water and drain well. Set aside.
3. In a large saucepan, melt the butter over medium heat. Whisk in the flour and cook for 2 minutes, stirring constantly. Gradually whisk in the milk and half-and-half, stirring until smooth after each addition. Add the mustard powder, onion powder, salt, and pepper, and continue whisking and cooking until the mixture begins to boil and thicken. Boil 1 minute more, whisking continuously.
4. Remove from the heat and stir in 3 cups (340g) cheddar cheese and the Parmesan cheese until melted.
5. Combine the cheese sauce with the cooked macaroni and spread into the prepared baking dish. Top with the remaining 1 cup (113g) cheddar cheese.
6. Bake for 18 to 24 minutes or until just browned and bubbly. Do not overcook. Cool 10 to 15 minutes before serving.

 **SERVING SUGGESTIONS**
This mac and cheese is nice and saucy and is great as a meal on its own with a tossed salad and crusty bread. It's also the perfect side dish next to The Best Ever Meatloaf (page 190) or pulled pork.

 **VARIATION**
I love this casserole topped with cheese, but if you'd like to top it with a crumb topping, combine ½ cup (25g) panko bread crumbs with 2 tablespoons melted butter and 1 tablespoon Parmesan cheese. Sprinkle over the casserole before baking.

 **MAKE AHEAD**
This mac and cheese can be assembled 48 hours ahead of time. Prepare as directed through step 4. Reserve the remaining 1 cup (113g) cheddar cheese in a separate dish. Combine the macaroni and sauce and spread into the prepared baking dish. Cool the casserole before covering and refrigerating.

Remove the casserole from the fridge 45 minutes before baking. Preheat the oven to 400°F (200°C). Bake the casserole for 20 minutes. Stir and add up to ½ cup (120ml) warm milk until the mixture is creamy. Top with the reserved 1 cup (113g) cheddar cheese and bake for 10 to 12 additional minutes or until heated through and lightly browned.

Prep time: 15 minutes
Total time: 30 minutes
Serves 4

1 large **lemon**, plus additional lemon wedges for serving

⅔ cup (140g) prepared **basil pesto sauce**

12oz (340g) **medium shrimp**, peeled and deveined

3 cloves **garlic**, minced

½ teaspoon **salt**

¼ teaspoon freshly ground **black pepper**

1 tablespoon **butter**

8oz (227g) **angel hair pasta**

2 tablespoons chopped **fresh parsley**

**FOR THE CRUMBS**

3 tablespoons **panko bread crumbs**

1 tablespoon **butter**

1 tablespoon freshly grated **Parmesan cheese**

½ teaspoon freshly ground **black pepper**

---

**Ingredient Swaps**

- Replace the shrimp with **Garlic Butter Chicken Bites** (see Something on the Side, page 119).
- **To make this dish vegetarian,** swap the shrimp for 8 ounces (227g) asparagus spears cut into 1-inch (2.5cm) pieces. Pan-fry them with garlic butter for 4 to 7 minutes or until tender-crisp before tossing with the pasta.

# Lemon-Pesto Shrimp Pasta
## with Pepper Parm Crumbs

This pasta is simple to make and has just the right amount of fancy and elegant in one bowl! A quick and zesty lemon-infused pesto is tossed with pasta and topped with garlic butter shrimp. Add a sprinkle of toasted pepper Parmesan crumbs for some extra crunch and yum. This dish comes together incredibly fast, so be sure to measure all of the ingredients before you begin.

1. **To make the crumbs,** heat a 10-inch (25cm) nonstick skillet over medium-high heat. Add the bread crumbs, butter, Parmesan cheese, and pepper. Cook, stirring frequently, for 3 to 4 minutes or until lightly browned and fragrant. Transfer the bread crumbs to a bowl and set aside.
2. Zest the lemon and cut it in half. Juice 3 tablespoons of lemon juice. Stir the zest and juice into the pesto and set aside.
3. In a small bowl, combine the shrimp, garlic, salt, and pepper.
4. In the skillet used for the bread crumbs, melt 1 tablespoon butter. Add half of the shrimp and stir, cooking until the shrimp becomes opaque, about 3 to 4 minutes. Transfer the shrimp to a bowl and repeat with the remaining shrimp. Set aside.
5. Bring a large pot of salted water to a boil and cook the pasta al dente according to package directions. Drain the pasta, reserving ¼ cup (60ml) pasta water. Do not rinse.
6. Add the pasta back to the warm pot. Add the lemon pesto, the shrimp with any juices, and the parsley. Toss to combine, adding pasta water 1 tablespoon at a time as needed to thin the sauce and coat the pasta.
7. Spoon the pasta into bowls and top with the toasted crumbs. Serve with lemon wedges, if desired.

**TIPS**

- Double the crumbs if you'd like; they're packed with flavor and are great sprinkled over salads, pasta, or casseroles.
- I prefer to leave the shrimp tails on for a prettier presentation, but for easier eating, they can be removed before cooking.
- Did you know that pesto should not be cooked? Pesto can be tossed with warm pasta but is intended to be eaten uncooked for the best flavor. Overheating pesto can cause it to separate and become oily.

**FEELING FANCY?**

If you've got lots of fresh herbs or greens, homemade pesto is easy to make! Experiment with different greens in place of basil (arugula, kale, or spinach are great options) and different types of nuts in place of pine nuts, like almonds or pistachios. Homemade pesto tends to be a little bit thicker than prepared varieties and may need a little bit of extra pasta water to coat the pasta.

*Scan for my Easy Homemade Pesto recipe.*

**Prep Time:** 5 minutes
**Total Time:** 35 minutes
**Serves** 4

---

1lb (454g) **bulk Italian sausage**
8oz (227g) **penne**
2½–3 cups (600–720ml) **chicken broth**
1 (14oz / 397g) can **crushed tomatoes**
¾ cup (180ml) **heavy whipping cream**
1 teaspoon **dried basil**
½ teaspoon **dried oregano**
¾ teaspoon **salt**
¼ teaspoon freshly ground **black pepper**
2 cups (80g) gently packed chopped **fresh spinach** (optional)
¼ cup (25g) freshly grated **Parmesan cheese**

### Ingredient Swap

If you don't have Italian sausage, you can easily make **homemade Italian sausage** with any type of ground meat and a handful of seasonings.

*Scan for my Homemade Italian Sausage recipe.*

# One-Pan Sausage & Penne
## in Creamy Rose Sauce

This sausage penne is fast and flavorful with a delicious creamy rose sauce. Layers of flavor are cooked right into the pasta using a few simple ingredients and one single pot—no strainer required. It's perfect for busy weeknights (you won't believe how easily it comes together), and with almost no cleanup, you'll be making it on repeat.

1. Heat a large, deep skillet or Dutch oven over medium-high heat. Add the Italian sausage, breaking up the meat with a spoon, and cook for 5 to 6 minutes or until no pink remains. Drain any fat.
2. Stir in the penne, 2½ cups (600ml) broth, crushed tomatoes, cream, basil, oregano, salt, and pepper. Bring to a boil over medium-high heat, then reduce to a simmer. Cook uncovered, stirring occasionally, for 14 to 18 minutes or until the pasta is tender, adding more broth or water if the sauce becomes too thick.
3. Remove from the heat and stir in the spinach, if using, and the Parmesan cheese.

---

 **SERVING SUGGESTIONS**

I love to serve pasta dishes with bread to sop up any bits of sauce in the bottom of the bowl, my Garlic Herb Bread (page 255) is the perfect addition. If you'd like to add a fresh salad, a vinaigrette like The Everyday Salad Dressing (page 252), complements this dish beautifully.

 **TIPS**

- If desired, ½ teaspoon red pepper flakes can be added to the sauce.
- Use heavy whipping cream for this recipe; half-and-half or light cream can curdle.

**Prep Time:** 10 minutes
**Total Time:** 30 minutes
**Serves** 4

6 cups (1.2kg) **cherry tomatoes**, halved
4 cloves **garlic**, minced
3 tablespoons **olive oil**
2 tablespoons **balsamic vinegar**
½ teaspoon **dried basil**
½ teaspoon **dried oregano**
½ teaspoon **salt**
¼ teaspoon freshly ground **black pepper**
1lb (454g) **spaghetti** or linguine
¼ cup (25g) freshly grated **Parmesan cheese**, to garnish
F**resh basil**, to garnish

# Kailey's Roasted Balsamic **Cherry Tomato Pasta**

This has been a favorite dish for my daughter Kailey since she was about 8 years old. Don't let the simplicity fool you—while this dish uses minimal ingredients, it's absolutely jam-packed with fresh flavor. Cherry tomatoes are roasted with seasonings, a splash of balsamic vinegar, and a drizzle of olive oil until tender and saucy. Toss them with pasta, Parmesan cheese, and basil for a new family favorite so ridiculously easy it'll earn a top spot in your regular rotation.

1. Preheat the oven to 425°F (220°C). Bring a large pot of salted water to a boil. Cover and reduce the heat to low.
2. Spray a rimmed baking sheet with cooking spray. Add the cherry tomatoes, garlic, oil, balsamic vinegar, dried basil, oregano, salt, and pepper, and toss to combine.
3. Roast for 15 minutes or until the tomatoes are tender. Meanwhile, bring the water back to a boil and cook the spaghetti according to the package directions. Reserve ½ cup (120ml) pasta water and drain the pasta without rinsing.
4. Add the drained pasta to the sheet pan and toss well to coat with the tomatoes and seasoning; add a few tablespoons of reserved pasta water if needed to achieve a saucy consistency.
5. Garnish with the Parmesan cheese and fresh basil before serving.

**SERVING SUGGESTIONS**
Top this dish with Perfect Baked Chicken Breasts (page 247) or grilled shrimp.

**TIP**
Replace the cherry tomatoes with another variety of fresh garden tomato. Cut the tomatoes into ½-inch (1.5cm) chunks and increase the roasting time by 10 to 15 minutes, for a total of 25 to 30 minutes. The tomatoes will appear juicy during the first half of cooking, but most of the liquid will evaporate. Remove them from the oven once tender and saucy; there should still be a very small amount of juice on the pan.

**Prep Time:** 10 minutes
**Total Time:** 25 minutes
**Serves** 4

4 tablespoons **unsalted butter**
2 cloves **garlic**, minced
2 cups (480ml) **heavy whipping cream**
¾ cup (75g) freshly grated **Parmesan cheese**
⅜ teaspoon **salt**
¼ teaspoon freshly ground **black pepper**
Pinch of **nutmeg**

# Fast! Homemade **Alfredo Sauce**

Alfredo sauce is a classic for good reason! With its super smooth and buttery texture, this sauce is incredibly rich and decadent. I love that it comes together in just minutes with only a handful of ingredients and can be tossed with fettuccine or other pasta shapes for a quick and easy dinner. Sneak in some veggies like peas, broccoli, or spinach.

1. In a 10-inch (25cm) nonstick skillet, melt the butter over medium heat. Stir in the garlic and cook just until fragrant, about 1 minute.
2. Add the heavy cream, increase the heat to medium-high, and bring to a boil. Reduce the heat to a gentle boil and cook uncovered, whisking occasionally, until slightly thickened, about 8 to 10 minutes.
3. Reduce the heat to low and whisk in the Parmesan cheese, salt, pepper, and nutmeg until smooth.

 **VARIATIONS**

| | |
|---|---|
| **Lemon Alfredo** | Stir the zest from 1 lemon plus 1 tablespoon fresh lemon juice into the thickened Alfredo sauce. |
| **Pesto Alfredo** | Stir ¼ cup (56g) prepared pesto into the thickened sauce before serving. |
| **Truffle Alfredo** | Stir 1 teaspoon truffle oil into the thickened sauce. The strength of truffle oil can vary by brand, so taste and add additional oil as needed. |
| **Bacon Alfredo** | Before preparing the Alfredo sauce, cook 4 slices of bacon in the skillet until crisp. Remove the bacon, leaving the fat in the pan. Add the butter to the bacon fat and prepare the recipe as directed. Finely chop the bacon and stir it into the Alfredo sauce before serving. |

 **SERVING SUGGESTIONS**

This recipe makes 2 cups of sauce, enough for 1 pound (454g) of pasta. Cook the pasta al dente according to the package directions. Drain the pasta well (do not rinse), reserving ¼ cup (60ml) pasta water. Toss the sauce, a little bit at a time, with the drained pasta. You may not use all of the sauce. Add reserved pasta water 1 tablespoon at a time to reach desired consistency. The sauce will thicken slightly as the pasta cools.

 **TIPS**

- For a smooth and flavorful Alfredo sauce, it's important to grate your own Parmesan cheese from a block using the finest side of a cheese grater or a food processor. If using purchased grated cheese, the sauce will still taste delicious, but depending on the brand, the sauce may not be as smooth.
- Use heavy whipping cream; lighter versions don't thicken well in this recipe.

 **MAKE AHEAD**

This sauce can be prepared ahead of time and refrigerated for up to 4 days before adding it to pasta or vegetables. Reheat the sauce in a skillet over low heat while whisking. The sauce will separate slightly as it begins to reheat; continue whisking over low heat until it is warmed and smooth. Alfredo sauce tossed with pasta does not reheat well.

**Prep Time:** 25 minutes
**Total Time:** 40 minutes
**Serves** 4

---

8oz (227g) **spaghetti**

1 tablespoon **vegetable oil**

12oz (340g) **medium shrimp,** peeled and deveined, tails removed, thawed if frozen

1½ teaspoons minced **fresh ginger**

2 cloves **garlic,** minced

¼ teaspoon **salt**

¼ teaspoon freshly ground **black pepper**

4 cups (260g) thinly sliced **green cabbage**

1 **red bell pepper,** thinly sliced

**Lime wedges,** for serving

**FOR THE SAUCE**

½ cup (120ml) **chicken broth**

2½ tablespoons **creamy peanut butter**

2 tablespoons **soy sauce**

2 tablespoons **honey**

1½ tablespoons freshly squeezed **lime juice**

2 teaspoons **toasted sesame oil**

1–3 teaspoons **garlic-chili paste** (sambal oelek)

---

**Ingredient Swaps**

- Replace the shrimp with 12 ounces (340g) thinly sliced **boneless, skinless chicken breast.**
- **To make this dish vegetarian,** replace the chicken broth with vegetable broth and exclude the shrimp. Add an additional 2 cups (125g) chopped vegetables such as broccoli or bell peppers. Add with the cabbage in step 5 and cook just until tender-crisp.

# Spicy-As-You-Like-It
# Shrimp Peanut Noodles

These creamy peanut noodles have been a family favorite for years. My daughter makes them all the time because they're both fast and fabulous—and my grandson Jaxson cannot get enough. A creamy, nutty sauce with tender noodles and shrimp, chicken, or veggies, it's the perfect balance of sweet and savory. And of course, make it *as spicy as you like it* with more or less chili paste.

1. **To make the sauce,** in a small bowl, combine the broth, peanut butter, soy sauce, honey, lime juice, sesame oil, and garlic-chili paste. Mix well and set aside.
2. In a large pot of boiling salted water, cook the spaghetti al dente according to the package directions. Drain well; do not rinse.
3. While the spaghetti is cooking, heat the vegetable oil in a 12-inch (30cm) skillet over medium-high heat.
4. In a medium bowl, toss the shrimp with the ginger, garlic, salt, and pepper. Add the shrimp to the preheated skillet and cook just until pink, about 3 minutes. Remove the shrimp from the skillet and set aside, lightly covered with foil.
5. Add the cabbage and red bell pepper to the skillet and cook until tender-crisp, about 3 to 4 minutes. Set aside with the shrimp.
6. Add the prepared sauce to the skillet and bring to a boil. Boil for 1 minute. Stir in the cooked spaghetti and shrimp with vegetables and toss well to combine. Cook just until heated through.
7. Serve with lime wedges.

---

 **SERVING SUGGESTIONS**
Garnish with fresh bean sprouts, crushed peanuts, green onions, and cilantro.

 **MAKE AHEAD**
This is a great recipe to prep ahead on the weekend for a quick meal during the week! Place the sauce ingredients in a jar with a lid and give it a quick shake before adding to the skillet. Veggies can be chopped and stored in the fridge up to 3 days ahead of time.

 **TIPS**
- Be sure to allow the skillet to preheat for the best sear on the shrimp.
- *Sambal oelek* is a flavorful garlic-chili paste found in the international food aisle of most grocery stores. If you don't have sambal on hand, replace it with sriracha or your favorite spicy chili sauce.
- You can adjust the heat level with as little or as much sambal oelek as you'd like. I like to use about 2 teaspoons.

**Prep Time:** 15 minutes
**Total Time:** 35 minutes
**Serves** 4

---

### FOR THE CHICKEN

4 **chicken cutlets**, ½ inch
(1.5cm) thick
¼ cup (56g) **mayonnaise**
⅜ teaspoon **salt**, divided
⅜ teaspoon freshly ground
**black pepper**, divided
⅓ cup (17g) **panko bread crumbs**
¼ cup (25g) freshly grated
**Parmesan cheese**
1 tablespoon **butter**, melted

### FOR THE PASTA

12oz (340g) **campanelle** or
medium pasta shells
1 (16oz / 454g) jar **roasted red
peppers,** drained
⅔ cup (160ml) **heavy whipping
cream**
1½ tablespoons **tomato paste**
⅛ teaspoon **salt**
1 tablespoon **olive oil**
2 cloves **garlic**, minced
1 teaspoon **dried basil**
½ cup (50g) shredded **Parmesan
cheese**
**Red pepper flakes** (optional),
to garnish

> **Ingredient Swap**
> Replace mayonnaise with **Greek
> yogurt,** if desired.

# Roasted Red Pepper Pasta
## with Crispy Parmesan Chicken

On the table in just over 30 minutes, this pasta is equal parts delicious and cozy. It starts with a super easy blender sauce that's both light and creamy with lots of sweet roasted red pepper flavor. Each serving is topped with the most tender chicken and crowned with a crispy, crunchy Parmesan crumb topping; it's the perfect weeknight meal.

1. Preheat the oven to 425°F (220°C).
2. **To make the chicken,** in a medium bowl, toss the cutlets with the mayonnaise, ¼ teaspoon salt, and ¼ teaspoon pepper.
3. In a separate small bowl, combine the bread crumbs, Parmesan cheese, butter, and the remaining ⅛ teaspoon each salt and pepper.
4. Place the chicken on a baking sheet, sprinkle the breadcrumb mixture over the top of the chicken, and gently press to adhere. Bake for 16 to 18 minutes or until they reach an internal temperature of 165°F (74°C).
5. Meanwhile, bring a large pot of salted water to a boil. Cook the pasta al dente according to the package directions. Reserve ½ cup (120ml) pasta water and drain well; do not rinse. Set aside.
6. **To make the sauce,** in a blender, combine the drained roasted red peppers, heavy cream, tomato paste, and salt. Blend until smooth and set aside.
7. In a 10-inch (25cm) skillet, heat the olive oil over medium heat. Add the garlic and basil and cook just until fragrant, about 1 minute. Stir in the blended red pepper mixture and let simmer for 5 to 6 minutes or until slightly thickened. Stir in the cooked pasta and Parmesan cheese, adding the reserved pasta water if needed to reach a creamy consistency. Season with additional salt and pepper to taste.
8. Divide the pasta among 4 bowls. Slice the chicken and add to each bowl. Garnish with red pepper flakes, if using.

---

**SERVING SUGGESTIONS**
This dish is fabulous served with fresh basil and parsley. If you're feeling particularly indulgent, tear some burrata and add a little bit to each serving.

**HEY! IT'S OKAY TO . . .**
Replace the chicken cutlets with prepared frozen crispy chicken strips. Bake them crispy according to the package directions, slice them up, and top the pasta for some added crunch.

**FEELING FANCY?**
Make your own roasted red peppers. Preheat the oven to 450°F (230°C). Place 2 whole red bell peppers on a rimmed baking sheet and roast for 35 minutes, flipping after 15 minutes. Once roasted, cover the peppers with foil or a lid and rest for 10 to 15 minutes or until cool enough to handle. Peel off the skin and cut the pepper open. Discard the seeds and stem.

**Prep Time:** 25 minutes
**Total Time:** 1 hour 25 minutes
**Serves** 8

3 tablespoons **olive oil**
1 small **yellow onion**, finely diced
2 ribs **celery**, finely diced
1 medium **carrot**, shredded
1lb (454g) **lean ground beef**
½lb (227g) **bulk Italian sausage**
4 cloves **garlic**, minced
1 (14oz / 397g) can **whole tomatoes**, with juices
1 (28oz / 794g) can **crushed tomatoes**
¾ cup (180ml) **water**
2 tablespoons **tomato paste**
1 teaspoon **granulated sugar**
1 teaspoon **dried oregano**
½ teaspoon **dried basil**
½ teaspoon **salt**
½ teaspoon freshly ground **black pepper**
2 **bay leaves**

### Ingredient Swap

Replace the ground beef or sausage with an equal amount of **ground meat** (any variety). If replacing the sausage with unseasoned ground meat, add ¾ teaspoon Italian seasoning (for homemade, see page 18) to the sauce.

# All-Purpose **Meaty Pasta Sauce**

I love the versatility of a great pasta sauce. As simple as it may seem, this sauce is thick, meaty, and packed with rich, zesty tomato flavor. It's perfect over pasta, layered with lasagna, or added to casseroles. Go ahead and make a double or triple batch—this sauce freezes beautifully for a quick from-scratch meal when time is short.

1. In a large 5-quart (4.7L) Dutch oven or heavy-bottomed saucepan, heat the oil over medium-high heat.
2. Add the onion, celery, and carrot, and cook, stirring occasionally, for 3 to 5 minutes until the onion is softened. Add the ground beef and sausage and cook, breaking up the meat with a spoon, for 5 to 6 minutes or until no pink remains. Drain any fat. Stir in the garlic and cook for 1 minute more.
3. Add the whole tomatoes with juices to the Dutch oven, breaking up the tomatoes with your hands as you add them. Scrape up any brown bits on the bottom of the pan.
4. Stir in the crushed tomatoes, water, tomato paste, sugar, oregano, basil, salt, pepper, and bay leaves. Cover and simmer for 15 minutes.
5. Uncover and simmer for an additional 45 minutes or until the sauce reaches the desired thickness. Remove and discard the bay leaves. Season with additional salt and pepper to taste.

### TO PREPARE IN A SLOW COOKER

If using a slow cooker, reduce the water to ½ cup (120ml) and omit the oil.

1. Heat a large skillet over medium-high heat. Cook the beef, sausage, and onion, breaking up the meat with a spoon, for 5 to 6 minutes until the beef is cooked and no pink remains. Drain any fat. Stir in the garlic and cook until fragrant, about 1 minute.
2. Transfer the browned meat to a 6-quart (5.7L) slow cooker. Add the celery, carrot, crushed tomatoes, ½ cup (120ml) water, tomato paste, sugar, oregano, basil, salt, pepper, and bay leaves. Break up the whole tomatoes with your hands and add them to the slow cooker.
3. Cook on low for 7 to 9 hours or on high for 3 to 4 hours. Discard the bay leaves before serving.

**SERVING SUGGESTIONS**
Pile this sauce over pasta, spoon it between layers of lasagna, or use it to stuff zucchini.

**TIPS**
- Brands or varieties of canned tomatoes can vary in acidity. If needed, add additional sugar, ¼ teaspoon at a time.
- This recipe yields approximately 7 cups (1.68L) of sauce.

**MAKE AHEAD**
Prepare the recipe as directed and cool completely. Once cooled, ladle into zipper-lock freezer bags or an airtight freezerproof container and freeze for up to 4 months.
To reheat, thaw in the fridge overnight and heat on the stovetop. If you're short on time, smaller portions can be thawed straight from the freezer in a saucepan on the stovetop over medium heat.

# Sheet Pan
## *Dinners*

**138**  Sticky Honey-Garlic Drumsticks with Peppers & Snap Peas

**141**  Crispy Oven Schnitzel Burgers with Zesty Dill Pickle Slaw

**142**  Sheet Pan Steak with Warm Potato Salad
& Horseradish Sauce

**145**  Bacon-Wrapped Pork Tenderloin
with Roasted Brussels Sprouts

**146**  Sheet Pan Cheeseburgers with Crispy Potato Wedges

**149**  One-Pan Smoked Sausage & Roasted Veggies

**150**  Lemon Herb-Crusted Salmon with Garlic Green Beans

**153**  Zucchini Turkey Meatballs with Roasted Tomato Sauce

**154**  Breakfast-for-Dinner Sheet Pan Chorizo Hash

**157**  Crunchy Pecan Chicken with Honey-Roasted
Sweet Potatoes

---

**FOR THE CHICKEN**

8 **chicken drumsticks**, about
    2lb (907g) total

½ teaspoon **salt**

½ teaspoon freshly ground
    **black pepper**

1 thinly sliced **green onion,**
    to garnish

**FOR THE SAUCE**

¼ cup (60ml) **soy sauce**

1 tablespoon **cornstarch**

½ cup (120ml) **honey**

1 tablespoon minced **fresh ginger**

6 cloves **garlic**, minced

1 **green onion**, thinly sliced

**FOR THE VEGETABLES**

1 **red bell pepper**, sliced ½ inch
    (1.5cm) thick

8oz (227g) **snap peas**, about
    3 cups

2 teaspoons **vegetable oil**

1 teaspoon **sesame seeds**

1 clove **garlic**, minced

¾ teaspoon **salt**

---

**Ingredient Swap**

Replace the drumsticks with
4 **boneless, skinless chicken
breasts.** Bake the chicken breasts
for 15 minutes. Baste both sides with
the sauce and add the vegetables to
the pan. Bake for an additional 10 to
15 minutes or until the chicken
reaches an internal temperature of
165°F (74°C). Broil for 1 minute more,
if desired.

# Sticky Honey-Garlic Drumsticks
## with Peppers & Snap Peas

This sheet pan dinner is everything you could ever want in a meal—sweet, sticky, delicious, fresh, and, best of all, easy! Chicken drumsticks are glazed with a quick homemade honey-garlic sauce and roasted until juicy inside with a sticky-crisp skin. The real MVP of this dish is the sauce; it's ready in less than 5 minutes and so finger-lickin' good, you'll want to eat it by the spoonful. With tender-crisp sesame veggies perfectly cooked on the same pan, cleanup is a breeze!

1. **To make the chicken,** preheat the oven to 400°F (200°C). Line a 13 × 18-inch (33 × 46cm) rimmed baking sheet with foil and spray generously with cooking spray.
2. Place the drumsticks on the prepared pan and season with ½ teaspoon each salt and pepper. Bake for 20 minutes.
3. Meanwhile, **to make the sauce,** in a small skillet, whisk together the soy sauce and cornstarch. Add the honey, ginger, garlic, and green onion and whisk until smooth. Place the skillet over medium-high heat and stir continuously until the mixture comes to a rolling boil. Reduce the heat to medium and boil for 3 to 4 minutes or until the mixture is thick. Remove from the heat.
4. **To make the vegetables,** in a medium bowl, mix the bell pepper, snap peas, oil, sesame seeds, garlic, and ¾ teaspoon salt.
5. Remove the baking sheet from the oven and brush the drumsticks with half of the sauce. Turn over the drumsticks and brush the other side with the remaining half of the sauce. Arrange the vegetables around the chicken.
6. Return the baking sheet to the oven and roast for an additional 12 to 15 minutes or until the chicken has reached an internal temperature of 165°F (74°C). Broil 4 inches (10cm) from the broiler for 1 to 2 additional minutes, if desired.
7. Let the chicken rest for 5 minutes before serving.

---

**SERVING SUGGESTIONS**

This chicken pairs well with white rice or Simply Seasoned Garlic Rice (page 259). For heartier appetites, double the sauce and drumsticks and divide the recipe over two pans (see Tips).

**TIPS**

- The sauce bakes up sticky and sweet in this recipe, which is great for the drumsticks but not so great for the baking sheet! Be sure to line the baking sheet with foil to catch all of the sauce and make cleanup a breeze.
- Avoid overcrowding the baking sheet or the veggies will steam, not roast. If you don't have a 13 × 18-inch (33 × 46cm) baking sheet (or if you're doubling the chicken and sauce), use two smaller sheets. The exact size of the baking sheet can vary; just ensure that there is enough space for the chicken to be arranged without the pieces touching one another.

**TO PREPARE IN AN AIR FRYER**

Preheat the air fryer to 400°F (200°C). There is no need to brown the bread crumbs if cooking in the air fryer. Instead, combine seasoned bread crumbs, panko, 2 tablespoons melted butter, ½ teaspoon salt, and pepper. Coat the pounded pork in flour, egg, and the bread crumb mixture. Air-fry in a single layer, in batches if needed, for 6 minutes, flipping after 3 minutes. Remove the schnitzel from the air fryer and warm the buns in the air fryer for 1 minute.

**Prep Time:** 25 minutes
**Total Time:** 45 minutes
**Serves** 4

---

**FOR THE SCHNITZEL**

2 tablespoons **butter**

⅔ cup (78g) **seasoned bread crumbs**

½ cup (25g) **panko bread crumbs**

1 teaspoon **salt**, divided

¼ teaspoon freshly ground **black pepper**

¼ cup (30g) **all-purpose flour**

1 **egg**, beaten

2 tablespoons freshly squeezed **lemon juice**

2 **center-cut pork chops**, ¾ inch (2cm) thick, about 1lb (454g) total

4 **lemon** wedges, to serve

**Mayonnaise** (optional), to serve

**FOR THE SLAW**

2 medium **dill pickles**

2 cups (182g) **coleslaw mix** or shredded cabbage

3 tablespoons **mayonnaise**

1 tablespoon **dill pickle juice**

½ teaspoon **granulated sugar**

⅛ teaspoon **salt**

**FOR THE BUNS**

4 **pretzel buns** or hamburger buns

2 tablespoons **butter**

¼ teaspoon **garlic powder**

---

**Ingredient Swap**

Replace the pork chops with 2 **boneless, skinless chicken breasts.** Cut the breasts in half horizontally and use the flat side of a meat mallet to pound to an even thickness of ¼ inch (0.6cm). Bake at 450°F (230°C) for 12 to 14 minutes; flip the breasts after 8 minutes.

# Crispy Oven Schnitzel Burgers
## with Zesty Dill Pickle Slaw

There's a local German restaurant on the beach near my house that serves up a crispy fried schnitzel that dreams are made of. Simple and incredibly delicious, this recipe skips the oil and the frying to create a totally craveable oven-baked schnitzel with a crispy, crunchy coating around tender pork. Tuck them into pretzel buns, add a squeeze of fresh lemon, and pile them high with zesty dill pickle slaw for the ultimate handheld bite.

1. Preheat the oven to 450°F (230°C). Arrange an oven-safe rack on a 13 × 18-inch (33 × 46cm) rimmed baking sheet.
2. **To prepare the buns,** butter the pretzel bun halves, sprinkle with garlic powder, and set aside.
3. **To make the schnitzel,** in a 10-inch (25cm) skillet, heat the butter over medium-low heat. Add the seasoned and panko bread crumbs to the skillet, and cook until golden brown, about 4 to 5 minutes. Transfer the bread crumbs to a shallow dish and add ½ teaspoon salt and the pepper. Cool completely.
4. Place the flour in a second shallow dish. In a third shallow dish, whisk together the egg and lemon juice. Set aside.
5. Trim any fat from the pork chops and cut them in half horizontally. Use the textured side of a meat mallet to pound to an even thickness of ¼ inch (0.6cm).
6. Pat the pork dry with a paper towel and season the pork with the remaining ½ teaspoon salt. Dip the pork in the dish of flour, followed by the egg mixture, and finally, the bread crumbs, pressing gently to adhere.
7. Place the schnitzel on the prepared baking sheet and bake for 8 minutes. Turn over the schnitzel, add the buns butter side up to the edges of the pan, and bake for an additional 4 to 6 minutes or until the pork reaches an internal temperature of 145°F (60°C).
8. Meanwhile, **to make the slaw,** use the large side of a box grater to grate the pickles. In a medium bowl, combine the coleslaw mix, grated dill pickles, mayonnaise, dill pickle juice, sugar, and salt.
9. To assemble, top each bun with ½ cup (50g) of the dill pickle slaw and 1 pork schnitzel. Squeeze fresh lemon juice over top and add a smear of mayonnaise, if you'd like.

---

**TIPS**
- Don't skip browning the bread crumbs; since this recipe cooks quickly, they won't brown in the oven. Browning the crumbs before baking ensures a perfectly crispy coating with tender pork.
- The baking sheet will be full; add the buns around the edges of the pan. It's okay if they overhang a little bit.

**SERVING SUGGESTIONS**
We love these burgers with a side of thick-cut kettle chips or french fries.

**Prep Time:** 10 minutes
**Total Time:** 50 minutes
**Serves** 4

_____

2 **striploin steaks**, cut 1 inch
   (2.5cm) thick
1 tablespoon **butter,** melted
1 tablespoon **steak seasoning**
¼ teaspoon **smoked paprika**
2lb (907g) **baby potatoes**, halved
1 tablespoon **olive oil**
1 teaspoon **garlic powder**
½ teaspoon **salt**
1 rib **celery** (optional), finely diced
2 **green onions**, thinly sliced
1 tablespoon **prepared**
   **horseradish**

**FOR THE SAUCE**
½ cup (120g) **sour cream**
¼ cup (56g) **mayonnaise**
1 tablespoon freshly squeezed
   **lemon juice**
¼ teaspoon **salt**
¼ teaspoon freshly ground
   **black pepper**

# Sheet Pan Steak
## with Warm Potato Salad & Horseradish Sauce

This sheet pan meal is literally the easiest steak dinner you'll ever make. My dad makes the best steaks, and one of his secrets to a great steak is adding butter to it before cooking. Not only does butter add flavor, but it also helps the seasonings stick. These steaks come out perfectly cooked and are served alongside a warm potato salad—all cooked on one pan.

1. Preheat the oven to 450°F (230°C). Line a rimmed baking sheet with foil.
2. Pat the steaks dry with a paper towel. Brush both sides of the steak with the melted butter and season with the steak seasoning and smoked paprika. Set aside.
3. Toss the potatoes with the oil, garlic powder, and ½ teaspoon salt. Spread evenly on the prepared baking sheet and roast for 15 minutes.
4. Meanwhile, **to make the sauce,** in a small bowl, whisk the sour cream, mayonnaise, lemon juice, ¼ teaspoon salt, and pepper.
5. After 15 minutes of roasting, stir the potatoes and move them to one side of the baking sheet. Place the steaks on the empty side of the baking sheet. Return the baking sheet to the oven and cook for 11 to 15 minutes or until the steaks reach the desired doneness. (For medium rare, cook 12 minutes for a 1-inch [2.5cm] steak.)
6. Remove the pan from the oven and place the steaks on a plate. Cover loosely with foil and set aside to rest for 5 to 7 minutes.
7. Meanwhile, transfer the roasted potatoes to a medium bowl and add the celery, if using, and green onions. Add ½ cup (120ml) of the sauce to the potatoes and toss to combine.
8. Mix the horseradish into the remaining sauce for serving with the steaks.
9. Cut the rested steaks into ½-inch (1.5cm) slices and serve with the warm potato salad and horseradish sauce.

**SERVING SUGGESTIONS**
This sheet pan dinner is a complete meal on its own, but feel free to add some sautéed mushrooms and a slice of garlic toast for serving.

**TIPS**
• The salt levels in steak seasoning can vary by brand. Taste a little bit of the seasoning, and if needed, add additional salt when seasoning the steak.
• For a browned crust on the steak, after resting, place the steak on a *new piece of foil* on the baking sheet. Broil on high 4 inches (10cm) from the heat for 2 to 3 minutes or until charred. Slice immediately as directed.
• Ensure that the steaks are 1 inch (2.5cm) thick for the best results. Thinner steaks will cook faster, while thicker steaks may need extra time.
• Steaks can be cooked to your desired doneness. Cook to these internal temperatures: medium rare (warm, red center) 135°F (57°C); medium (warm, pink center) 145°F (63°C); medium well (slightly pink center) 150°F (66°C). Remove the steak from the heat about 3°F to 4°F (1–2°C) before it reaches the desired temperature since the temperature will continue to rise as it rests.

**LOVE YOUR LEFTOVERS**

Leftover steak makes a great steak sandwich. Brush sourdough or artisan bread with softened garlic butter and place bread 4 inches (10cm) under the broiler and broil until golden, about 2 to 3 minutes per side. In a medium skillet, heat 1½ teaspoons olive oil over medium-high heat. Add the slices of leftover steak and cook just until heated through, about 2 to 3 minutes. Spread the toast with Dijon mustard, add the steak strips, top with a slice of provolone cheese, and broil again, if desired. Serve open-faced.

**Prep Time:** 15 minutes
**Total Time:** 40 minutes
**Serves** 4

1lb (454g) **pork tenderloin**
1 teaspoon **garlic powder**, divided
1 teaspoon **salt**, divided
½ teaspoon freshly ground
   **black pepper**, divided
8 slices uncooked **bacon**
1½ tablespoons **brown sugar**
1lb (454g) fresh **Brussels sprouts**
1½ tablespoons **olive oil**

# Bacon-Wrapped Pork Tenderloin
## with Roasted Brussels Sprouts

This pork tenderloin is incredibly simple to prepare, but it'll make you look like a gourmet chef! Lean, tender pork is wrapped in crisp, brown-sugared bacon and roasted with Brussels sprouts until perfectly juicy. This is a delicious weeknight meal but elegant enough for special occasions. No one will ever guess how easy it is to prepare!

1. Preheat the oven to 400°F (200°C) and line a 13 × 18-inch (33 × 46cm) rimmed baking sheet with foil.
2. Remove any silverskin from the pork tenderloin and pat it dry with a paper towel. Sprinkle the pork with ½ teaspoon garlic powder, ½ teaspoon salt, and ¼ teaspoon pepper.
3. Wrap the bacon slices around the pork tenderloin, ensuring the bacon slices are slightly overlapping, and secure them by weaving toothpicks into the ends of the bacon as needed.
4. In a 12-inch (30cm) skillet over medium-high heat, cook the bacon-wrapped tenderloin for about 3 minutes per side or until the bacon begins to brown.
5. Place the browned tenderloin on the prepared baking sheet and rub the brown sugar over the bacon on all sides. Roast in the oven for 10 minutes.
6. Meanwhile, cut the Brussels sprouts in half lengthwise if they are larger than 1 inch (2.5cm) in diameter. Toss them with the oil and remaining ½ teaspoon garlic powder, ½ teaspoon salt, and ¼ teaspoon pepper. Add the Brussels sprouts to the sheet pan with the pork.
7. Roast for an additional 10 to 13 minutes or until the pork tenderloin reaches an internal temperature of 145°F (63°C) at the thickest part.
8. Remove the baking sheet from the oven and transfer the pork to a plate to rest for 5 to 7 minutes.
9. Remove the toothpicks from the pork and slice it into 1-inch (2.5cm) pieces. Serve with the Brussels sprouts.

**TIPS**

- Pork tenderloin has a shiny membrane (called *silverskin*) which should be removed because it can be tough. Place a small sharp knife under the silverskin and slide it along the skin to remove this. If your pork tenderloin has any fatty bits, they can be removed as well.
- The Brussels sprouts cook quickly because the pan is hot when you add them. Check them with a fork when

removing the pork from the oven; they should be tender. They will continue to cook slightly on the hot pan while the pork rests.
- For heartier appetites or planned leftovers, two pork tenderloins can be cooked at the same time. Ensure you use a large baking sheet, so it isn't overcrowded and there is space between the tenderloins.

**MAKE AHEAD**

- Season the pork and wrap it in bacon up to 48 hours in advance and store it tightly covered in the fridge. Remove it from the fridge at least 15 minutes before cooking. Brown the bacon just before baking.
- The Brussels sprouts can be washed, cut, and refrigerated for up to 3 days before cooking. Add oil and season just before roasting.

# Sheet Pan Cheeseburgers
## with Crispy Potato Wedges

**Prep Time:** 20 minutes
**Total Time:** 50 minutes
**Serves** 4

---

### FOR THE POTATO WEDGES
1½lb (680g) unpeeled **russet potatoes,** about 3 medium potatoes
3 tablespoons **olive oil**
1 teaspoon **garlic powder**
1 teaspoon **seasoned salt**
½ teaspoon **dried rosemary,** crushed

### FOR THE BURGER PATTIES
1lb (454g) **lean ground beef**
¼ cup (28g) **seasoned bread crumbs**
1 **egg**
2 teaspoons **Worcestershire sauce**
1 teaspoon **onion powder**
½ teaspoon **garlic powder**
½ teaspoon **smoked paprika**
½ teaspoon **salt**
¼ teaspoon freshly ground **black pepper**

### FOR SERVING
4 slices **cheddar cheese,** about 4oz (113g) total
4 **hamburger buns**
**Additional toppings,** as desired

*Scan for instructions to prepare in an air fryer.*

These easy sheet pan cheeseburgers are a complete meal in one pan, and you'll be amazed at how juicy they are! The secret to really great baked cheeseburgers lies in adding a little sprinkle of breadcrumbs to the meat mixture; it ensures they stay extra juicy and helps them hold their shape, no flipping required. Best of all, they're baked alongside crispy potato-wedge fries for a perfect dinner duo that the whole family will love.

1. Preheat the oven to 400°F (200°C). Line a 13 × 18-inch (33 × 46cm) baking sheet with parchment paper.
2. **To make the potato wedges,** scrub the potatoes and cut them in half lengthwise. Cut each half, lengthwise, into 4 wedges. Toss the potatoes with the oil, 1 teaspoon garlic powder, seasoned salt, and rosemary. Place them in a single layer on the prepared baking sheet. Bake for 20 minutes.
3. **To make the burger patties,** while the potatoes are baking, in a medium bowl, combine the ground beef, bread crumbs, egg, Worcestershire sauce, onion powder, ½ teaspoon garlic powder, smoked paprika, salt, and pepper. Form the mixture into four patties, 4½ inches (11.5cm) in diameter. Use your thumb or the back of a measuring spoon to press a ½-inch (1.5cm) indent into the center of each patty.
4. Remove the baking sheet from the oven, turn the potatoes over, and move them to one side. Add the beef patties to the other side of the baking sheet and cook for an additional 9 to 12 minutes or until the center of each patty reaches 160°F (71°C) on an instant-read thermometer.
5. Remove the baking sheet from the oven and immediately add a cheddar slice on top of each patty. Let the patties and potatoes rest on the baking sheet for 5 minutes, allowing the cheese to melt.
6. **To serve,** place the burger patties on buns and add desired toppings. Serve with potato wedges.

---

 **TIP**
The cooking time for the burger patties is dependent on starting with a hot pan from cooking the potato wedges. If you are cooking the beef without the potatoes, preheat an empty baking sheet in the oven for 5 to 7 minutes before adding the patties.

 **MAKE AHEAD**
Prepare the burger patties and place them in a sealed container separated by parchment paper. Store them in the fridge for up to 48 hours before cooking. Potato wedges can be cut up to 24 hours ahead of time and stored in cold water in the fridge. Pat them very dry with paper towels before cooking. Remove the burgers from the fridge and let them rest at room temperature for at least 20 minutes before baking.

**Prep Time:** 15 minutes
**Total Time:** 55 minutes
**Serves** 4

---

1lb (454g) **red potatoes**, peeled
and cut into 1-inch (2.5cm)
pieces

2 medium **carrots**, cut into
½-inch (1.5cm) slices

2 **ears corn**, cut into 2-inch (5cm)
pieces

1 **red bell pepper**, cut into 1-inch
(2.5cm) pieces

8oz (227g) **cremini mushrooms**,
halved if large

1lb (454g) **smoked sausage**, cut
into ¾-inch (2cm) slices

**Fresh herbs,** such as oregano or
parsley (optional), to garnish

**FOR THE SAUCE**

¾ cup (180ml) **barbecue sauce**,
divided

¼ cup (56g) **mayonnaise**

**FOR THE SEASONING MIX**

3 tablespoons **olive oil**

2 cloves **garlic**, minced

1 teaspoon **dried oregano**

1 teaspoon **salt**

½ teaspoon freshly ground
**black pepper**

---

**Ingredient Swap**

Swap the smoked sausage for your
favorite brand of **frozen cooked
meatballs.** Toss 1 pound (454g)
meatballs with ½ cup (120ml)
barbecue sauce and add them to the
pan 15 minutes after the potatoes.
Add the remaining vegetables
15 minutes later.

# One-Pan Smoked Sausage
## & Roasted Veggies

I find it incredibly satisfying when a whole meal can be prepared on a single pan, and this one amazes everyone with how easy it is to prep. In fact, this meal is so delicious it's been voted a Spend with Pennies favorite by everyone on the team. Sausage and potatoes roast alongside seasoned veggies, all on one pan. It's served with a simple sauce so good you'll want to dip and dunk everything in it.

1. Preheat the oven to 425°F (220°C). Line a 13 × 18-inch (33 × 46cm) rimmed baking sheet with foil and spray with cooking spray.
2. **To make the sauce,** in a small bowl, mix ¼ cup (60ml) barbecue sauce with the mayonnaise. Refrigerate until ready to serve.
3. **To make the seasoning mix,** in a small bowl, combine the olive oil, garlic, oregano, salt, and pepper.
4. In a medium bowl, toss half of the seasoning mix with the potatoes and carrots. Spread them evenly on the prepared baking sheet and roast for 20 minutes.
5. In the same bowl, toss the corn, bell pepper, and mushrooms with the remaining seasoning mix and set aside.
6. In a separate medium bowl, toss the smoked sausage with the remaining ½ cup (120ml) barbecue sauce.
7. Remove the potatoes from the oven and stir. Increase the temperature to 450°F (230°C) and add the sausage and all remaining vegetables to the pan. Drizzle any barbecue sauce in the bottom of the bowl over the vegetables.
8. Roast for 15 minutes more or until the vegetables are tender. Stir and roast for 5 minutes more. If desired, place 6 inches (15cm) under the broiler and broil for 2 minutes.
9. Garnish with fresh herbs, if desired, and serve with the sauce for dipping.

---

**TIP**

Select a thick barbecue sauce for the best results. I love Sweet Baby Ray's Original for flavor and price.

**Prep Time:** 20 minutes
**Total Time:** 30 minutes
**Serves** 4

---

1 **lemon**
¼ cup (13g) **panko bread crumbs**
1 clove **garlic**, minced
2 tablespoons chopped **fresh parsley**
1 tablespoon chopped **fresh basil**
½ teaspoon **salt**, divided
1 tablespoon **butter**, melted
4 **salmon fillets**, 6oz (170g) each
½ teaspoon freshly ground **black pepper**

**FOR THE BEANS**

1lb (454g) **fresh green beans**, trimmed
1 tablespoon **olive oil**
1 clove **garlic**, finely minced
¼ teaspoon **salt**, or to taste

---

**Ingredient Swaps**

- Replace 2 tablespoons chopped fresh parsley with 2 teaspoons **dried parsley.**
- Replace 1 tablespoon chopped fresh basil with 1 teaspoon **dried basil.**
- Replace green beans with 1 pound (454g) **fresh broccolini.**

# Lemon Herb-Crusted Salmon
## with Garlic Green Beans

We live on the West Coast, and my husband has a yearly fishing trip that results in a generous bounty of fish, including salmon. It's so incredibly delicious and fresh, so when preparing it, we love to keep the flavors light and simple with just a hint of lemon and a vibrant herby topping. I round out this meal with a generous serving of roasted, garlicky green beans.

1. Preheat the oven to 400°F (200°C). Line a 13 × 18-inch (33 × 46cm) rimmed baking sheet with parchment paper or grease the sheet well.
2. Zest 1 teaspoon of lemon zest and juice 2 tablespoons of lemon juice.
3. In a small bowl, combine the bread crumbs, garlic, parsley, basil, lemon zest, and ¼ teaspoon salt. Add the melted butter and stir to combine.
4. Pat the salmon dry and drizzle with 2 tablespoons lemon juice. Season the salmon with the remaining ¼ teaspoon salt and the pepper.
5. Place the salmon skin side down on the prepared baking sheet and sprinkle the bread crumb mixture over top.
6. **To make the beans,** in a medium bowl, combine the beans, olive oil, garlic, and ¼ teaspoon salt, and toss well to coat.
7. Arrange the beans around the salmon on the baking sheet, and bake uncovered for 8 to 12 minutes or until the salmon is cooked through and flakes easily. Broil for 1 minute.
8. Transfer the salmon to serving plates. Stir the beans and bake or broil for an additional 2 to 5 minutes or until tender-crisp.

---

 **SERVING SUGGESTIONS**
Pair this salmon with our favorite Simply Seasoned Garlic Rice (page 259) or rice pilaf.

 **TIP**
Thicker 1-inch (2.5cm) salmon fillets will need to bake for closer to 12 minutes, while thinner, flatter ½-inch (1.5cm) fillets will need closer to 9 minutes.

 **FEELING FANCY?**
We like to serve the salmon with additional lemon wedges, and roasting the lemon softens the bite. Cut a lemon in half lengthwise, and place the halves cut side down on the baking sheet, and cook them along with the rest of the meal. The lemon halves can also be browned in a small nonstick skillet over medium heat for 2 to 3 minutes. Cut the halves into wedges and serve.

### SOMETHING ON THE SIDE

Our favorite crusty Garlicky Toast is delicious with these meatballs. Brush slices of artisan or sourdough bread with olive oil and season with a sprinkle of salt. Place under the broiler about 4 inches (10cm) from the heat, and broil until golden brown, about 1 to 2 minutes per side. Cut a clove of garlic in half and rub the toasted bread with the cut side of the garlic.

**Prep Time:** 25 minutes
**Total Time:** 1 hour 20 minutes
**Serves** 4

1 medium **zucchini**, about
    8oz (227g)

2 teaspoons **salt**, divided

3lb (1.4kg) ripe **Roma tomatoes** or
    beefsteak tomatoes

2½ tablespoons **olive oil**, divided

¾ teaspoon **dried oregano**

6 cloves **garlic**, peeled

1lb (454g) **ground turkey**

½ cup (56g) **seasoned bread
    crumbs**

1 **egg**

3 tablespoons **prepared pesto**

Chopped **fresh basil and parsley**,
    to garnish

---

**Ingredient Swap**
Replace the ground turkey
with **lean ground beef.**

# Zucchini Turkey Meatballs
## with Roasted Tomato Sauce

This rustic dish is incredibly fresh, flavorful, and entirely craveable. Oven-roasted tomatoes create the easiest-ever roasted garlic tomato sauce that will rival any fresh restaurant tomato sauce. It's paired with turkey meatballs that just might be the most tender and flavor-packed you've ever had. Once you try this recipe, you'll be making it on repeat.

1. Use the large side of a box grater to shred the zucchini and toss with ½ teaspoon salt. Let it drain in a colander for 10 minutes.
2. Preheat the oven to 425°F (220°C). Line a 13 × 18-inch (33 × 46cm) rimmed baking sheet with parchment paper.
3. Cut the tomatoes in half crosswise and remove and discard the seeds. On the prepared baking sheet, toss the tomatoes with 2 tablespoons oil, the oregano, and 1¼ teaspoons salt.
4. Wrap the garlic cloves and the remaining 1½ teaspoons olive oil in a small square of foil and place on the pan with the tomatoes. Roast for 25 minutes.
5. Meanwhile, to make the meatballs, squeeze excess liquid from the zucchini using a clean towel or cheesecloth.
6. In a medium bowl, mix the drained zucchini, ground turkey, bread crumbs, egg, pesto, and remaining ¼ teaspoon salt. Shape the mixture into 24 1-inch (2.5cm) meatballs.
7. Lower the oven temperature to 400°F (200°C), stir the tomatoes, and move them to one side of the baking sheet. Add the meatballs to the other side of the baking sheet.
8. Return the pan to the oven and roast for an additional 18 to 21 minutes or until the meatballs reach an internal temperature of 165°F (74°C).
9. Remove any loose tomato skins with tongs. Transfer the roasted garlic to a medium bowl and mash with a fork. Add the tomatoes, and mash to make a chunky sauce. Season with additional salt and pepper to taste.
10. Serve the meatballs and sauce, garnished with fresh basil and parsley, with toasted or grilled bread or over pasta.

 **TIPS**

- I prefer using Roma or beefsteak tomatoes, although any ripe variety will work. Garden-fresh or heirloom tomatoes may have more liquid. The sauce can be lightly drained once mashed if needed.
- For this recipe, I like a rustic, chunky-style tomato sauce. However, if a smoother sauce is more to your taste, feel free to pulse the tomatoes and garlic a couple of times in a food processor or blender.
- If serving over pasta, cook 12 ounces (340g) long pasta (I like pappardelle) according to package directions, and drain well, reserving ½ cup (120ml) pasta water. Toss the pasta with the roasted tomato sauce, adding pasta water if needed.

**Prep Time:** 20 minutes
**Total Time:** 1 hour
**Serves** 4

---

8oz (227g) **ground chorizo**
1½lb (680g) **sweet potatoes**,
    peeled and cut into ½-inch
    (1.5cm) cubes, about
    1 large sweet potato
1 cup (135g) **frozen corn**
1 small **red onion**, diced
1 **red bell pepper**, diced
3 cloves **garlic**, minced
1½ tablespoons **olive oil**
¾ teaspoon **salt**
½ teaspoon **dried thyme leaves**
¼ teaspoon freshly ground
    **black pepper**
8 large **eggs**
3 tablespoons chopped **fresh
    cilantro** or flat-leaf parsley
1 **avocado**, sliced

**Ingredient Swap**
Replace chorizo with **hot Italian
sausage.** Remove the casings
and brown in a skillet.

# Breakfast-for-Dinner
# Sheet Pan Chorizo Hash

My kids have always loved breakfast for dinner (aka *brinner*), whether it's pancakes or a hashbrown casserole. This chorizo hash is an elevated, grown-up version of breakfast for dinner; sweet potatoes, peppers, and onions are roasted until tender with bits of crisped chorizo. Crack some eggs into the hash during the last few minutes of roasting for a great weeknight brinner or a delicious Sunday brunch.

1. Preheat the oven to 425°F (220°C). Line a 13 × 18-inch (33 × 46cm) rimmed baking sheet with parchment paper.
2. In a 10-inch (25cm) skillet over medium-high heat, brown the chorizo, breaking up the meat with a spoon, for 5 to 6 minutes or until fully cooked. Drain any fat.
3. On the prepared baking sheet, combine the cooked chorizo, sweet potatoes, corn, onion, red bell pepper, garlic, olive oil, salt, thyme, and pepper. Toss well to combine.
4. Place the baking sheet in the oven and roast for 15 minutes, stir, and cook for 15 minutes more or until the sweet potatoes are tender.
5. Remove the baking sheet from the oven and stir the vegetables. Create 8 wells. Crack an egg into each well and season the eggs with salt and pepper to taste.
6. Return the pan to the oven, and cook for 5 to 8 minutes or until the eggs are done to your liking. Broil for 1 additional minute, if desired.
7. Remove the pan from the oven, and immediately transfer the eggs to a plate.
8. Top the hash with the chopped parsley or cilantro and avocado.

---

 **SERVING SUGGESTIONS**
This hash is a full meal in itself. We love to serve it with salsa, sour cream, and whole-grain toast or warmed tortillas.

 **HEY! IT'S OKAY TO . . .**
Skip the chopping! Check the produce area of your local grocery store; many stores have cubed sweet potatoes, which can be used in this recipe.

 **TIP**
The eggs will continue to cook once removed from the oven, so be sure not to overcook them, and transfer them to a plate immediately after baking.

 **LOVE YOUR LEFTOVERS**
Leftovers make great breakfast burritos. Chop leftover eggs and stir them into the hash. Spoon ¾ cup (125g) hash into a 10-inch (25cm) flour tortilla and top with 1 tablespoon salsa and shredded cheese, if desired. Fold the edges in and roll tightly.

Wrap the burritos in foil and store them in a zipper-lock freezer bag. To reheat frozen burritos, thaw in the fridge overnight. Remove the burrito from the foil, place on a plate, and cover with a damp paper towel. Microwave for 3 minutes or until heated through.

**Prep Time:** 20 minutes
**Total Time:** 1 hour 5 minutes
**Serves** 4

---

**FOR THE CHICKEN**

4 boneless, skinless **chicken breasts**, about 6oz (170g) each

3 tablespoons **mayonnaise**

2 tablespoons **Dijon mustard**

¾ teaspoon **salt**, divided

½ teaspoon **garlic powder**

½ teaspoon freshly ground **black pepper**

½ cup (62g) finely chopped **pecans**

⅓ cup (17g) **panko bread crumbs**

1 tablespoon **butter**, melted

½ teaspoon **smoked paprika**

**FOR THE SWEET POTATOES**

1½lb (680g) **sweet potatoes**, peeled and cut into ½-inch (1.5cm) cubes

3 tablespoons **honey**, divided

1 tablespoon **olive oil**

1 teaspoon **salt**

½ teaspoon **ground cinnamon**

---

**Ingredient Swap**

For a lighter version, replace the mayonnaise with **Greek yogurt**.

---

*Scan for instructions to prepare in an air fryer.*

# Crunchy Pecan Chicken with Honey-Roasted Sweet Potatoes

This sheet pan meal is the perfect combination of salty, sweet, and savory. Dijon-marinated chicken breasts are topped with crunchy pecan-panko crumbs and roasted alongside cinnamon-spiced sweet potatoes. It's finished off with a glistening honey glaze for big flavor in a single pan.

1. Preheat the oven to 425°F (220°C). Line a 13 × 18-inch (33 × 46cm) rimmed baking sheet with parchment paper.
2. **To make the chicken,** place the chicken breasts between two sheets of plastic wrap and use the flat side of a meat mallet or a rolling pin to pound to an even thickness of ½ inch (1.5cm).
3. In a medium bowl, combine the mayonnaise, Dijon mustard, ¼ teaspoon salt, garlic powder, and pepper. Add the chicken breasts and toss to coat. Refrigerate for at least 20 minutes or up to 4 hours.
4. **To make the sweet potatoes,** in a large bowl, toss the cubed potatoes, 1 tablespoon honey, oil, 1 teaspoon salt, and cinnamon, and set aside.
5. For the chicken topping, in a small bowl, mix the pecans, bread crumbs, melted butter, smoked paprika, and the remaining ½ teaspoon salt.
6. Place the chicken on one side of the baking sheet and top each chicken breast with the pecan mixture. Gently press the topping to adhere.
7. Arrange the sweet potatoes on the other side of the baking sheet, discarding any liquid at the bottom of the bowl.
8. Roast for 15 to 18 minutes or until the chicken reaches an internal temperature of 165°F (74°C). Transfer the chicken to a plate to rest. Stir the potatoes, drizzle with the remaining 2 tablespoons honey, and spread the potatoes evenly on the baking sheet. Return the potatoes to the oven and roast for an additional 5 to 6 minutes or until lightly browned.

---

 **SERVING SUGGESTIONS**

While it's perfect all year, this dish has cozy fall vibes and is great served alongside roasted Brussels sprouts (page 262) or Garlic Green Beans (page 150).

 **TIP**

Pecans can be quickly chopped with a pulse in a food processor or blender; however, my favorite way to chop nuts is to place them in a zipper-lock freezer bag, squeeze out as much air as possible when sealing the bag, and gently break the nuts with the flat side of a meat mallet or a rolling pin.

# Casseroles Bring
## *the Comfort*

**160**   Three-Cheese Scalloped Potato & Beef Gratin

**163**   Melt-in-Your-Mouth Pork Steaks
in Creamy Mushroom Sauce

**164**   Salsa Verde Chicken Enchilada Casserole

**167**   Savory Ham & Cheese Bread Pudding

**168**   Baked Chicken Spaghetti

**171**   Lazy Day Bacon & Pea Oven Risotto

**172**   From-Scratch Tuna Noodle Casserole

**175**   Cozy Chicken, Broccoli & Wild Rice Casserole

**176**   Hearty Baked Chili with Cornmeal Drop Biscuits

**179**   Cheesy Herbed-Ricotta Baked Ziti

# Three-Cheese
# Scalloped Potato & Beef Gratin

**Prep Time:** 45 minutes
**Total Time:** 2 hours 15 minutes
**Serves** 8

---

1lb (454g) **lean ground beef**
4 cloves **garlic**, minced
1 large **white onion**, chopped into
 ½-inch (1.5cm) pieces
2½lb (1.1kg) **Yukon Gold potatoes**,
 about 8 medium potatoes
1 teaspoon **salt**
½ teaspoon freshly ground
 **black pepper**
½ cup (57g) freshly grated
 **cheddar cheese**
¼ cup (25g) freshly grated
 **Parmesan cheese**

**FOR THE SAUCE**
4 tablespoons **butter**
¼ cup (30g) **all-purpose flour**
1 teaspoon crushed **dried
 rosemary**
1½ cups (360ml) **milk**
¾ cup (180ml) **chicken broth**
1½ cups (170g) freshly grated
 **Swiss cheese**
1 cup (113g) freshly grated
 **cheddar cheese**
½ cup (50g) freshly grated
 **Parmesan cheese**
1 teaspoon **mustard powder**
¼ teaspoon **salt**
¼ teaspoon freshly ground
 **black pepper**

Nothing says comfort food like a bubbling pan of cheesy, carby scalloped potatoes. This recipe transforms our favorite scalloped potatoes from a side dish to a full meal deal. Tender slices of potato and seasoned ground beef are layered in a creamy, totally dreamy three-cheese sauce and baked under a blanket of cheese until golden brown. It's the ultimate cozy casserole, and while this recipe takes a bit of time, the results are definitely worth it.

1. Preheat the oven to 350°F (175°C), and grease a 9 × 13-inch (22 × 33cm) baking dish.
2. In a 10-inch (25cm) skillet, over medium-high heat, cook the ground beef, garlic, and onion, breaking up the beef with a spoon, for 5 to 6 minutes or until the beef is cooked and no pink remains. Drain any fat.
3. **To make the sauce,** in a medium saucepan, melt the butter over medium heat. Add the flour and rosemary, and cook for 1 minute. Gradually add the milk and chicken broth, continuously whisking, until the mixture is smooth. Continue cooking until the sauce begins to boil and becomes thick and bubbly. Boil for 1 minute.
4. Remove the saucepan from the heat, and stir in the Swiss cheese, 1 cup (113g) cheddar cheese, ½ cup (50g) Parmesan cheese, mustard powder, ¼ teaspoon salt, and ¼ teaspoon pepper. Set aside.
5. Scrub the potatoes and cut them into ¼-inch (0.6cm) slices.
6. To prepare the casserole, place half the potatoes in the prepared baking dish, and sprinkle with ½ teaspoon salt and ¼ teaspoon pepper. Layer half of the ground beef and half of the sauce over the potatoes. Repeat the layers with the remaining potatoes, salt, pepper, beef, and sauce.
7. Cover the baking dish with foil and bake for 45 minutes.
8. Uncover, and top with ½ cup (57g) cheddar cheese and ¼ cup (25g) Parmesan cheese. Bake uncovered for an additional 30 minutes or until the cheese is browned and bubbly and the potatoes are tender.
9. Cool for at least 15 minutes before serving.

---

**SERVING SUGGESTIONS**
This is a full meal in itself, but if you'd like to add a side, this hearty casserole pairs well with a fresh salad topped with The Everyday Salad Dressing (page 252) or a simple pan of fresh green beans (page 264).

**TIP**
Mild cheddar cheese melts into a smoother, creamier sauce; an aged cheddar has great flavor but can sometimes break down and become a bit oily when baked for long periods of time.

**HEY! IT'S OKAY TO . . .**
Replace the sauce with our shortcut sauce! Combine 2 (10.5oz / 298g) cans cream of mushroom soup, 1 cup (240ml) milk, 1 teaspoon crushed dried rosemary, and 2 cups (226g) shredded Swiss cheese. Layer the potatoes, cooked ground beef, and sauce in a casserole dish according to the recipe, and bake as directed.

**Prep Time:** 20 minutes
**Total Time:** 2 hours 35 minutes
**Serves** 4

---

2lb (907g) **Yukon Gold potatoes,**
    about 8 medium potatoes
1 teaspoon **salt,** divided
1 teaspoon freshly ground
    **black pepper,** divided
1 tablespoon **butter**
2 medium **yellow onions,** sliced
    ¼ inch (0.6cm) thick
2lb (907g) **pork steaks,** cut ¾ inch
    (2cm) thick
¼ cup (30g) **all-purpose flour**
1 tablespoon **vegetable oil**
8oz (227g) **cremini mushrooms,**
    sliced
2 (10.5oz / 298g) cans **condensed**
    **cream of mushroom soup**

# Melt-in-Your-Mouth Pork Steaks
## in Creamy Mushroom Sauce

This is one of the very few recipes in this book that doesn't have a "from-scratch" version, but trust me, it's perfect as is. This is a version of my mom's recipe; a favorite dish from my childhood that we had often, and to this day, it remains my sister Candace's absolute favorite meal. Thick pork steaks are baked in the oven until they're so tender, they literally melt in your mouth. Paired with potatoes and a delicious mushroom gravy, it's the very definition of comfort food.

1. Preheat the oven to 350°F (175°C). Grease a deep 9 × 13 × 3-inch (22 × 33 × 7.5cm) baking dish.
2. Scrub the potatoes and cut them in half lengthwise. (Quarter if large.) Toss them with ½ teaspoon each salt and pepper, and place them cut side down in a single layer in the prepared baking dish.
3. In a 12-inch (30cm) skillet, melt the butter over medium heat. Add the onions and cook, stirring occasionally, for 5 to 7 minutes, or until the onions begin to soften. Transfer the onions to the baking dish with the potatoes.
4. While the onions are cooking, check the pork steaks for bits of bone or debris. Pat the pork steaks dry with a paper towel and season with the remaining ½ teaspoon salt and ½ teaspoon pepper. Place the flour on a plate and gently press the seasoned steaks into the flour, ensuring that they are lightly coated on all sides. Shake off any excess flour.
5. In the same skillet used for the onions, heat the oil over medium-high heat. Add the pork steaks in batches and sear until browned, about 3 minutes per side. Place the pork on top of the potatoes.
6. Add the sliced mushrooms on top of the pork and spread the condensed mushroom soup over the mushrooms.
7. Cover tightly with aluminum foil and bake for 2 hours. Peel back a corner of the foil and use a fork to check if the pork is fork-tender; it should pull apart very easily. If it is not tender, cover it and cook for an additional 30 minutes.
8. Remove from the oven, uncover, and let the casserole rest for at least 15 minutes to thicken the sauce.

---

**SERVING SUGGESTIONS**
This casserole is rich and delicious; I love to pair it with a light, fresh side like Grandma Mary's Simple Green Salad.

*Scan for my Simple Green Salad recipe.*

**TIPS**
- This recipe needs a deeper baking dish so everything can fit without bubbling over; I find 3 inches (7.5cm) deep to be just right. If you don't have a deep dish, skip the potatoes or roast them on the side.
- Use Yukon Gold, yellow, or red-skinned potatoes. The thin skins don't require peeling and keep the potatoes from overcooking. Russet or baking potatoes are starchier and fall apart when baked for a long time.
- Skip lean chops in this recipe; they'll dry out. Instead, look for packages labeled blade chops, shoulder chops, sirloin chops, or pork steaks. Choose thick-cut, well-marbled steaks with a fat cap on one end.

---

1 tablespoon **olive oil**

1 small **yellow onion**, finely diced

1 **green bell pepper**, finely diced

2 cloves **garlic**, minced

4oz (113g) **cream cheese**, softened

½ teaspoon **ground cumin**

2 cups (250g) shredded **cooked chicken**

**Salt** and freshly ground **black pepper** (optional), to taste

16oz (454g) **salsa verde**

½ cup (114g) **sour cream**

9 (6in / 15cm) **corn tortillas** or flour tortillas

1½ cups (170g) shredded **pepper Jack cheese**, divided

¼ cup (14g) finely chopped **fresh cilantro** (optional), to garnish

# Salsa Verde
# Chicken Enchilada Casserole

Enchiladas of any kind are right at the top of my list, and this recipe is a whole new level of amazing. Cozy, creamy, and delicious, a family favorite is transformed into an easy "no rolling required" casserole with layers of tortillas and shredded chicken in a tangy salsa verde sauce. It's all topped off with cheese and baked to bubbly perfection for a Tex-Mex meal that your family will request on repeat.

1. Preheat the oven to 375°F (190°C). Grease a 9 × 9-inch (23 × 23cm) baking dish.
2. In a large skillet, heat the oil over medium heat. Add the onion, green pepper, and garlic. Cook until softened, about 3 to 4 minutes.
3. Add the cream cheese and cumin to the skillet. Stir until the cream cheese is melted and smooth. Stir in the shredded chicken, and season with salt and pepper, to taste. Remove from the heat and set aside.
4. To make the sauce, in a medium bowl, whisk the salsa verde and sour cream until smooth.
5. Spread ½ cup (120ml) of the sauce in the bottom of the prepared baking dish.
6. Place 3 tortillas over the sauce, cutting them in half as needed.
7. Layer half of the chicken mixture, ½ cup (57g) cheese, 3 tortillas, and half of the remaining sauce. Repeat the layers, finishing with the remaining 3 tortillas and the remaining sauce.
8. Sprinkle the remaining ½ cup (57g) cheese over the top.
9. Bake for 23 to 27 minutes or until the cheese is melted and bubbly and the casserole is heated through.
10. Remove from the oven and let rest for 5 minutes. Garnish with chopped cilantro before serving, if using.

---

**SERVING SUGGESTIONS**
This casserole pairs well with a fresh and flavorful coleslaw or even a simple side of corn.

**MAKE AHEAD**
Cover and freeze the unbaked casserole for up to 4 months. Thaw in the fridge overnight. Remove from the fridge at least 30 minutes before baking and bake as directed, adding up to 10 minutes to the cooking time if needed.

**FEELING FANCY?**
Salsa verde is delicious, and it's easy to make at home with just a handful of ingredients.

*Scan for my Salsa Verde recipe.*

**Prep Time:** 30 minutes
**Total Time:** 1 hour 40 minutes
**Serves** 8

6 **eggs**
2½ cups (600ml) **milk**
½ cup (120ml) **heavy cream**
1½ tablespoons **Dijon mustard**
1 teaspoon **garlic powder**
½ teaspoon **ground sage**
½ teaspoon **dried thyme leaves**
½ teaspoon freshly ground
  **black pepper**
¼ teaspoon **salt**
12 cups (458g) cubed **hearty
  artisan bread**, 1-inch (2.5cm)
  cubes
2 cups (276g) diced **ham**, ½-inch
  (1.5cm) cubes
4 **green onions**, thinly sliced
1½ cups (170g) shredded **Swiss
  cheese**, divided
1½ cups (170g) shredded **sharp
  cheddar cheese**, divided

**Ingredient Swaps**
- Replace the ham with 1 pound
  (454g) **cooked sausage** or 1 pound
  (454g) **cooked bacon,** crumbled.
- If you're out of Swiss cheese, **any
  type of shredded cheese** can be
  substituted.
- **To make this dish vegetarian,**
  omit the ham, and pan-fry
  8 ounces (227g) mushrooms and
  2 cloves minced garlic in
  1 tablespoon butter. Stir in an
  additional ¼ teaspoon salt.

# Savory Ham & Cheese
# **Bread Pudding**

Ham and Cheese Bread Pudding is inspired by one of my favorite family recipes, and it's so good, I stash the leftovers in the back of the fridge so I don't have to share. This casserole is fully loaded with smoky ham and a duo of cheeses baked into a delicious eggy bread pudding—perfect for brunch or dinner. Best of all, it's a great make-ahead recipe for every day or for entertaining; whip it up on the weekend and bake it right away or a couple of days later.

1. Preheat the oven to 350°F (175°C) and grease a 9 × 13-inch (23 × 33cm) baking dish.
2. In a large bowl, combine the eggs, milk, cream, mustard, garlic powder, sage, thyme, pepper, and salt.
3. Add the bread cubes, ham, green onions, 1 cup (113g) Swiss cheese, and 1 cup (113g) cheddar cheese and toss gently to combine.
4. Let the bread rest for 15 minutes to soak up the egg mixture, gently tossing it a couple of times.
5. Transfer the mixture to the prepared baking dish and top with the remaining ½ cup (57g) Swiss cheese and ½ cup (57g) cheddar cheese.
6. Bake uncovered for 45 to 55 minutes or until the casserole has puffed and a butter knife inserted in the center comes out clean.
7. Rest for 10 minutes before serving.

**MAKE AHEAD**
Prepare the casserole as directed and cover tightly with plastic wrap. Refrigerate for up to 48 hours. Remove the casserole from the fridge and let it rest on the counter for at least 30 minutes while preheating the oven to 350°F (175°C). Bake uncovered for 50 to 60 minutes or until a butter knife inserted in the center comes out clean.

**VARIATION**
Add some veggies! Stir in 2 cups (226g) leftover roasted veggies, 2 cups (220g) lightly steamed asparagus, or 1 cup (85g) thawed frozen peas.

# Baked **Chicken Spaghetti**

**Prep Time:** 20 minutes
**Total Time:** 1 hour
**Serves** 6

---

8oz (226g) **spaghetti**
2 cups (250g) shredded **cooked chicken**
1 (14.5oz / 411g) can **petite-diced tomatoes** or diced tomatoes with chiles (such as Rotel), drained

**FOR THE SAUCE**
4 tablespoons **butter**
1 medium **yellow onion**, chopped
1 **clove garlic**, minced
½ **green bell pepper**, chopped
¼ cup (30g) **all-purpose flour**
1 teaspoon **Italian seasoning** (for homemade, see page 18)
1 cup (240ml) **chicken broth**
1 cup (240ml) **half-and-half** or light cream
½ cup (50g) freshly grated **Parmesan cheese**
2 cups (226g) freshly grated **sharp cheddar cheese**, divided
¼ teaspoon **salt**
¼ teaspoon freshly ground **black pepper**

Can we take a moment to appreciate the way a perfect bowl of pasta takes you from stressed to soothed with every spoonful? Some nights just call for creamy, carby goodness, and this dish hits all the right spots. Spaghetti is tossed with tender chunks of chicken and diced tomatoes in a cheesy sauce. If you've got time, I highly recommend the homemade sauce. (It's pretty quick.) However, if real life is calling and you've got hungry bellies to fill, skip straight to the shortcut sauce because it's still super delicious!

1. Preheat the oven to 375°F (190°C). Grease a 9 × 13-inch (22 × 33cm) baking dish.
2. Bring a large pot of salted water to a boil and cook the spaghetti al dente according to package directions. Drain well; do not rinse. Set aside.
3. Meanwhile, **to make the sauce,** in a 12-inch (30cm) skillet, melt the butter over medium heat. Add the onion, garlic, and bell pepper and cook until tender. Stir in the flour and Italian seasoning and cook for 1 to 2 minutes.
4. Gradually add the broth and half-and-half, whisking until smooth, and bring to a boil. Boil for 1 minute or until thick and bubbly.
5. Remove the skillet from the heat and whisk in the Parmesan cheese, 1 cup (113g) cheddar cheese, salt, and pepper until smooth. Taste and season with additional salt and pepper, if desired.
6. In the prepared baking dish, combine the cooked spaghetti, shredded chicken, drained tomatoes, and sauce. Mix well and top with the remaining 1 cup (113g) cheddar cheese.
7. Bake 25 to 30 minutes or until hot and bubbling.

**TIPS**
- Cook the pasta just until tender; it will continue to cook as the dish bakes in the oven.
- Preshredded cheddar cheese can be used, but shredding cheese from a block will make a smoother sauce.

**HEY! IT'S OKAY TO . . .**
Skip the from-scratch sauce and make a shortcut sauce. In a large skillet, heat 1 tablespoon butter over medium heat. Add 1 chopped yellow onion and ½ chopped green bell pepper; stir, and cook until softened. Stir in ¾ pound (340g) diced processed cheese, such as Velveeta, and 1 (10.5oz / 298g) can condensed cream of mushroom soup or cream of chicken soup. Cook until melted and creamy. You can top the casserole with 1 cup (113g) shredded cheddar cheese if you'd like or skip it—the shortcut sauce is plenty cheesy!

**Prep Time:** 15 minutes
**Total Time:** 1 hour 5 minutes
**Serves** 6

---

6 slices uncooked **bacon**, chopped
1½ cups (285g) **arborio rice**
1 small **yellow onion**, finely diced
2 cloves **garlic**, minced
½ cup (120ml) **dry white wine**
4 cups (960ml) **reduced-sodium chicken broth**, at room temperature
2 **bay leaves**
½ teaspoon **dried thyme leaves**
½ cup (50g) freshly grated **Parmesan cheese**
¼ cup (60ml) **half-and-half** or light cream, warmed
¾ cup (64g) **frozen peas**, thawed
**Salt** and freshly ground **black pepper**, to taste
1 tablespoon **fresh parsley**, to garnish

> **Ingredient Swap**
> Replace the peas with chopped steamed **asparagus** or steamed **broccoli florets,** if you'd prefer.

# Lazy Day
# Bacon & Pea Oven Risotto

If you've never made risotto before, it's a labor of love that involves small additions of warm broth and lots of standing over the stove stirring. This oven risotto is just as creamy and delicious, but it's so easy, it practically makes itself. Rice, broth, and seasonings are baked until tender in a richly flavored broth. It's finished with Parmesan cheese, peas, and crumbled bacon for a creamy rice dish as beautiful as it is delicious.

1. Preheat the oven to 350°F (175°C).
2. Heat a 4-quart (3.8L) Dutch oven or ovenproof saucepan with a lid over medium-high heat. Add the bacon and cook uncovered until crisp. Remove the bacon with a slotted spoon and set aside, leaving the drippings in the pan.
3. Reduce the heat to medium and add the rice, onion, and garlic. Cook until the onion begins to soften and some of the rice begins to lightly brown, about 3 minutes.
4. Add the white wine, a little at a time, and simmer until evaporated, about 2 minutes.
5. Stir in the broth, bay leaves, and thyme. Cover with a tight-fitting lid and bake for 35 to 40 minutes or until the rice is just tender. (Do not overcook.) The risotto will appear to have a lot of liquid at this point. As long as the rice is tender, remove it from the oven.
6. Let the risotto rest uncovered, stirring occasionally, for 5 to 7 minutes or until the liquid is absorbed.
7. Stir in the Parmesan cheese, half-and-half, and peas, adding more hot broth or hot water if needed to reach desired consistency. Season with salt and pepper to taste.
8. Garnish with the reserved bacon and the parsley. Top with additional Parmesan cheese, if desired.

---

 **SERVING SUGGESTIONS**
This is a delicious and rich risotto recipe that is a full meal. If you'd like to add some extra protein, top it with seared scallops or grilled shrimp.

 **TIPS**
- It is important that the broth is at room temperature before baking.
- Ensure the lid to your Dutch oven or saucepan has a tight seal. If it doesn't, cover it with foil before adding the lid.

 **VARIATION**
To make mushroom risotto, replace the bacon and peas with 12 ounces (340g) thinly sliced cremini or white mushrooms and use regular chicken broth in place of reduced-sodium chicken broth. Cook the mushrooms in 2 tablespoons butter for 3 to 4 minutes before adding the onions and rice in step 3.

**Prep Time:** 25 minutes
**Total Time:** 45 minutes
**Serves** 6

8oz (227g) **wide egg noodles**
⅔ cup (112g) **frozen peas**, thawed
1 cup (113g) **shredded cheddar cheese**
1 tablespoon chopped **fresh parsley**
2 (5oz / 142g) cans **solid white tuna in water**, drained

**FOR THE SAUCE**
3 tablespoons **butter**
3 ribs **celery**, finely diced
4oz (113g) **mushrooms**, finely diced (about 1⅓ cups)
1 teaspoon **onion powder**
1 teaspoon **garlic powder**
½ teaspoon **dried thyme leaves**
3 tablespoons **all-purpose flour**
1 cup (240ml) **evaporated milk**
¾ cup (180ml) **chicken broth**
½ teaspoon **salt**
¼ teaspoon freshly ground **black pepper**

**FOR THE TOPPING**
½ cup (57g) **shredded cheddar cheese**
½ cup (25g) **panko bread crumbs**
1 tablespoon **butter**, melted

---

**Ingredient Swaps**
- I prefer solid white tuna in this recipe as it has bigger, heartier pieces, but **chunk light tuna** will work as well; however, the pieces are smaller.
- Canned tuna can be replaced with **canned chicken** or **canned salmon.**

# From-Scratch **Tuna Casserole**

Tuna casserole is a classic that has graced tables since the '40s, and it's a Spend with Pennies reader favorite. This "from-scratch" version replaces the canned mushroom soup with a creamy homemade sauce. It's tossed with tender egg noodles and tuna, and baked until bubbling under a buttery crumb topping. Don't worry; I've also included the classic shortcut version for busy weekdays!

1. Preheat the oven to 400°F (200°C). Grease a 9 × 13-inch (23 × 33cm) baking dish.
2. Bring a large saucepan of salted water to a boil. Cook the egg noodles al dente according to package directions. Drain and rinse under cold water.
3. Meanwhile, **to make the sauce,** in a 10-inch (25cm) skillet, melt the butter over medium heat. Add the celery, mushrooms, onion powder, garlic powder, and thyme. Cook until the celery is tender, about 5 minutes.
4. Stir in the flour and cook for 1 minute. Gradually add the evaporated milk and broth, and bring to a boil over medium heat. Boil for 1 minute or until thickened. Stir in the salt and pepper.
5. In a large bowl, combine the cooked noodles, sauce, peas, 1 cup (113g) cheddar cheese, and parsley. Gently fold in the tuna. Spread the mixture into the prepared baking dish.
6. **To make the topping,** in a small bowl, combine ½ cup (57g) cheddar cheese, bread crumbs, and melted butter. Sprinkle over the casserole.
7. Bake for 18 to 22 minutes or until the edges are bubbling and the topping is browned.

---

 **HEY! IT'S OKAY TO . . .**
Skip the from-scratch sauce and opt for a quick and classic mushroom-soup sauce! Increase the egg noodles to 12 ounces (340g) and add 1 cup (100g) sliced celery to the boiling water during the last 2 minutes of cooking. To make the shortcut sauce, combine 2 (10.5oz / 298g) cans condensed cream of mushroom soup with ½ cup (120ml) whole milk, and ¾ teaspoon onion powder. This shortcut version serves 8.

4 cups (300g) **fresh broccoli**, chopped into bite-size pieces

1 tablespoon **olive oil**

1 small **yellow onion**, diced

12oz (340g) boneless, skinless **chicken breasts**, cut into bite-size pieces

1 teaspoon **salt**

¼ teaspoon freshly ground **black pepper**

⅔ cup (160ml) **chicken broth**

4oz (113g) **cream cheese**, softened

1½ teaspoons **curry powder**

⅓ cup (80ml) **milk**

1¼ teaspoons **cornstarch**

⅓ cup (76g) **sour cream**

2½ cups (500g) warm cooked **wild rice blend** (cook in broth for best flavor)

¼ cup (28g) **seasoned bread crumbs**

1 tablespoon **butter,** melted

---

### Ingredient Swaps

- Replace the chicken breast with 2 cups (600g) cubed **cooked chicken.**
- You can use 3 cups (336g) **cooked 100% wild rice** in place of the wild rice blend.

# Cozy Chicken, Broccoli & **Wild Rice Casserole**

Few things say love from the oven like a rich, creamy chicken and rice casserole. Growing up, my mom served a broccoli wild rice casserole for every holiday meal that I absolutely love. This recipe is every bit as delicious with a homemade sauce and a hint of curry for a cozy casserole that I could eat every day.

1. Preheat the oven to 400°F (200°C). Grease a 2-quart (1.9L) baking dish.
2. In a 10-inch (25cm) skillet, bring ½ cup (120ml) water to a simmer over medium-high heat. Add the broccoli and cook for 3 to 4 minutes or until tender-crisp. Drain well and add to the prepared baking dish.
3. In the same skillet over medium heat, add the olive oil and onion and cook until the onion is softened, about 3 to 4 minutes.
4. Add the chicken, salt, and pepper. Cook until the chicken is lightly browned and cooked through, about 6 minutes. Transfer the chicken and onions to the baking dish.
5. Add the broth to the skillet and scrape up any brown bits. Stir in the cream cheese and curry, and cook until smooth and melted.
6. In a small bowl, combine the the milk and cornstarch and add to the skillet with the sauce mixture. Cook until the mixture comes to a boil. Remove from the heat and whisk in the sour cream until smooth.
7. Add the sauce and cooked rice to the baking dish and toss with the chicken and broccoli. Spread into an even layer.
8. In a small bowl, combine the bread crumbs and butter and sprinkle over the casserole.
9. Bake uncovered for 15 to 20 minutes or until heated through and the topping is lightly browned.

---

 **TIP**
Wild rice blends vary by brand. For best results, follow the package directions for cooking (discard seasoning packet, if present) and measure out 2½ cups (500g) of the cooked wild rice blend to use in the recipe. You will likely need about ⅔–1 cup (130–200g) dry wild rice blend before cooking.

 **HEY! IT'S OKAY TO . . .**
Replace the homemade sauce with an easy pantry sauce. In a medium bowl, combine 1 (10.5oz / 298g) can cream of chicken soup, ½ cup (113g) sour cream, ⅓ cup (80ml) milk, and 1½ teaspoons curry powder. Add to the chicken, broccoli, and rice in step 7.

---

## FOR THE CHILI
1lb (454g) **lean ground beef**
1 medium **yellow onion**, diced
1 **green bell pepper**, diced
1½ tablespoons **chili powder**
2 cloves **garlic**, minced
½ teaspoon **ground cumin**
2 (10oz / 283g each) cans **diced tomatoes with chiles**, such as Rotel, with juices
1 (15.5oz / 439g) can **kidney beans**, drained and rinsed
1 (14.5oz / 411g) can **crushed tomatoes**
½ cup (120ml) **water**
1 teaspoon **granulated sugar**
½ teaspoon **salt**

## FOR THE BISCUITS
1⅓ cup (160g) **all-purpose flour**
½ cup (80g) **cornmeal**
2 tablespoons **granulated sugar**
2 teaspoons **baking powder**
1 teaspoon **salt**
4 tablespoons cold **butter**
1 cup (113g) shredded **sharp cheddar cheese**
1 **egg**, beaten
¾ cup (180ml) **buttermilk** or soured milk

---

### Ingredient Swap
It's easy to make your own **buttermilk substitute.** Place 2 teaspoons white vinegar in a liquid measuring cup and top to ¾ cup (180ml) with milk. Stir and let sit for 5 minutes.

# Hearty Baked Chili
# with Cornmeal Drop Biscuits

Chili is at the very top of my husband's list of favorites, and it's one of the most popular recipes at Spend with Pennies. Packed with ground beef and beans, this hearty dish is a zesty oven version of our favorite chili recipe. It's topped with easy, cheesy cornmeal biscuits and baked like a casserole until the chili is thick and bubbly and the biscuits are golden and fluffy. If you're short on time, skip the biscuits and let the chili simmer for a few extra minutes on the stove.

1. Preheat the oven to 375°F (190°C). Grease a 9 × 13-inch (23 × 33cm) baking dish.
2. To make the chili, heat a 12-inch (30cm) nonstick skillet over medium-high heat. Add the ground beef and onion and cook, breaking the beef up with a spoon, for 5 to 6 minutes or until no pink remains. Drain any fat.
3. Stir in the bell pepper, chili powder, garlic, and cumin and cook for 3 minutes more.
4. Add the diced tomatoes with juices, beans, crushed tomatoes, water, sugar, and salt. Bring to a simmer over medium heat and simmer uncovered for 5 minutes, stirring occasionally.
5. Meanwhile, **to make the biscuits,** in a medium bowl, combine the flour, cornmeal, sugar, baking powder, and salt. Use a fork to cut in the cold butter until small crumbs form, about the size of peas. Stir in the cheese.
6. Create a well in the center of the dry mixture and add the egg and buttermilk. Mix just until combined.
7. Transfer the chili to the prepared baking dish. Spoon the batter over the chili in large spoonfuls to make 16 biscuits. Bake uncovered for 22 to 27 minutes or until the biscuits are browned and cooked through. Rest for 10 minutes before serving.

---

 **SERVING SUGGESTIONS**
This is a full meal in itself; however, I love setting out toppings and garnishes like shredded cheddar cheese, diced white onion, sliced jalapeños, and sour cream.

 **HEY! IT'S OKAY TO . . .**
Skip the biscuits and the baking. Prep this easy chili on the stovetop by adding an additional ½ cup (120ml) water and simmer the chili uncovered for a total of 15 to 20 minutes to blend the flavors.

**Prep Time:** 35 minutes
**Total Time:** 1 hour 5 minutes
**Serves** 8

---

1lb (454g) bulk **hot Italian sausage**
1 small **yellow onion**, diced
2 cloves **garlic**, minced
1 (28oz / 794g) can **crushed tomatoes**
1 (14.5oz / 411g) can **diced tomatoes**, with juices
¼ cup (60ml) **water**
2 tablespoons **tomato paste**
2 teaspoons **Italian seasoning** (for homemade, see page 18)
½ teaspoon **granulated sugar**
¼ teaspoon **salt**, plus more **to taste**
Freshly ground **black pepper**, to taste
1lb (454g) **ziti** or another tubular pasta
15oz (425g) **ricotta cheese**
1 **egg**
2 tablespoons chopped **fresh parsley**
2 tablespoons chopped **fresh basil**
2 cups (226g) shredded **mozzarella cheese**, divided
¼ cup (25g) grated **Parmesan cheese**

**Ingredient Swaps**
- Replace the ricotta cheese with 15 ounces (425g) **cottage cheese.**
- Replace the fresh parsley and fresh basil with 1½ teaspoons each of **dried basil** and **dried parsley.**

# Cheesy Herbed-Ricotta Baked Ziti

There's something truly irresistible about a hearty dish of saucy pasta with golden cheese and crispy edges—it's one of my son Tyler's favorites! This baked ziti has layers of pasta nestled in a rich, meaty sauce with pockets of creamy herbed ricotta cheese throughout. It's all baked under a layer of bubbly, browned cheese for a meal that's perfect to feed a crowd or to make ahead and freeze for another day.

1. Preheat the oven to 375°F (190°C). Grease a 9 × 13-inch (23 × 33cm) baking dish.
2. Heat a large 12-inch (30cm) nonstick skillet over medium-high heat. Add the sausage, onion, and garlic, and cook, breaking up the meat with a spoon, for 5 to 6 minutes or until no pink remains. Drain any fat.
3. Add the crushed tomatoes, diced tomatoes with juices, water, tomato paste, Italian seasoning, sugar, and salt. Simmer uncovered for 10 to 12 minutes or until thickened. Season with salt and pepper to taste.
4. Meanwhile, bring a large pot of salted water to a boil. Add the ziti and cook al dente according to package directions. Drain well.
5. In a medium bowl, mix the ricotta, egg, parsley, basil, 1 cup (113g) mozzarella cheese, and Parmesan cheese.
6. Spread 1 cup (240ml) of the meat sauce in the prepared dish. Layer half of the ziti, all of the ricotta mixture, and half of the remaining meat sauce. Add the remaining ziti and the remaining meat sauce. Sprinkle with the remaining 1 cup (113g) mozzarella cheese.
7. Bake uncovered for 25 to 30 minutes or until golden and bubbly.

---

**SERVING SUGGESTIONS**
We love to serve this pasta with crusty bread and a fresh salad.

**TIP**
If desired, this casserole recipe can be halved for 4 servings and prepared in an 8-inch (20cm) baking dish. Bake for 18 to 20 minutes or until heated through.

**MAKE AHEAD**
To make Baked Ziti ahead of time, prepare as directed, reserving the 1 cup (113g) of mozzarella for the topping from step 6 in a separate container. Cover the dish and refrigerate for up to 48 hours or freeze for up to 4 months. If frozen, thaw in the fridge overnight. Remove the dish from the fridge 30 minutes before baking. Bake at 375°F (190°C) for 25 minutes, top with the remaining mozzarella cheese, and bake for an additional 20 to 25 minutes or until hot and bubbly.

# Slow-Down Sunday *Suppers*

**182**    Grandma Mary's Pierogi

**185**    My Mom's Best Ever Pork Roast & Gravy

**188**    Homestyle Roast Chicken Dinner

**190**    The Best Ever Meatloaf

**193**    Grandma Mary's Rouladen with Mushroom Gravy

**194**    Creamy Clam Chowder with Mini Cheddar Biscuits

**197**    Slow Cooker Pot Roast with Root Veggies & Gravy

**198**    Three-Cheese Creamy Chicken & Mushroom Lasagna

**201**    Rustic Beef & Veggie Pot Pie

**202**    Slow Cooker Sticky Honey-Garlic Ribs

# Grandma Mary's **Pierogi**

**Prep Time:** 2 hours 15 minutes
**Total Time:** 2 hours 45 minutes
**Makes** 65 pierogi

---

### FOR THE DOUGH

6 cups (720g) **all-purpose flour**
2 large **eggs**, beaten
6 tablespoons **vegetable oil**
2 teaspoons **kosher salt**
1½ cups (360ml) cold **water**, more
  as needed

### FOR THE FILLING

3¾lb (1.7kg) **russet potatoes** or
  baking potatoes
6 tablespoons **butter**, softened,
  divided
1 medium **white onion**, finely
  diced
4½ cups (504g) finely shredded
  **cheddar cheese**
¾ teaspoon **salt**
¼ teaspoon ground **white pepper**

### FOR COOKING AND SERVING

3 tablespoons **butter**, plus more
  as needed
1 **white onion**, finely diced
**Sour cream**

> **Ingredient Swap**
> **Black pepper** can be used in
> place of white pepper.

This recipe is near and dear to my heart, as I very fondly remember the days spent next to my Grandma Mary making pierogi. Tender dough filled with buttery, cheesy mashed potatoes; these were a favorite for all nineteen of us grandchildren. Homemade pierogi are a labor of love worth every second, so set aside an afternoon, invite your friends or family over, and create some new memories. These can be prepared in large batches and frozen for quick meals throughout the week.

1. **To make the dough,** add the flour to a large bowl. Add the beaten eggs, oil, kosher salt, and water. Mix with a spoon to form a dough, adding more water if needed for the dough to pull together.
2. Turn out the dough onto a clean work surface and knead until smooth and pliable, about 4 to 5 minutes. Cover with plastic wrap and allow the dough to rest at room temperature for 1 hour.
3. **To make the filling,** peel the potatoes and cut them into 2-inch (5cm) pieces. Place them in a large pot of salted water and bring to a boil over medium-high heat. Cook for 15 minutes or until the potatoes are fork-tender.
4. Meanwhile, in a medium skillet, melt 2 tablespoons butter over medium-low heat. Add the onion and cook for 4 to 6 minutes until tender without browning.
5. Once potatoes are cooked, drain well and place in a large bowl. Mash the potatoes with a hand masher. Add the cooked onion, cheese, remaining 4 tablespoons butter, salt, and pepper. Continue mashing until the potatoes are very smooth and slightly cooled.
6. To assemble pierogi, divide the dough in half, leaving one half covered. Roll the dough to ⅛ inch (0.33cm) thick. Using a 3-inch (7.5cm) cookie cutter or biscuit cutter, cut out circles. Reroll the scraps and repeat to make about 65 circles of dough.
7. Scoop 1½ tablespoons of the mashed potato filling and roll it into a ball. Place the potato ball in one of the dough circles, fold the dough over to form a semicircle, and pinch the edges closed. Place prepared pierogi on a parchment-lined baking sheet. Repeat with the remaining dough. (Prepared pierogi can be cooked, or frozen and then cooked at a later date.)
8. To cook pierogi, in a large skillet over medium-low heat, melt the butter. Add the onion and cook for 4 to 6 minutes until tender without browning. Remove the onion from the pan and set aside for serving.
9. Bring a large pot of salted water to a boil. Add pierogi and cook until they float, about 3 minutes (or 5 minutes for frozen pierogi). Remove with a slotted spoon.
10. Transfer the boiled pierogi to the hot skillet, adding more butter if needed, and cook over medium-low heat until browned on each side, about 5 minutes.
11. Serve warm with onions and sour cream.

---

**MAKE AHEAD**
Freeze uncooked pierogi in a single layer on a parchment-lined baking sheet. Once frozen, transfer to a zipper-lock freezer bag or an airtight freezerproof container for up to 3 months.

**TIPS**

- Knead the dough just until it's smooth and pliable. If you overwork the dough, it will become tough and too elastic; this will cause it to spring back when rolled out.
- When sealing the dough, ensure it's pinched to the same thickness as the rest of the pierogi for even cooking. The edges of the dough can be trimmed with kitchen scissors, if desired.

5–9lb (2.3–4.1kg) **pork shoulder butt roast**

4 medium cloves **garlic**, thinly sliced

2¼ teaspoons **salt**, divided

1 teaspoon freshly ground **black pepper**

2 large **yellow onions**, sliced into ½-inch (1.5cm) rings

½lb (227g) **cremini mushrooms**, thinly sliced

3 cups (720ml) **chicken broth**

6 medium **Yukon Gold potatoes**

¼ cup (60ml) **olive oil**

3 tablespoons **cornstarch**

3 tablespoons **cold chicken broth** or water

# My Mom's Best Ever
# Pork Roast & Gravy

This is my favorite meal of all time, and it has been voted "most loved" by my sisters and my dad too. My mom has made this pork roast so many times that she no longer uses a recipe. Years ago, I followed her around the kitchen, documenting her every move so I could re-create it. Twenty-five years and countless pork roast dinners later, it's still my favorite meal. The succulent pork is so tender and buttery it melts in your mouth, and the rich brown gravy is so good that I could literally drink it. You absolutely must try it; it's perfection on a plate.

1. Place one rack on the bottom of the oven and one rack in the center of the oven. Preheat the oven to 450°F (230°C).

2. If the pork roast has a thick fat cap, use a sharp knife to trim it down. Pat the pork dry with a paper towel. Use a paring knife to poke slits around the pork roast and insert a slice of garlic into each slit.

3. Season the pork with 1½ teaspoons salt and 1 teaspoon pepper, and place the roast fat side up in a large dark roasting pan. Place the pan on the center rack in the oven, and cook uncovered for 30 minutes.

4. Separate the rings of the onions and, after 30 minutes of cooking, place half of the onions on top of the roast. Reduce the heat to 325°F (165°C), cover the roast with a lid or foil, and cook for 2 hours.

5. After 2 hours, remove the pan from the oven, uncover, move the onions to the bottom of the roasting pan, and add the mushrooms and chicken broth to the pan. Flip the roast over and add the remaining sliced onions on top of the roast, re-cover, and cook for an additional 3 to 3½ hours (see cooking times by weight).

6. Meanwhile, line a rimmed baking sheet with foil and place a piece of parchment paper on top of the foil. Cut the potatoes in half lengthwise, leaving their skins on. Toss the potatoes with the oil and the remaining ¾ teaspoon salt. Place the potatoes, flat side down, on the baking sheet. Place the pan on the bottom rack of the oven 60 minutes before you expect the roast to be done cooking.

7. Remove the roasting pan from the oven, leaving the potatoes to continue roasting for another 30 minutes while you prepare the gravy. Remove the roast from the juices and place it on a large platter to rest for at least 30 minutes.

8. To make the gravy, skim any fat off the juices in the roasting pan. Use a spatula to scrape up any brown bits on the bottom or sides of the roasting pan. Place the roasting pan directly on the stovetop (or transfer the juices to a large saucepan) and bring to a boil over medium-high heat.

9. In a small bowl or liquid measuring cup, whisk the cornstarch with the cold broth to make a slurry. Drizzle the slurry slowly into the simmering juices while whisking until you reach the desired consistency for gravy. (You might not use all of the slurry or you might need more, depending on how much juice is in the pan.)

10. Remove the potatoes from the oven. Slice the roast into 1-inch (2.5cm) slices and serve with potatoes and gravy.

*Recipe continues next page.*

## SERVING SUGGESTIONS

My mom often serves this meal with roasted potatoes as written here, but we also love to serve it with cavatappi. Skip the potatoes and boil the noodles in salted water according to the package directions, drain, and smother with a generous serving of gravy.

## TIPS

- Cut the potatoes right before baking so they don't oxidize (turn brown).
- If the potatoes are ready early, tender with a crisp bottom on the flat side, turn the oven off while the roast rests and leave them in the oven until serving.
- The onion that is added first may blacken, which will add extra flavor to the gravy. The dark onion pieces can be removed before serving if you'd like.
- If you'd like extra gravy, add up to 2 cups (480ml) additional broth to the juices when simmering the gravy. You may need extra cornstarch slurry for thickening.
- The roast is incredibly tender, so be sure to cut the slices thick or they will fall apart. I use an electric knife to make cutting easy.

## APPROXIMATE COOKING TIMES

Cook the roast at 450°F (230°C) for 30 minutes and then for an additional 40 to 45 minutes per pound at 325°F (165°C).

| Weight of Roast | Cook Time at 450°F (230°C) | Cook Time at 325°F (165°C) | Total Cook Time |
|---|---|---|---|
| 5lb (2.3kg) | 30 minutes | 3 hours 20 minutes to 3 hours 45 minutes | 3 hours 50 minutes to 4 hours 15 minutes |
| 6lb (2.7kg) | 30 minutes | 4 hours to 4 hours 30 minutes | 4 hours 30 minutes to 5 hours |
| 7lb (3.2kg) | 30 minutes | 4 hours 40 minutes to 5 hours 15 minutes | 5 hours 10 minutes to 5 hours 45 minutes |
| 8lb (3.6kg) | 30 minutes | 5 hours 20 minutes to 6 hours | 5 hours 50 minutes to 6 hours 30 minutes |
| 9lb (4.1kg) | 30 minutes | 6 hours to 6 hours 45 minutes | 6 hours 30 minutes to 7 hours 15 minutes |

Homestyle Roast Chicken Dinner, page 188

**Prep Time:** 35 minutes
**Total Time:** 2 hours 40 minutes
**Serves** 6

---

1 **whole chicken**, 4–6lb (1.8–2.7kg)
2 tablespoons **olive oil**, divided
1¾ teaspoons **salt**, divided
1 teaspoon freshly ground **black pepper**, divided
1 teaspoon **dried rosemary**, crushed
1 teaspoon **poultry seasoning** (for homemade, see page 18)
1 large **yellow onion**, cut into 1-inch (2.5cm) wedges
6 **carrots**, cut into 1-inch (2.5cm) pieces
2 ribs **celery**, cut into 1-inch (2.5cm) pieces

**FOR THE STUFFING**
5 tablespoons **butter**
1 small **yellow onion,** finely diced
2 ribs **celery,** finely diced
1 teaspoon **poultry seasoning** (for homemade, see page 18)
8 cups (190g) **dried bread cubes**
1 tablespoon **chopped fresh parsley**
¾ teaspoon **salt**
¼ teaspoon freshly ground **black pepper**
1½–2 cups (360–520ml) **reduced-sodium chicken broth**

**FOR THE GRAVY**
1½ cups (360ml) **reduced-sodium chicken broth,** or as needed
4 tablespoons **butter**
¼ cup (30g) **all-purpose flour**

# Homestyle
# **Roast Chicken Dinner**

My mom makes a really great roast chicken dinner, and growing up, it was a wholesome meal that graced our dinner table frequently. In this recipe, a whole seasoned chicken is surrounded by veggies and roasted until moist and juicy with crispy skin. It's served with the best homemade stuffing and a rich chicken gravy. While this dinner takes a little time to make, it's actually pretty easy to prepare, and most of the cooking time is hands off.

1. Preheat the oven to 450°F (230°C). Remove the chicken from the fridge 30 minutes before cooking.
2. Pat the chicken dry with a paper towel and rub it with 1 tablespoon olive oil, 1½ teaspoon salt, ½ teaspoon pepper, rosemary, and poultry seasoning. Remove the giblets and the neck from inside the cavity if present, and place two onion wedges inside the chicken's cavity. Reserve the neck and giblets to cook with the chicken or discard, as desired. Tie the legs together with kitchen twine and tuck the wings underneath.
3. To the bottom of a metal roasting pan or 12-inch (30cm) cast-iron skillet, add the remaining onion wedges, carrots, and celery. Toss these with the remaining 1 tablespoon olive oil, remaining ¼ teaspoon salt, and remaining ½ teaspoon pepper.
4. Place the chicken, breast side up, on top of the vegetables. Add the neck and giblets to the roasting pan, if desired. Roast uncovered for 15 minutes. Reduce the temperature to 350°F (175°C) and roast for an additional 18 to 20 minutes per pound or until the chicken reaches 165°F (74°C) in the thickest part of the thigh.
5. Meanwhile, **to make the stuffing,** in a large skillet over medium heat, melt the butter. Add the onion, celery, and poultry seasoning and cook over medium-low heat until tender (do not brown), about 10 to 12 minutes.
6. In a large bowl, combine the bread cubes, onion mixture, parsley, salt, and pepper. Add the broth, a little bit at a time, just until the cubes are moist but not soggy, and gently toss. Let the cubes rest for 5 minutes and toss again, adding more broth if needed. You may not need all the broth.
7. Transfer the stuffing to an 8 × 8-inch (20 × 20cm) baking dish and cover with foil. Place the stuffing in the oven with the chicken (they can sit on the same rack) and bake for 25 minutes. Remove the foil and bake for 20 to 25 minutes more or until browned on top.
8. Transfer the chicken and vegetables to a serving platter, leaving any juices in the bottom of the pan. Allow the chicken to rest, lightly covered, for 20 minutes before carving.
9. **To make the gravy,** use a spatula to scrape up any brown bits in the roasting pan. Transfer the drippings to a liquid measuring cup and add the broth to make a total of 2 cups (480ml). You might need more or less broth depending on the quantity of drippings.
10. In a medium saucepan over medium heat, combine the butter and flour. Cook for 3 to 4 minutes or until the butter lightly browns. Gradually add the broth mixture, whisking until smooth after each addition. Let boil for 3 to 4 minutes. Season with additional salt and pepper to taste.
11. Carve the chicken and serve with the vegetables, stuffing, and gravy.

**SERVING SUGGESTIONS**

To round out the meal, make Garlicky Mashed Potatoes (page 256) and some fresh dinner rolls.

**TIPS**

- Ensure the bread is dry throughout (like a crouton) before adding broth; any type of bread or leftover buns will work. If possible, purchase the bread a few days early, tear it or cut it into ¾-inch (2cm) cubes, and dry it on a pan at room temperature.
- If needed, fresh bread cubes can be dried in the oven at 300°F (150°C) for about 10 minutes. If drying fresh bread in the oven, the stuffing will need less broth.
- Stuffing can be assembled up to 3 days in advance. Remove from the fridge 30 minutes before baking. Additional baking time may be needed.

**APPROXIMATE COOKING TIMES**

- Roast the chicken at 450°F (230°C) for 15 minutes and then for an additional 18 to 20 minutes per pound at 350°F (175°C).
- Cook times can vary slightly if your chicken is cold out of the fridge. For the best results, use a meat thermometer inserted into the thickest part of the thigh without touching the bone and ensure it reaches 165°F (74°F).

| Weight of Chicken | Cook Time at 450°F (230°C) | Cook Time at 350°F (175°C) | Total Cook Time |
|---|---|---|---|
| 4lb (1.8kg) | 15 minutes | 1 hour 20 minutes | 1 hour 35 minutes |
| 5lb (2.3kg) | 15 minutes | 1 hour 40 minutes | 1 hour 55 minutes |
| 6lb (2.7kg) | 15 minutes | 2 hours | 2 hour 15 minutes |

*Scan for how to prepare chicken for roasting.*

# The Best Ever **Meatloaf**

**Prep Time:** 15 minutes
**Total Time:** 1 hour 15 minutes
**Serves** 6

---

## FOR THE MEATLOAF

½ medium **yellow onion**, finely diced

1 teaspoon **butter**

2 **eggs**

¾ cup (180ml) **whole milk**

¾ cup (84g) **seasoned bread crumbs**

2lb (907g) **lean ground beef**

1 tablespoon **ketchup**

1 tablespoon **Worcestershire sauce**

1 teaspoon **Italian seasoning** (for homemade, see page 18)

2 tablespoons chopped **fresh parsley**

¾ teaspoon **salt**

½ teaspoon freshly ground **black pepper**

## FOR THE SAUCE

½ cup (120ml) **Heinz chili sauce** (see Tip)

½ cup (120ml) **ketchup**

2 tablespoons **brown sugar**, optional

---

### Ingredient Swaps

- If you don't have chili sauce, use extra **ketchup** with 1 tablespoon cider vinegar added or swap for **barbecue sauce**.
- Replace 2 tablespoons chopped fresh parsley with 2 teaspoons **dried parsley**.

---

Classic and unfussy, meatloaf has always had a special place in my heart—and my kids dub it their childhood favorite too. It's incredibly delicious, easy to make, and it reheats well. (Although we rarely have leftovers.) The real secret to a perfect meatloaf is skipping the loaf pan so you get a delicious crust on the outside. The zesty topping finishes it off; it's next level. This is the last meatloaf recipe you'll ever need because, honestly, it's the best.

1. Preheat the oven to 350°F (175°C). Line a rimmed baking sheet with foil and spray with cooking spray.
2. **To make the meatloaf,** in a 6-inch (15cm) skillet, cook the onions and butter over medium heat just until softened, about 4 minutes. Cool completely.
3. In a medium bowl, combine the eggs, milk, and bread crumbs. Let sit for 5 minutes.
4. Add the ground beef, cooled onions, ketchup, Worcestershire sauce, Italian seasoning, parsley, salt, and pepper to the bread crumb mixture. Mix until just combined.
5. Form the meatloaf mixture into an 8 × 4-inch (20 × 10cm) loaf and place on the prepared baking sheet. Bake for 40 minutes.
6. **To make the sauce,** while the meatloaf is cooking, combine the chili sauce, ketchup, and brown sugar, if using.
7. Spread the sauce over the meatloaf and bake for an additional 10 to 15 minutes or until the meatloaf has reached an internal temperature of 160°F (71°C) in the center. Broil for 1 to 2 minutes, if desired.
8. Let the meatloaf rest for 10 minutes before slicing and serving.

---

 **SERVING SUGGESTIONS**
Serve this meatloaf alongside Garlicky Mashed Potatoes (page 256) or My All-Time Favorite Mac & Cheese (page 120). Add a side of fresh veggies like broccoli or green beans (page 262).

 **TIP**
Chili sauce is not spicy; it has a tangy flavor, similar to ketchup, but with more zing and less sweetness. It's my favorite part of this meatloaf and worth adding to your grocery list! I prefer Heinz chili sauce, which can be found near the ketchup in most grocery stores.

 **HEY! IT'S OKAY TO . . .**
Save some time and make mini meatloaves instead! Prepare the meatloaf mixture as directed but instead of forming one large loaf, form the meat mixture into 8 mini meatloaves, each 2 × 3 inches (5 × 7.5cm). Place them on the prepared baking sheet and top with the sauce. Bake at 400°F (200°C) for 20 to 24 minutes or to an internal temperature of 160°F (71°C).

## TIPS

- 2 pounds (907g) beef should yield 6 to 8 rouladen. You will need one pickle and one slice of bacon per rouladen.
- Each piece of beef should be about 9 × 4½ inches (23 × 11.5cm) and ¼ inch (0.6cm) thick. If the beef strips aren't long enough, it's okay to overlap two shorter pieces.
- Even if your beef is thinly cut, it should be pounded with a meat mallet to tenderize.
- If you do not have a Dutch oven, brown the rouladen in a large skillet and transfer them to a metal roasting pan with a lid to cook in the oven.

**Prep Time:** 45 minutes
**Total Time:** 2 hours 45 minutes
**Serves** 6

---

2lb (907g) **thin-cut beef round** or flank steak
½ teaspoon **salt**
¼ teaspoon freshly ground **black pepper**
3 tablespoons **yellow mustard**
8 slices uncooked **bacon**
1 medium **yellow onion**, very thinly sliced
8 **dill pickles**
1 tablespoon **butter**
2 cups (480ml) **reduced-sodium beef broth**
4oz (114g) sliced **white mushrooms**
¼ cup (60ml) **dill pickle juice**
4 tablespoons **cornstarch**, plus more as needed
4 tablespoons **cold water**
Cooked **elbow macaroni**, for serving

# Grandma Mary's Rouladen
## with Mushroom Gravy

Visiting my Grandma Mary's house is one of my most cherished memories of childhood. Her basement smelled of pickles, and her kitchen was always filled with the aroma of cabbage rolls and rouladen slow cooking in the oven. This recipe for my grandma's rouladen—an age-old dish of stuffed rolled beef—holds a special place in my heart. I've made it many times over the years, and each time it feels as though she is right there with me. Tender beef rolls filled with bacon, onion, and a dill pickle are slow cooked to perfection and served with a rich, brown mushroom gravy.

1. Preheat the oven to 325°F (165°C).
2. Lay out the beef slices and use the textured side of a meat mallet to pound and tenderize each piece. Ensure the meat is an even thickness of ¼ inch (0.6cm).
3. Season each piece of beef with salt and pepper and spread with a thin layer of mustard.
4. Place a piece of uncooked bacon over each piece of beef and top with the sliced onions. Add a dill pickle to one end and roll up the meat and onions around the pickle, jelly-roll style. Secure with a toothpick or kitchen twine.
5. In a 5-quart (4.7L) Dutch oven over medium heat, melt the butter. Working in batches, brown the beef rolls on all sides and set aside. Add the broth to the Dutch oven, scraping up any brown bits in the bottom of the pan. Return the beef rolls to the Dutch oven and add the mushrooms and pickle juice. Bring to a boil. Once boiling, cover with a lid and remove from the heat.
6. Carefully transfer the Dutch oven to the oven and cook for 60 minutes. Flip the beef rolls over, replace the lid, and cook for 30 to 60 minutes more until the beef becomes tender. To check for doneness, use a fork to pull off a piece of beef. If it's not tender yet, replace the lid and cook for an additional 20 minutes and then check again.
7. Remove the rouladen from the juices, transfer to a plate, and cover to keep warm.
8. To make the gravy, place the Dutch oven on the stovetop and bring the juices to a boil over medium-high heat. Use a spoon or spatula to scrape any brown bits from the sides and bottom.
9. In a small bowl or liquid measuring cup, whisk the cornstarch with the cold water to make a slurry. Drizzle the slurry slowly into the simmering juices while whisking until it reaches the desired consistency. (You might not use all of the slurry.) Season with salt and pepper to taste.
10. Serve rouladen over elbow macaroni and topped with gravy.

---

**SERVING SUGGESTIONS**
Rouladen is often served with spätzle, a small egg noodle, or dumplings. In my family, my mom always served it over elbow macaroni and smothered in gravy—and that's exactly how I serve it here—but mashed potatoes are another great option.

**Prep Time:** 15 minutes
**Total Time:** 1 hour
**Serves** 6

### FOR THE CHOWDER

6 slices uncooked **thick-cut bacon**, chopped

1 medium **yellow onion**, finely diced

2 ribs **celery**, finely diced

¼ cup (30g) **all-purpose flour**

1 teaspoon **Old Bay seasoning**

½ teaspoon **dried thyme leaves**

½ teaspoon **salt**

½ teaspoon freshly ground **black pepper**

3 (6.5oz / 184g) cans **chopped clams**, with juices

⅔ cup (160ml) **clam juice**, or as needed

1lb (454g) **russet potatoes**, peeled and cut into ½-inch (1.5cm) cubes

1½ cups (360ml) **reduced-sodium chicken broth**

2 **bay leaves**

¾ cup (180ml) **half-and-half** or light cream

1½ teaspoons chopped **fresh parsley**

### FOR THE BISCUITS

1½ cups (180g) **self-rising flour**

¾ teaspoon **Old Bay seasoning**

¾ teaspoon **garlic powder**

4½ tablespoons cold **butter**

⅓ cup (37g) shredded **sharp cheddar cheese**

¾ cup (180ml) **milk**, or as needed

---

### Ingredient Swap

To make **homemade self-rising flour**, whisk together 1½ cups (180g) all-purpose flour, 2¼ teaspoons baking powder, and ½ teaspoon salt.

---

# Creamy Clam Chowder
# with Mini Cheddar Biscuits

My husband can't resist a creamy bowl of clam chowder, and while this version isn't a traditional New England clam chowder, it is his favorite and it's a favorite of everyone who tries it. A creamy potato-clam broth is perfectly seasoned and simmered with a handful of vegetables, plenty of chopped clams, and a sprinkle of smoky bacon. Pair it with fluffy bite-size mini cheddar biscuits for dipping, dunking, and savoring every spoonful. Bake the biscuits while the chowder is simmering or make them ahead of time.

1. Heat a 4-quart (3.8L) Dutch oven or saucepan over medium heat. Add the bacon and cook until browned. Remove the bacon with a slotted spoon, leaving the drippings in the pot, and set aside.
2. Add the onion and celery and cook for 3 to 4 minutes or until the onions are tender.
3. Stir in the flour, Old Bay seasoning, thyme, salt, and pepper. Cook for 2 minutes while stirring.
4. Drain the juice from the clams into a liquid measuring cup. Add additional clam juice to make 1½ cups (360ml).
5. Add the clam juice, potatoes, broth, and bay leaves to the Dutch oven. Bring to a boil over medium-high heat, reduce the heat and simmer covered for 12 to 14 minutes or until the potatoes are very tender. (While the chowder is simmering, you can prepare the dough for the biscuits.)
6. Once the potatoes are tender, stir in the half-and-half and simmer uncovered for 5 minutes or until thickened. If desired, mash some of the potatoes using a potato masher to thicken the chowder.
7. Remove and discard the bay leaves, and stir in half of the cooked bacon along with the clams and parsley. Turn off the heat and let rest for 3 minutes.
8. Ladle into bowls and garnish with the remaining bacon and additional parsley, if desired.

### FOR THE BISCUITS

1. Preheat the oven to 400°F (200°C). Line a large baking sheet with parchment paper (or grease it well) and set aside.
2. In a medium bowl, whisk the flour, Old Bay seasoning, and garlic powder.
3. Cut in the cold butter with a fork or pastry cutter until the butter is slightly smaller than the size of peas. Stir in the cheddar cheese.
4. Add the milk a bit at a time, stirring after each addition to make a dough that is sticky and can be dropped with a spoon. You may not need all of the milk.
5. Drop the dough by slightly heaping teaspoons, ½ inch (1.5cm) apart onto the prepared baking sheet to create 36 mini biscuits. Bake for 7 to 10 minutes or lightly browned.

**FEELING FANCY?**

Check your local grocery store or bakery for bread bowls. Bake in a 400°F (200°C) oven for 7 to 10 minutes or until heated through and crisp. To serve, cut 1-inch (2.5cm) off the top of the loaf and hollow the loaf out, leaving a ½-inch (1.5cm) shell inside. Fill with clam chowder and serve the top and insides for dipping.

**Prep Time:** 20 minutes
**Total Time:** 8 hours 20 minutes
**Serves** 6

---

3½–4lb (1.6–1.8kg) **chuck roast**

1½ teaspoons **salt**

1 teaspoon freshly ground
**black pepper**

1 tablespoon **vegetable oil**

1 tablespoon **butter**

1 large **yellow onion**, cut into
1-inch (2.5cm) pieces

½ cup (120ml) **red wine**

1 cup (240ml) **beef stock**

1½ tablespoons **soy sauce**

4 cloves **garlic**, chopped

1 teaspoon **dried rosemary**,
crushed

½ teaspoon **dried thyme leaves**

1 **bay leaf**

1lb (454g) **yellow- or red-skinned
potatoes** (about 4 medium),
cut into 2-inch (5cm) pieces

4 **carrots**, cut into 2-inch (5cm)
pieces

3 ribs **celery**, cut into ½-inch
(1.5cm) pieces

**FOR THE GRAVY**

3 tablespoons **cornstarch**

3 tablespoons **cold water**

1 or 2 **beef bouillon cubes**,
if needed

---

**Ingredient Swaps**
The red wine can be replaced with
additional **beef stock**.

---

*Scan for instructions
to prepare in oven.*

# Slow Cooker Pot Roast
## with Root Veggies & Gravy

A hearty pot roast is an unfussy, almost effortless kind of meal that just tastes like home. Cooked low and slow in either a slow cooker or the oven, beef roast becomes melt-in-your-mouth tender and delicious. Served with root veggies and smothered in a rich brown gravy, this really is the ultimate Sunday supper.

1. Pat the roast dry with a paper towel and season with salt and pepper.
2. In a large skillet, heat the oil over medium-high heat. Add the roast to the skillet and sear on each side until browned, about 4 minutes per side. Transfer the roast to a 6-quart (5.7L) slow cooker.
3. Reduce the stovetop heat to medium, and add the butter and onion to the skillet. Cook for 3 to 4 minutes or until the onion begins to soften. Transfer the onion to the slow cooker.
4. Add the wine to the skillet, scraping up any browned bits, and let simmer for 2 minutes. Stir in the beef stock, soy sauce, garlic, rosemary, and thyme. Pour the sauce over the roast and add the bay leaf. Arrange the potatoes, carrots, and celery around the roast.
5. Cover the slow cooker, set to low, and cook for 8 to 10 hours or until the roast is fork-tender.
6. Remove the roast and vegetables to a platter and cover with foil to rest. Discard the bay leaf.
7. **To make the gravy,** pour the juices from the slow cooker into a medium saucepan and heat to boiling over medium-high heat. In a small bowl, whisk the cornstarch and water to make a slurry. Slowly add the slurry to the boiling juices, while whisking, to reach desired consistency; you might not need all the cornstarch mixture. Taste the gravy and if it is light in flavor, add 1 bouillon cube and whisk to combine. Taste and add a second bouillon cube, if needed. Boil for 1 minute. Season with additional salt and pepper to taste.

---

 **TIPS**

- The liquid added in step 4 will not cover the roast; the roast will release juices as it cooks.
- A 4-pound (1.8kg) roast will need closer to 9 to 10 hours. If the roast is over 4 pounds, cut it in half if cooking in the slow cooker and check it at 8 hours.
- Whether cooking in the slow cooker or the oven, to test the roast for doneness, stick a fork in the center of the roast; it should go in very easily, and you should be able to twist it with almost no effort. If there is any resistance, cook the roast a little bit longer.
- It is not recommended to cook this in the slow cooker on high as the meat will be most tender when cooked low and slow.

**Prep Time:** 1 hour
**Total Time:** 2 hours 15 minutes
**Serves** 12

9 **lasagna noodles**
2 tablespoons **butter**
2 cloves **garlic**, minced
1lb (454g) **white mushrooms**,
   sliced ¼ inch (0.6cm) thick
1lb (454g) **cremini mushrooms**,
   sliced ¼ inch (0.6cm) thick
8oz (227g) fresh spinach, coarsely
   chopped
½ teaspoon **salt**
3 cups (375g) shredded **cooked
   chicken**, divided
3 cups (339g) shredded
   **mozzarella cheese**, divided
¼ cup (25g) shredded **Parmesan
   cheese**

**FOR THE SAUCE**
6 tablespoons **butter**
1 small **yellow onion**, finely diced
2 cloves **garlic**, minced
⅓ cup (40g) **all-purpose flour**
1½ teaspoons **Italian seasoning**
   (for homemade, see page 18)
2 cups (480ml) **whole milk**
1½ cups (360ml) **chicken broth**
1 cup (113g) shredded **mozzarella
   cheese**
1 cup (113g) shredded **Gouda
   cheese**
½ cup (50g) shredded **Parmesan
   cheese**
½ teaspoon **salt**
½ teaspoon freshly ground
   **black pepper**
Pinch of **nutmeg**

---

### Ingredient Swaps

- Swap out the white and cremini mushrooms for 4 cups (575g) of **any cooked vegetable.** Steamed broccoli, cauliflower, and asparagus are all great in this recipe.
- Use **any shredded cheese** you have on hand in place of Gouda, but be sure to keep the mozzarella; it adds just the right texture to the sauce.

# Three-Cheese Creamy
# **Chicken & Mushroom Lasagna**

I've always had a deep love for cheesy pasta, so it's no surprise that this creamy lasagna tops my list. Heaps of garlicky mushrooms and shredded chicken are smothered in a rich, homemade cheese sauce and baked together under a layer of bubbly browned cheese. When I make this, my kids lick their plates clean— a total win in my book. There are a few steps to this recipe, but it's worth the effort, and leftovers reheat beautifully. Perfection.

1. Preheat the oven to 350°F (175°C). Grease a 9 × 13-inch (23 × 33cm) baking dish and set aside.
2. In a large pot of salted water, cook the lasagna noodles according to the package directions. Drain well and set aside.
3. In a large 12-inch (30cm) skillet, melt 2 tablespoons butter over medium-high heat. Add the garlic and white and cremini mushrooms. Cook, stirring occasionally, for 10 to 12 minutes or until the juices have been released and almost evaporated. Stir in the spinach and cook for 2 minutes more or until wilted. Season with ½ teaspoon salt. Remove from the heat and set aside.
4. **To make the sauce,** in a medium saucepan, melt 6 tablespoons butter over medium heat. Stir in the onion and garlic; cook until tender without browning, about 4 minutes.
5. Whisk in the flour and Italian seasoning, and cook for 1 minute or until bubbly. Gradually stir in the milk and broth, whisking until smooth after each addition. Increase the heat to medium-high and bring the mixture to a boil, while whisking constantly, and boil for 2 minutes or until slightly thickened.
6. Remove the saucepan from the heat and whisk in the mozzarella cheese, Gouda cheese, ½ cup (50g) Parmesan cheese, ½ teaspoon salt, pepper, and nutmeg.
7. To assemble the lasagna, spread 1 cup (240ml) sauce in the bottom of the prepared baking dish. Top the sauce with 3 cooked lasagna noodles. Layer half of the shredded chicken and half of the mushroom mixture over the noodles. Sprinkle with ½ cup (57g) mozzarella cheese and top with 1 cup (240ml) sauce. Repeat these layers once more with 3 noodles, remaining chicken and mushrooms, ½ cup (57g) mozzarella, and 1 cup (240ml) sauce.
8. Top with the remaining 3 lasagna noodles and the remaining sauce.
9. Cover the lasagna with foil and bake for 30 minutes.
10. Remove the foil and top with the remaining 2 cups (226g) mozzarella cheese and the Parmesan cheese. Bake for 25 to 30 minutes more or until bubbly. Broil for 2 to 3 minutes to brown the top, if desired.
11. Rest for at least 15 minutes before cutting and serving.

---

**TIP**
Use shredded rotisserie chicken in this recipe or shredded Perfect Baked Chicken Breasts (page 247).

**VARIATION**
To make this recipe vegetarian, replace the shredded chicken with additional cooked vegetables, and replace the chicken broth with vegetable broth.

✓

**HEY! IT'S OKAY TO . . .**

Save some time and swap the homemade sauce for
our fave shortcut sauce. In a medium bowl, combine
1 (10.5oz / 298g) can condensed cream of mushroom
soup, 1 (15oz / 425g) jar of your favorite Alfredo
sauce, and ⅓ cup (80ml) whole milk. Season with
salt and pepper. Stir in 1 cup (113g) shredded
mozzarella, 1 cup (113g) shredded Gouda, and
½ cup (50g) shredded Parmesan cheese.

# Rustic **Beef & Veggie Pot Pie**

**Prep Time:** 1 hour
**Total Time:** 3 hours 50 minutes
**Serves** 6

---

4 slices uncooked **bacon**, chopped
2lb (908g) **chuck roast**
1 teaspoon **salt**
½ teaspoon freshly ground **black pepper**
1 large **yellow onion**, chopped
12oz (340g) **cremini mushrooms**, quartered
¼ cup (30g) **all-purpose flour**
½ cup (120ml) **ale** or dark beer
1¾ cups (420ml) **beef stock**
2 tablespoons **tomato paste**
1½ tablespoons **Worcestershire sauce**
2 **bay leaves**
½ teaspoon **dried thyme leaves**
1 teaspoon **dried rosemary**
4 medium **carrots**, cut into ¾-inch (2cm) pieces
2 ribs **celery**, sliced
½ cup (64g) **frozen peas**
1 sheet **frozen puff pastry,** thawed in the refrigerator overnight
1 **egg**

## Ingredient Swaps

- The ale or dark beer adds depth and flavor to the gravy but does not taste of beer once cooked; however, ale can be replaced with additional **beef stock.**
- **Stewing beef** can be used in place of chuck roast, but it might need an additional 30 minutes of cooking time before adding the vegetables.

This recipe marries the traditional goodness of a classic beef pot pie with a savory gravy inspired by British ale pie. It's slow cooked in the oven to create a richly flavored deep brown gravy, beef so tender it practically melts in your mouth, and hearty roasted veggies. Baked under a layer of flaky puff pastry, this is exactly what a warm, cozy Sunday supper is all about.

1. Preheat the oven to 325°F (165°C).
2. In a 5-quart (4.7L) Dutch oven, cook the bacon over medium-high heat until the fat is rendered, about 4 minutes. Transfer the bacon to a plate, reserving 1 tablespoon bacon grease in the Dutch oven and reserving the rest in a bowl.
3. Trim the beef, cut it into 1-inch (2.5cm) cubes, and toss with salt and pepper. Brown the beef in batches in the bacon grease over medium-high heat, adding more grease if needed. Transfer to a bowl.
4. Add the onion to the Dutch oven and cook for 3 minutes or until it begins to soften. Add the chopped mushrooms and cook until they begin to release their liquid, about 4 minutes. Stir in the flour and cook for 1 minute more.
5. Add the ale and beef stock, scraping up any browned bits. Stir in the browned beef with any accumulated juices, tomato paste, Worcestershire sauce, bay leaves, thyme, rosemary, and cooked bacon. Bring to a boil, cover, and transfer to the oven. Cook in the oven for 60 minutes. Stir in the carrots and celery, cover, and continue cooking for an additional 45 to 60 minutes or until the beef and vegetables are tender.
6. Remove the Dutch oven from the oven. Transfer the beef mixture to a 9 × 13-inch (23 × 33cm) baking dish. Remove and discard the bay leaves. Stir in the frozen peas, taste the sauce, and season with additional salt and pepper, if desired.
7. Increase the oven temperature to 400°F (200°C).
8. On a lightly floured work surface, use a rolling pin to roll the puff pastry into a 10 × 14-inch (26 × 36cm) rectangle.
9. Top the beef mixture with the puff pastry, tucking any excess pastry up the sides of the baking dish, and cut a few slits in the pastry to allow steam to escape. Whisk the egg with 1 tablespoon water and lightly brush over the puff pastry.
10. Bake for 35 to 40 minutes or until the filling is bubbly and the crust is a deep golden brown. Rest 10 minutes before serving.

---

**SERVING SUGGESTIONS**
While this is a complete feast on its own, as with most saucy recipes, I love a good chunk of bread to sop up any bits in the bottom of the bowl.

**TIP**
If you don't have a Dutch oven, prepare the filling in a large, deep skillet and then roast the mixture in a 9 × 13-inch (23 × 33cm) baking dish tightly covered with heavy-duty foil. If cooking in a baking dish, you may need to add additional cooking time.

**MAKE AHEAD**
Prepare the filling up to 48 hours in advance. If the filling is cold from the fridge, warm it in the oven for 15 minutes before adding the puff pastry. The baking time may need to be increased slightly.

**Prep Time:** 15 minutes
**Total Time:** 4 hours 25 minutes
**Serves** 4

2 racks of **pork ribs**, about 2½–3lb
  (1.1–1.4kg) total
1 teaspoon **salt**
½ teaspoon freshly ground
  **black pepper**
½ cup (120ml) **water**
1 medium **yellow onion**, cut into
  ¼-inch (0.6cm) slices
4 cloves **garlic**, sliced

**FOR THE SAUCE**
1 teaspoon **vegetable oil**
4 cloves **garlic**, minced
⅓ cup (80ml) **honey**
¼ cup (60ml) **soy sauce**
2 teaspoons minced **fresh ginger**
½ teaspoon **red pepper flakes**
⅓ cup (80ml) **cold water**
1 tablespoon **cornstarch**

# Slow Cooker Sticky **Honey-Garlic Ribs**

You won't believe how easy these tender, fall-off-the-bone ribs are to make. With just minutes of prep, the slow cooker transforms ribs into a tender, melt-in-your-mouth, finger-lickin' favorite. Simply add the ribs to the slow cooker, set it, and forget it. Just before serving, brush the ribs with the sticky honey-garlic sauce and give them a flash broil for a couple of minutes. No grill required.

1. Remove the silverskin membrane from the back of the ribs if present. Cut each slab in half and pat dry with a paper towel. Season both sides of the ribs with salt and pepper.

2. Place the ribs upright in a 6-quart (5.7L) slow cooker and add the water, onion, and garlic. Cover and cook on high for 4 hours or on low for 8 hours or until fork-tender.

3. Meanwhile, **to make the sauce,** in a 6-inch (15cm) skillet, heat the oil over medium heat. Add the garlic and cook for 2 minutes or until fragrant without browning.

4. Add the honey, soy sauce, ginger, and red pepper flakes to the skillet and bring to a boil. Boil for 1 minute.

5. In a small bowl, mix the water and cornstarch. While whisking, add the cornstarch mixture to the sauce and boil for 2 minutes more.

6. Line a rimmed baking sheet with foil and spray with cooking spray. Remove the ribs from the slow cooker and place them on the prepared baking sheet. Discard the onions and garlic.

7. Preheat the broiler to high and arrange a baking rack 6 inches (15cm) from the heat.

8. Brush the thickened sauce over both sides of the ribs and broil for 2 to 3 minutes per side or until lightly charred.

**SERVING SUGGESTIONS**
These ribs pair well with baked or roasted sweet potatoes, a fresh cucumber salad, and a big side of coleslaw.

**TIPS**
• Any type of pork ribs can be used in this recipe. Baby back ribs or back ribs are typically the most tender and flavorful option, but they can be pricier. Side ribs or spareribs will also yield tender and delicious results; they are a bit meatier in texture and have great flavor.

• Ribs have a very thin membrane located on the back. It's okay to cook ribs with the membrane on, but I personally prefer to remove it. To remove the membrane, simply slide a knife under it, grip it with a paper towel if needed, and pull it off. If you don't see a membrane, it may have been removed already.

**VARIATION**
You can replace the sauce with my favorite sticky barbecue sauce. Combine ¼ cup (60ml) ketchup, ½ cup (120ml) Heinz chili sauce, and ½ cup (120ml) of your favorite barbecue sauce. Generously brush the sauce over the ribs before broiling. Be sure you're choosing a tangy chili sauce like Heinz, which is sold near the ketchup, and not a hot or spicy chili sauce.

# What to Do with *Ground Beef*

**206**   Beefed-Up Busy Day Lasagna

**209**   Better-Than-Take-Out Cheeseburger Sloppy Joes

**210**   Spicy Hoisin Beef with Garlic Ramen Noodles

**213**   Baked Beef Pinwheels

**214**   Feta Meatballs with Lemon Orzo & Cucumber Salsa

**217**   Mushroom & Swiss–Stuffed Mini Meatloaf

**218**   Ground Beef Barley Soup

**221**   Melty French Onion Meatballs

**222**   Layered Tex-Mex Tortilla Bake

**225**   Hearty Homemade Goulash

**Prep Time:** 10 minutes
**Total Time:** 1 hour 30 minutes
**Serves** 8

---

1lb (454g) **lean ground beef**
1 medium **yellow onion**, diced
3 cloves **garlic**, minced
24oz (710ml) **marinara sauce**
1 (14.5 oz / 411g) can **diced tomatoes**, drained
1½ teaspoons **Italian seasoning** (for homemade, see page 18)
25oz (709g) **frozen cheese ravioli**
5oz (142g) **fresh spinach**, stems removed and coarsely chopped (optional)
2½ cups (284g) shredded **mozzarella cheese**, divided
¼ cup (25g) freshly grated **Parmesan cheese**

*Scan for instructions to prepare in a slow cooker.*

# Beefed-Up Busy Day **Lasagna**

Who doesn't love layer upon layer of rich lasagna deliciousness? Let's be real: a traditional lasagna, while incredibly delicious, is time-consuming (and often reserved for weekends). With a couple of quick shortcuts, you can have all the goodness you crave from a traditional lasagna any night of the week! Layers of pasta, heaps of gooey cheese, and a rich and hearty meaty sauce are topped off with beautifully browned cheese. The best part? It's all cooked in just one pot (including the sauce) until golden and bubbly.

1. Preheat the oven to 375°F (190°C).
2. For the sauce, heat a 4-quart (3.8L) Dutch oven over medium heat. Add the ground beef, onion, and garlic and cook, breaking up the meat with a spoon, for 5 to 6 minutes or until no pink remains. Drain any fat.
3. Add the marinara sauce, diced tomatoes, and Italian seasoning. Simmer uncovered over medium heat, stirring occasionally, for 5 to 7 minutes or until slightly thickened.
4. Remove the Dutch oven from the heat. Remove 4 cups (960ml) of the sauce and set aside.
5. Arrange half of the ravioli over the sauce left in the Dutch oven. Top with half of the spinach (if using), ¾ cup (85g) mozzarella cheese, and 2 cups sauce.
6. Repeat the layers with the remaining ravioli, remaining spinach (if using), ¾ cup (85g) mozzarella cheese, and remaining 2 cups (480ml) sauce.
7. Place the lid on the Dutch oven and bake for 35 minutes.
8. Top with the remaining 1 cup (113g) mozzarella cheese and the Parmesan cheese. Bake uncovered for an additional 15 to 20 minutes or until bubbly.
9. Let rest for 15 minutes before serving.

**TO PREPARE IN A BAKING DISH**

1. Grease a 9 × 13-inch (23 × 33cm) baking dish with cooking spray.
2. Add 1 cup (240ml) sauce to the bottom of the dish and layer half the ravioli, half the spinach (if using), 2 cups (480ml) marinara sauce, and half the mozzarella cheese.
3. Add the remaining ravioli, remaining spinach (if using), and the remaining sauce. Cover with foil and bake for 30 minutes.
4. Uncover, top with the remaining 1¼ cups (141g) mozzarella cheese and the Parmesan cheese. Bake for an additional 10 to 15 minutes or until hot and bubbly.

---

 **SERVING SUGGESTIONS**
Garnish with fresh basil or parsley and additional Parmesan cheese, if desired. This dish pairs well with a fresh salad and crusty bread or warm Garlic Herb Bread (page 255).

**Prep Time:** 10 minutes
**Total Time:** 25 minutes
**Serves** 4

---

¼ cup (60ml) **barbecue sauce**

2 tablespoons **ketchup**

1 tablespoon **yellow mustard**

1½ teaspoons **Worcestershire sauce**

¾ teaspoon **steak seasoning**

1lb (454g) **lean ground beef**

⅔ cup (160ml) **beef broth**

2oz (57g) **cream cheese**

1½ teaspoons **onion powder**

¾ cup (85g) shredded **medium cheddar cheese**

4 large **sesame seed buns**

1 cup (60g) shredded **iceberg lettuce**

½ cup (75g) **sliced pickles**

# Better-Than-Take-Out
# Cheeseburger Sloppy Joes

I love a good cheeseburger with all the fixin's and lots of pickles. This meal is a super easy way to serve up some of that cheesy goodness—sloppy-joe style! Lean ground beef is browned and smothered in a zesty cheese sauce and then spooned into a soft sesame seed bun. Pile it high with pickles and shredded lettuce for a new weeknight favorite.

1. In a small bowl, combine the barbecue sauce, ketchup, mustard, Worcestershire sauce, and steak seasoning. Set aside.
2. Heat a 10-inch (25cm) skillet over medium-high heat. Add the ground beef and cook, breaking up the meat with a spoon, for 5 to 6 minutes or until no pink remains. Drain any fat.
3. Stir in the broth, cream cheese, and onion powder and cook until the cream cheese is melted. Add the barbecue sauce mixture and simmer until slightly thickened, about 5 to 6 minutes.
4. Remove the skillet from the heat and stir in the cheddar cheese until melted.
5. Spoon the beef mixture over the bottom buns, and top with the shredded lettuce and pickles.

---

**TIPS**
- If you are shredding your own cheese to use in this recipe, allow the filling to cool for 3 to 4 minutes before stirring in the cheese.
- Toasting the buns will take these sloppy joes to the next level.

**VARIATION**
If you're looking for a classic sloppy joe, look no further.

*Scan for my Easy Sloppy Joe recipe.*

**FEELING FANCY?**
Make Homemade Quick Pickles in about 15 minutes!

1. In a glass bowl, combine ½ an English cucumber, thinly sliced, and 2 slices of white onion.
2. In a small saucepan, combine ½ cup (120ml) water; ⅓ cup (80ml) white vinegar; 2 teaspoons coarse salt; 1 teaspoon granulated sugar; 1 teaspoon dried dill; and 1 clove garlic, sliced. Boil for 1 minute.
3. Pour the hot brine over the cucumbers and onions and let cool to room temperature, about 10 to 15 minutes. The pickles can be eaten immediately or refrigerated for up to 2 weeks.

**Prep Time:** 15 minutes
**Total Time:** 40 minutes
**Serves** 4

# Spicy Hoisin Beef
## with Garlic Ramen Noodles

This easy recipe transforms a pound of ground beef into a craveable weeknight dinner that's on the table faster than delivery! The sticky hoisin beef is the real star of this dish with a little bit of sweet, a little bit of heat, and a whole lotta flavor. We love to serve it piled high over garlic ramen noodles, but for a fun, hands-on kind of meal, skip the noodles and serve the beef in lettuce wraps with your favorite toppings.

**FOR THE BEEF**

1lb (454g) **lean ground beef**
2 **green onions**, sliced, white and green parts separated
2 teaspoons minced **fresh ginger**
½ cup (120ml) **hoisin sauce**
1 tablespoon **water**
2 teaspoons **sriracha**
1 teaspoon **rice vinegar**
¼ teaspoon **red pepper flakes**
**Sesame seeds**, to garnish

**FOR THE NOODLES**

2 medium **carrots**
2 (3oz / 85g) **packages ramen noodles**, seasoning mixes discarded
1 teaspoon **vegetable oil**
6 cups (390g) thinly sliced **green cabbage**
2 cups (227g) **fresh bean sprouts**
2 cloves **garlic**, minced
3 tablespoons **soy sauce**
2 teaspoons **rice vinegar**
1¾ teaspoons **toasted sesame oil**

1. Using a spiralizer or a vegetable peeler, cut the carrots into long, thin strips, enough to make 2 cups (113g) when gently packed. Set aside.
2. **To make the beef,** heat a 10-inch (25cm) nonstick skillet over medium-high heat. Add the beef to the skillet and cook for 2 to 3 minutes without stirring to form a crust. Continue cooking, now breaking up the meat with a spoon, for 4 to 5 minutes or until no pink remains. Drain any fat.
3. Add the whites of the green onions and the ginger and cook for 1 minute. Add the hoisin, water, sriracha, rice vinegar, and red pepper flakes. Continue cooking over medium-high heat, stirring occasionally, until the sauce is caramelized and begins to crisp and brown, about 3 to 4 minutes. Transfer the beef to a bowl and cover lightly with foil.
4. Meanwhile, **to make the noodles,** cook the ramen according to the package directions, drain well, and set aside.
5. Wipe out the skillet with a paper towel and add the vegetable oil. Add the cabbage and carrot strips and cook until tender, about 3 to 4 minutes. Stir in the bean sprouts and garlic and cook for 2 minutes more.
6. Add the soy sauce, rice vinegar, and sesame oil. Stir in the cooked ramen noodles, toss to coat, and cook for 2 minutes more or until the sauce is absorbed and the noodles are heated through.
7. Place the noodles in bowls and top with the crispy beef. Garnish with the green onion tops and sesame seeds.

**Ingredient Swap**
Replace the carrots, cabbage, and bean sprouts with 16oz (454g) **coleslaw mix**.

 **TIP**
Hoisin is a sweet Chinese condiment that can be found in almost any grocery store near the soy sauce. It's a must-have for this recipe, and it's also great for replacing sugar in marinades, drizzling on lettuce wraps, or stirring into a stir-fry.

 **VARIATION**
Skip the noodles entirely and serve the beef mixture as lettuce wraps. Cook the hoisin beef as directed and add your favorite toppings, like fresh bean sprouts and julienned cucumbers. Drizzle with additional hoisin sauce, if desired.

# Baked Beef Pinwheels

**Prep Time:** 20 minutes
**Total Time:** 1 hour
**Serves** 4

1 **egg**
⅓ cup (39g) **seasoned bread crumbs**
¼ cup (60ml) **marinara sauce**
2 tablespoons chopped **fresh parsley**
1 clove **garlic**, minced
½ teaspoon **dried oregano**
¼ teaspoon **dried basil**
¼ teaspoon **salt**
¼ teaspoon freshly ground **black pepper**
1lb (454g) **lean ground beef**
3oz (85g) thinly sliced **ham**
½ cup (57g) shredded **mozzarella cheese**
2 tablespoons shredded **Parmesan cheese**

These Beef Pinwheels are a fun twist on a traditional meatloaf recipe. This recipe was inspired by a retro-style Sicilian Meat Roll recipe that is in many of my church cookbooks from the '60s and '70s. Seasoned ground beef is layered with ham and cheese, rolled, and sliced into pinwheels. These little bundles are packed with flavor, cook quickly, and make a beautiful presentation.

1. In a medium bowl, combine the egg, bread crumbs, marinara sauce, parsley, garlic, oregano, basil, salt, and pepper. Add the ground beef and gently mix just until combined.
2. Place the beef mixture on a sheet of plastic wrap and press it into a 12 × 8-inch (30 × 20cm) rectangle. Layer the ham on the beef, leaving a 1-inch (2.5cm) space on the short end, and sprinkle with the mozzarella and Parmesan cheeses. Starting with the short end, roll the meat as you would a jelly roll to create a log that is 8 inches (20cm) across. Wrap tightly in plastic wrap, twisting the ends of the wrap to seal, and refrigerate for 15 minutes.
3. Meanwhile, preheat the oven to 350°F (175°C). Line a rimmed baking sheet with parchment paper.
4. Using a serrated knife, cut the roll into four pinwheels, each 2 inches (5cm) wide. Place the pinwheels cut side up on the prepared baking sheet, and seal the pinched edge of the roll with a toothpick.
5. Bake for 20 to 25 minutes or until the center of each roll reaches an internal temperature of 160°F (71°C). Remove the toothpick and discard before serving.

 **SERVING SUGGESTIONS**
For heartier appetites, this recipe can be doubled. Just like with meatloaf, these pinwheels are great with our Garlicky Mashed Potatoes (page 256). We also love to pair them with a simple side dish of spaghetti and marinara sauce.

 **TIPS**
- Pinch the seam well and seal each edge with a toothpick so the rolls do not unwrap.
- If any of the rolls unwrap while baking, immediately squeeze them together with tongs after removing from the oven, while they are still warm.

 **VARIATIONS**
If you'd like to cook these with a sauce, add 1½ cups (360ml) of prepared marinara sauce to a 9-inch (23cm) square baking dish. Increase the cooking time to 28 to 32 minutes.

**Prep Time:** 20 minutes
**Total Time:** 50 minutes
**Serves** 4

---

**FOR THE MEATBALLS**
1lb (454g) **lean ground beef**
¼ cup (28g) **bread crumbs**
¼ cup (28g) finely crumbled
   **feta cheese**
1 **egg**
2 tablespoons **milk**
2 tablespoons minced **red onion**
2 cloves **garlic**, minced
1 tablespoon **dried parsley**
1½ teaspoons **dried oregano**
½ teaspoon **salt**
1 tablespoon **olive oil**

**FOR THE ORZO**
2¼ cups (540ml) **chicken broth**,
   plus more as needed
1 cup (170g) **orzo**
½ teaspoon **dried oregano**
2 tablespoons **lemon juice**
2 tablespoons crumbled
   **feta cheese**

**FOR THE SALSA**
½ **English cucumber**, finely diced
2 tablespoons minced **red onion**
1 tablespoon **olive oil**
2 teaspoons **red wine vinegar**
¼ teaspoon freshly ground
   **black pepper**
⅛ teaspoon **salt**

# Feta Meatballs with Lemon Orzo & Cucumber Salsa

These meatballs are inspired by my fave Greek meatballs from the farmers' market, and they're so good, I do a little happy dance as I fill my plate! This whole meal is totally flavor packed, and everything cooks in just one skillet making cleanup a total breeze. These juicy feta meatballs are perfect paired with fresh lemon orzo, but they can also be cooked on their own and served in a pita with lemon wedges. Fresh cucumber salsa is the perfect topper and can be made days ahead of time.

1. **To make the meatballs,** in a large bowl, combine the ground beef, bread crumbs, feta, egg, milk, red onion, garlic, parsley, oregano, and salt. Gently mix until combined. Roll the mixture into 24 meatballs.
2. In a 12-inch (30cm) nonstick skillet, heat 1 tablespoon olive oil over medium heat. Add the meatballs to the skillet and cook for 5 to 7 minutes, turning occasionally, until they are browned on the outsides.
3. **To make the orzo,** increase the heat to medium-high and add the broth to the skillet with the meatballs, scraping any browned bits from the bottom. Add the orzo and oregano to the skillet. Bring to a boil.
4. Reduce the heat to medium-low so the liquid is at a gentle boil and simmer uncovered, stirring occasionally, for 10 to 15 minutes or until the orzo is tender and the meatballs are cooked through, adding more liquid if needed.
5. Meanwhile, **to make the salsa,** in a small bowl, combine the cucumber, red onion, olive oil, red wine vinegar, pepper, and salt. Set aside.
6. Once the orzo is tender, turn the heat off, stir in the lemon juice and feta cheese, and let rest for 5 minutes to thicken. Season with additional salt to taste.
7. Serve the orzo and meatballs with cucumber salsa.

**TO PREPARE IN AN AIR FRYER**
Prepare the meatball mixture and divide it into 16 meatballs. Preheat the air fryer to 380°F (190°C). Cook the meatballs in a single layer for 12 to 15 minutes while the orzo cooks.

---

 **SERVING SUGGESTIONS**
This meal is perfect on its own, but to stretch it a bit further, add some tzatziki (cucumber yogurt dip) and warmed Greek pita. For a quick side dish, grab a Greek salad from the grocery store.

 **TIP**
Brands of orzo can vary in both the amount of liquid needed and cooking time. Start with 2¼ cups (540ml) broth, and if needed, add additional broth or water ¼ cup (60ml) at a time to create a creamy consistency. The orzo will thicken as it rests.

 **HEY! IT'S OKAY TO . . .**
Swap out the homemade meatballs with frozen meatballs. Cook 1 pound (454g) frozen meatballs according to the package directions. Prepare the orzo as directed in the recipe and increase the oregano to 1½ teaspoons and the feta cheese to ¼ cup (57g). Serve with cucumber salsa.

**MAKE AHEAD**

Prepare the meatballs as directed without baking them and place them on a baking sheet lined with parchment paper. Freeze on the baking sheet, and once frozen, transfer the meatballs to a zipper-lock freezer bag or an airtight freezerproof container for up to 3 months. Thaw the meatballs in the fridge overnight and cook as directed.

Cucumber salsa can be prepared up to 3 days before serving.

---

4oz (113g) **Swiss cheese**, divided
1lb (454g) **lean ground beef**
⅓ cup (39g) **seasoned bread crumbs**
1 **egg yolk**
2 tablespoons **milk**
1 tablespoon grated **yellow onion**
1 tablespoon **olive oil**
1 ½ teaspoons **Dijon mustard**
¾ teaspoon **salt**
½ teaspoon **garlic powder**
¼ teaspoon **dried thyme leaves**
¼ teaspoon freshly ground **black pepper**

**FOR THE FILLING**
1 tablespoon **butter**
6oz (170g) sliced **white mushrooms** or cremini mushrooms
1 clove **garlic**, minced
⅛ teaspoon **salt**

# Mushroom & Swiss–Stuffed Mini Meatloaf

Our family loves meatloaf; it's a classic dinner that never goes out of style! In this quickie recipe, a seasoned beef mixture is stuffed with a cheesy mushroom and Swiss filling, and while these may be mini, they pack a big flavor. These bake up in no time at all, making them a perfect weeknight meal. Good things really do come in small packages!

1. Preheat the oven to 400°F (200°C). Line a rimmed baking sheet with parchment paper and set aside.
2. Cut 3 ounces (85g) of the Swiss cheese into 4 cubes, shred the remaining 1 ounce (28g) Swiss cheese, and set both aside.
3. **To make the filling,** in a 10-inch (25cm) skillet, melt the butter over medium-high heat. Add the mushrooms and cook until they start to release liquid. Stir in the garlic and salt and continue cooking until tender, about 4 minutes. Cool completely.
4. While the mushrooms are cooling, in a medium bowl, combine the ground beef, bread crumbs, egg yolk, milk, grated onion, oil, mustard, salt, garlic powder, thyme, and pepper, and mix well.
5. Divide the meat mixture into 4 portions, flatten each into a 4-inch (10cm) circle, and top with a cube of Swiss cheese and one-quarter of the mushroom mixture.
6. Gently wrap the meat around the filling, ensuring it is sealed. Shape the meat into a mini meatloaf, about 3 × 2 inches (7.5 × 5cm). Repeat with remaining 3 meat portions.
7. Place the loaves, seam sides down, on the prepared baking sheet. Divide the shredded Swiss cheese evenly over the top of the loaves.
8. Bake for 22 to 25 minutes or until the meatloaves have reached an internal temperature of 165°F (74°C).
9. Cool for 5 minutes before serving.

---

**SOMETHING ON THE SIDE**
- Turn this meal into a sheet pan dinner by adding veggies to the pan. Toss 2 cups (240g) baby carrots, halved lengthwise, and 2 cups (320g) quartered baby potatoes (any color) with 1 tablespoon olive oil and ½ teaspoon each of salt and black pepper. Add them to the sheet pan along with the meatloaves.
- Quick-cooking vegetables, like sliced peppers, mushrooms, or zucchini, can be added during the last 15 minutes of cooking time; see page 262 for roasting preparation.

**MAKE AHEAD**
These mini meatloaves can be prepared up to 48 hours in advance. Store them in a sealed container in the fridge. Take them out of the fridge and let them sit at room temperature for at least 15 minutes, while the oven preheats, before baking.

**Prep Time:** 20 minutes
**Total Time:** 1 hour
**Serves** 4

---

8oz (227g) **lean ground beef**
½ medium **yellow onion**, diced
1 clove **garlic**, minced
1 rib **celery**, sliced
1 **carrot**, sliced
2oz (56g) sliced **cremini mushrooms**
3 cups (720ml) **reduced-sodium beef broth**
½ cup (120ml) **vegetable juice**, such as V8, or tomato juice
½ cup (120ml) **water**
1 cup (30g) finely chopped, gently packed **kale** (optional)
⅓ cup (60g) **pearl barley**
1½ teaspoons **Worcestershire sauce**
1 teaspoon **soy sauce**
¼ teaspoon **dried thyme leaves**
¼ teaspoon freshly ground **black pepper**, plus more to taste
1 **bay leaf**
**Salt**, to taste

**Ingredient Swaps**

**To make the soup vegetarian,** skip the ground beef and increase the mushrooms to 8 ounces (227g). Swap the beef broth for mushroom or vegetable broth. Skip the Worcestershire sauce and increase the soy sauce to 1 tablespoon.

# Ground Beef **Barley Soup**

Beef barley is a feel-good soup, and there's nothing fussy about it. The secret ingredient here is vegetable juice—it makes the soup taste like it's been simmering all day long—and starches from the barley give the broth a rich, silky texture, perfect for dunking crusty bread. Use this recipe as an opportunity to clean out the produce drawer: toss in that last handful of green beans, the kernels from a leftover ear of corn, or the tomato that's on its last leg. It's like a warm hug from Grandma's kitchen!

1. In a large saucepan over medium-high heat, cook the beef, onion, and garlic, breaking up the beef with a spoon, for 5 to 6 minutes or until no pink remains. Drain any fat.
2. Add the celery, carrot, and mushrooms to the beef and cook for 2 to 3 minutes or until the mushrooms begin to release liquid.
3. Add the broth, vegetable juice, water, kale (if using), barley, Worcestershire sauce, soy sauce, thyme, pepper, and bay leaf.
4. Increase the heat to high and bring to a boil. Reduce the heat to medium-low, cover, and simmer for 30 to 35 minutes until the barley is just tender.
5. Remove the bay leaf, taste, and season with salt and additional pepper, if desired.

 **VARIATION**

To make a beef soup with rice or pasta instead of barley, prepare the soup as directed, omitting the water and the barley in step 3. In step 4, reduce the cooking time and simmer for 15 to 20 minutes or just until the vegetables are tender. Cook 4 servings of pasta or rice according to the package directions, add a serving to each bowl, and ladle the hot soup over the pasta or rice.

 **MAKE AHEAD**

- Leftover beef barley soup can be stored in the refrigerator for up to 3 days. The barley will soak up some of the broth over time, so you may need to add a little bit of extra broth or water when reheating.
- This recipe doubles easily and freezes well. Prepare as directed and cool the soup, then ladle it into zipper-lock freezer bags or airtight freezerproof containers, leaving 1 inch (2.5cm) of space at the top. Freeze for up to 4 months. Thaw the soup in the fridge overnight and heat it on the stovetop, adding a bit of water or broth as needed.

**Prep Time:** 25 minutes
**Total Time:** 55 minutes
**Serves** 6

---

2 tablespoons **butter**

1lb (454g) **sweet onion**, about
   2 large, sliced ¼ inch (0.6cm)
   thick

½ teaspoon light or dark
   **brown sugar**

2⅔ cups (640ml) **beef broth**,
   divided

⅓ cup (80ml) **dry white wine**

1½ tablespoons **cornstarch**

1 tablespoon **Worcestershire
   sauce**

1 **bay leaf**

½ teaspoon **dried thyme leaves**

¼ teaspoon freshly ground
   **black pepper**

½ cup (57g) freshly grated
   **Gruyère cheese**

½ cup (57g) freshly grated
   **mozzarella cheese**

**FOR THE MEATBALLS**

1lb (454g) l**ean ground beef**

½ cup (56g) **seasoned bread
   crumbs**

¼ cup (60ml) **milk**

1 teaspoon **Italian seasoning**
   (for homemade, see page 18)

1 **egg**

2 tablespoons finely chopped
   **fresh parsley**

2 tablespoons shredded
   **Parmesan cheese**

¼ teaspoon **salt**

---

**Ingredient Swap**
The wine can be replaced with
additional **beef broth**.

# Melty **French Onion Meatballs**

French onion soup is one of my husband's all-time favorites, with a rich, sweet onion broth under a layer of browned, bubbly cheese. This recipe channels those cozy French onion vibes and turns them into a hearty meal with tender beef meatballs, lots of caramelized onions, and a deep brown gravy. As you'd expect, it's topped with a blanket of browned, bubbly cheese.

1. Preheat the oven to 425°F (220°C).
2. In a 12-inch (30cm) skillet over medium-high heat, melt the butter. Add the onion and brown sugar and stir until the onion begins to soften and brown. Add ⅓ cup (80ml) broth 2 tablespoons at a time, stirring frequently, and cook until the onions are caramelized, about 15 to 17 minutes.
3. Meanwhile, **to make the meatballs,** in a medium bowl, combine the ground beef, bread crumbs, milk, Italian seasoning, egg, parsley, Parmesan cheese, and salt. Roll the mixture into 24 meatballs, each about 1 inch (2.5cm) in diameter.
4. Place the meatballs in a 2-quart (1.9L) baking dish and bake uncovered for 14 minutes.
5. Stir the white wine into the caramelized onions and cook over medium-high heat until the wine is almost evaporated.
6. Whisk the remaining 2⅓ cups (560ml) broth with the cornstarch and Worcestershire sauce. Add it to the skillet along with the bay leaf, thyme, and pepper. Bring to a boil and simmer for 5 minutes or until slightly thickened. Discard the bay leaf.
7. Pour the sauce and onions over the meatballs, top with the Gruyère and mozzarella cheeses, and bake for an additional 8 to 12 minutes or until the meatballs have reached an internal temperature of 165°F (74°C) and the cheese is browned and bubbly.
8. Rest for 5 minutes before serving.

---

**SERVING SUGGESTIONS**
Serve these meatballs over thick slices of garlic toast, mashed potatoes, or egg noodles. We love green beans (see page 264) with these meatballs for a fresh and easy side dish.

**HEY! IT'S OKAY TO . . .**
- Replace the homemade meatballs with 1 pound (454g) frozen cooked meatballs. Preheat the oven to 400°F (200°C), prepare the sauce as directed, and place the meatballs in a 2-quart (1.9L) baking dish. Bake the meatballs for 14 minutes. Add the sauce and sprinkle with the mozzarella and Gruyère cheeses. Bake for 8 to 12 minutes more.
- Make a shortcut sauce: Omit the caramelized onions and in a small saucepan, whisk together 1 (10.5oz / 298g) can condensed French onion soup, ¼ cup (60ml) water, 2 tablespoons heavy whipping cream, and 2 teaspoons cornstarch. Bring to a boil over medium-high heat.

# Layered Tex-Mex **Tortilla Bake**

**Prep Time:** 25 minutes
**Total Time:** 1 hour 10 minutes
**Serves** 8

1lb (454g) **lean ground beef**
½ medium **red onion**, finely diced
1 **green bell pepper**, diced
1 **red bell pepper**, diced
2¾ cups (660ml) **red enchilada sauce**, divided
1 (15.25oz / 432g) can **black beans**, drained and rinsed
1 (10oz / 283g) can **diced tomatoes with chiles**, such as Rotel, drained
1 cup (144g) **frozen corn**, thawed
2 tablespoons **taco seasoning** (for homemade, see page 18)
½ teaspoon **salt**
12 (6in / 15cm) **flour tortillas** or corn tortillas
3 cups (339g) shredded **Mexican cheese blend**, divided

I love all Tex-Mex-inspired dishes, especially when they include enchilada sauce. This crowd-pleasing casserole has layers of tortillas, seasoned beef, beans, and a whole rainbow of vegetables. It's all smothered in zesty enchilada sauce and baked until browned and bubbly. This casserole can be prepared and baked immediately or prepped on the weekend and baked a couple of days later for an easy weeknight meal.

1. Preheat the oven to 350°F (175°C). Grease a 9 × 13-inch (23 × 33cm) baking dish.
2. Heat a large 12-inch (30cm) skillet over medium-high heat. Add the ground beef and onion and cook, breaking up the meat with a spoon, for 5 to 6 minutes or until no pink remains. Drain any fat.
3. Add the green and red bell peppers to the skillet and cook for 3 to 4 minutes until softened. Stir in 1½ cups (360ml) enchilada sauce and the black beans, tomatoes, corn, taco seasoning, and salt. Simmer for 5 minutes.
4. Spread ½ cup (120ml) enchilada sauce in the bottom of the baking dish. Layer 4 tortillas over the sauce, cutting them in half as needed.
5. Add half of the meat mixture and 1 cup (113g) shredded cheese. Repeat the layers with 4 tortillas, the remaining meat mixture, and 1 cup (113g) shredded cheese.
6. Top with the last 4 tortillas and the remaining ¾ cup (180ml) enchilada sauce.
7. Cover tightly with foil and bake for 30 minutes. Uncover, top with the remaining 1 cup (113g) cheese, and bake for 10 to 15 minutes more or until browned and bubbly. Rest for 10 minutes before serving.

---

**SERVING SUGGESTIONS**
This is a full meal; set out bowls of your favorite taco-style toppings for a fun dinner. We love sour cream, shredded lettuce, jalapeños, tomatoes, and green onions.

**TIPS**
- When layering tortillas, cut them in half and place the straight edge along the edges of the pan and the rounded edge toward the center for the best fit.
- This recipe can be halved and baked in an 8-inch (20cm) square baking dish for 4 servings. Bake covered for 15 minutes. Uncover, add the remaining cheese, and bake uncovered for 20 minutes more or until browned and bubbly.

**FEELING FANCY?**
Did you know that it's really easy to make homemade enchilada sauce? You'll need just a handful of ingredients, some spices, and about 15 minutes.

*Scan for my Homemade Enchilada Sauce recipe.*

→

**MAKE AHEAD**

Prepare as directed up to step 6 reserving 1 cup (113g) shredded cheese in a separate container. Cover the unbaked casserole tightly with plastic wrap and refrigerate for up to 3 days. Remove from the refrigerator 30 minutes before baking. Remove the plastic wrap and cover the dish with foil. Bake covered for 30 minutes. Uncover, sprinkle the reserved cheese over top, and bake for 15 to 20 minutes more or until heated through and bubbly.

**Prep Time:** 20 minutes
**Total time:** 45 minutes
**Serves** 6

---

1lb (454g) **lean ground beef**

1 large **yellow onion,** finely diced

2 cloves **garlic,** minced

2 cups (480ml) **marinara sauce**

2 cups (480ml) **beef broth**
or water

1 (14oz / 397g) can **diced
tomatoes,** with juices

3 tablespoons **tomato paste**

1½ teaspoons **Italian seasoning**
(for homemade, see page 18)

½ teaspoon **granulated sugar**

½ teaspoon **salt,** plus more to
taste

¼ teaspoon freshly ground **black
pepper,** plus more to taste

8oz (227g) **elbow macaroni,**
about 1½ cups

---

**Ingredient Swap**
Replace the ground beef with **any
variety of ground meat.**

# Hearty Homemade **Goulash**

When I'm looking for something easy and super satisfying, this childhood favorite is a go-to. It's easy to see why this was always on the table—the ingredients are usually on hand, everyone loves it, and just one pan means easy cleanup. It's a versatile dish, so feel free to change up the seasonings or add in a handful of veggies if you'd like.

1. Heat a deep 12-inch (30cm) skillet over medium-high heat. Add the beef, onion, and garlic and cook, breaking up the meat with a spoon, for 5 to 6 minutes or until no pink remains. Drain any fat.
2. Stir in the marinara sauce, broth, diced tomatoes with juices, tomato paste, Italian seasoning, sugar, salt, and pepper.
3. Bring to a boil over medium-high heat and add the elbow macaroni. Reduce the temperature to medium-low, cover, and simmer for 10 minutes, stirring occasionally. Remove the lid and simmer uncovered for 5 to 10 minutes more or until the pasta is tender.
4. Remove from the heat and let rest uncovered for 5 minutes before serving. Season with additional salt and pepper to taste.

**TIPS**

- Some brands of pasta may require a little bit of extra liquid. Add additional broth or water if needed to maintain a saucy consistency. The mixture will thicken as it cools.
- This recipe can easily be doubled to feed a crowd, and it reheats well.

**VARIATIONS**

- Stir in 1 cup (113g) shredded cheddar after the mixture has rested.
- Add 1 diced green bell pepper along with the diced tomatoes.

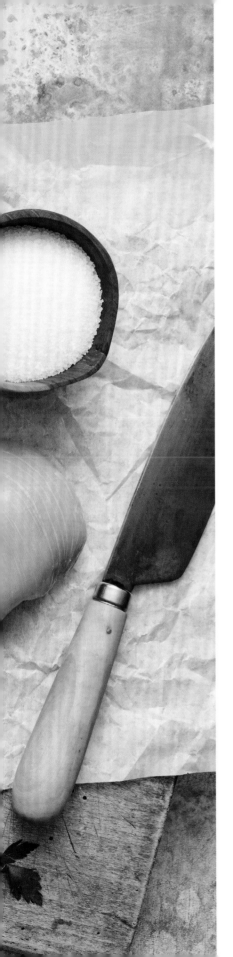

# When All You Have
## *Is Chicken*

**228** One-Pan Chicken Pomodoro Skillet

**231** Choose-Your-Own-Adventure Chicken Stir-Fry

**232** Slow Cooker Homestyle Chicken & Vegetable Chowder

**235** Pimento Cheese–Stuffed Chicken Breasts with Honey Corn

**236** Grilled Greek Chicken Wraps with Feta Mint Sauce

**239** Easy Salsa Chicken Power Bowls

**240** Skillet Chicken & Gravy

**243** Cozy Chicken, Mushroom & Rice Soup

**244** Cowboy Chopped Chicken Salad

**247** Perfect Baked Chicken Breasts

4 boneless, skinless **chicken breasts**, about 6oz (170g) each
1¼ teaspoon **salt**, divided
¾ teaspoon freshly ground **black pepper**, divided
1 tablespoon **olive oil**
4 cloves **garlic**, minced
¼ cup (60ml) **water**
1 (28oz / 794ml) can **whole San Marzano tomatoes**, with juices
½ teaspoon **granulated sugar**
¼ teaspoon **dried basil**
¼ teaspoon **dried oregano**
2 **Roma tomatoes**, diced
8 to 10 **fresh basil leaves**, thinly sliced, to garnish

# One-Pan
# Chicken Pomodoro Skillet

This is one of those dishes where a handful of the simplest of ingredients come together and create a beautiful, fresh-tasting meal that's worthy of a great Italian restaurant. In just one skillet, tender chicken breasts are gently simmered in an easy homemade tomato sauce. This meal requires only a few minutes of prep, and it's on the table in about a half hour.

1. Layer the chicken breasts between two sheets of plastic wrap and use the flat side of a meat mallet to pound to an even thickness of ½ inch (1.5cm). Season with 1 teaspoon salt and ½ teaspoon pepper.
2. In a 10-inch (25cm) skillet, heat the oil over medium-high heat. Add the chicken and cook for 2 to 3 minutes per side or until browned; it does not need to be cooked through. Remove the chicken from the pan and set it aside on a plate. Reduce the heat to medium.
3. Add the garlic to the pan and cook just until fragrant, about 1 minute. Add the water and scrape up any browned bits with a spatula.
4. Add the canned tomatoes with juices to the pan, breaking up the tomatoes with your hands as you add them. Stir in the sugar, dried basil, and oregano. Return the chicken to the skillet and turn to coat with the sauce.
5. Cover and cook over medium heat for 11 to 14 minutes or until the chicken is cooked through and reaches 165°F (74°C). Remove the chicken from the sauce and let rest for 5 minutes.
6. While the chicken is resting, stir in the diced Roma tomatoes and cook until heated through, about 3 minutes. Season with the remaining ¼ teaspoon each salt and pepper or to taste. Serve the sauce over the chicken and sprinkle with fresh basil.

 **SERVING SUGGESTIONS**
This is an incredibly fresh-tasting dish. The sauce is great served over pasta or polenta. Roasted zucchini (page 262) makes a perfect side dish, along with some crusty bread to sop up any sauce.

 **TIP**
The tomatoes in this recipe account for a lot of the flavor, so if possible, I recommend using San Marzano tomatoes since they're less acidic than other varieities and have a sweet, vibrant flavor. If you don't have San Marzano tomatoes, this recipe is also great with any variety of canned whole tomatoes. Taste the sauce before serving and add a very small pinch of sugar if you find it to be tart.

**Prep Time:** 10 minutes
**Total Time:** 35 minutes
**Serves** 4

---

1lb (454g) boneless, skinless
  **chicken breasts**, cut into
  ¾-inch (2cm) pieces
2½ tablespoons **cornstarch**,
  divided
¼ teaspoon **salt**
¼ teaspoon freshly ground
  **black pepper**
4 teaspoons **vegetable oil**, divided
6 cups (600g) **chopped**
  **vegetables of choice**
  (see table)
2 cloves **garlic**, minced
1 teaspoon grated **fresh ginger**
2 tablespoons **cold water**
2 cups (280g) **cooked rice**
**Sesame seeds** (optional),
  for garnish

**FOR THE SAUCE**
½ cup (120ml) **juice of choice**
  (see table)
¼ cup (60ml) **chicken broth**
3 tablespoons **sweetener of**
  **choice** (see table)
3 tablespoons **soy sauce**
1½ teaspoons **toasted sesame oil**

# Choose-Your-Own-Adventure
# Chicken Stir-Fry

Sweet and savory with lots of healthy goodness, this stir-fry is the perfect way to enjoy the veggies that have been forgotten in the back of the produce drawer. Tender chunks of chicken and mixed vegetables come together quickly with an easy sweet and sour–style sauce. Pick and choose your additions based on what you have on hand. This recipe is so versatile; you'll have a new stir-fry adventure every time.

1. In a medium bowl, toss the chicken with ½ tablespoon cornstarch, salt, and pepper. Set aside.
2. In a 12-inch (30cm) nonstick skillet, heat 2 teaspoons oil over medium-high heat until it shimmers. Add the chicken and cook for 6 to 8 minutes or just until cooked through. Transfer to a bowl and cover to keep warm.
3. Reduce the heat to medium and add 1 teaspoon oil. Add any firm vegetables and 1 tablespoon water and cook for 3 minutes. Stir in any more delicate vegetables and cook for an additional 4 minutes or until tender-crisp.
4. Move the vegetables to one side of the pan and add the remaining 1 teaspoon oil, garlic, and ginger to the pan. Cook for 1 minute or until fragrant and then stir the garlic and ginger into the vegetables. Transfer the vegetables to the bowl with the chicken.
5. **To make the sauce,** return the pan to the stovetop and increase the heat to medium-high. Add the juice, chicken broth, sweetener, soy sauce, and sesame oil, and bring to a boil. Boil for 1 to 2 minutes.
6. In a small bowl, mix the remaining 2 tablespoons cornstarch with the cold water to make a slurry. While whisking, drizzle the slurry a little bit at a time into the sauce to thicken. You may not need all of the slurry.
7. Add the chicken and vegetables along with any juices to the pan and stir to coat with the sauce. Cook for about 2 minutes or until heated through.
8. Serve over rice and sprinkle with sesame seeds, if using.

| Chopped Vegetables<br>Use a mix of your favorite veggies and keep firm and delicate vegetables separate. | Juice<br>Choose one option. | Sweetener<br>Choose one option. |
|---|---|---|
| • **Firm veggies:** onion, broccoli florets, carrots, celery, cauliflower florets<br>• **Delicate veggies:** bell pepper, zucchini, snap peas, mushrooms, shredded cabbage, bok choy | • Pineapple<br>• Orange<br>• Apple<br>• Cranberry | • Honey<br>• Apricot jam<br>• Grape jelly<br>• Brown sugar |

**Prep Time:** 15 minutes
**Total Time:** 4 hours 15 minutes
**Serves** 8

---

1 tablespoon **butter**
1 large **yellow onion,** chopped
1lb (454g) boneless, skinless
    **chicken breasts**
2 medium **sweet potatoes,**
    peeled and cut into 1-inch
    (2.5cm) pieces
2 medium **carrots,** sliced into
    ½-inch (1.5cm) pieces
3 ribs **celery,** chopped
2 cups (288g) **frozen corn,** thawed
1 (15oz / 425g) can **chickpeas,**
    drained and rinsed
3 cups (720ml) **chicken broth**
2 **bay leaves**
1 teaspoon **salt,** plus more to taste
1 teaspoon **garlic powder**
½ teaspoon **dried thyme leaves**
½ teaspoon **ground sage**
½ teaspoon freshly ground **black**
    **pepper,** plus more to taste
1 cup (240ml) **heavy cream**
2 tablespoons **cornstarch**

---

**Ingredient Swap**

For a lighter version, replace the
heavy cream with **evaporated milk.**

# Slow Cooker Homestyle
# Chicken & Vegetable Chowder

This homestyle chicken vegetable chowder is a wholesome meal where feel good meets good for you. Packed with tender chicken and lots of fresh veggies, it's both satisfying and nourishing; plus, it's so easy, it practically makes itself! Simply toss everything into the slow cooker and let it work its magic. Just before serving, shred the chicken and add it back into the soup. It's the perfect cozy dinner at the end of a long day and a great way to up your veggie intake.

1. In a small 8-inch (20cm) skillet, melt the butter over medium heat. Add the onion and cook just until softened, about 4 minutes.
2. Place the raw chicken in the bottom of a 6-quart (5.6L) slow cooker.
3. Add the onions, sweet potatoes, carrots, celery, corn, chickpeas, chicken broth, bay leaves, salt, garlic powder, thyme, sage, and pepper.
4. Cook on high for 3 to 4 hours or on low for 7 to 8 hours or until the vegetables are tender.
5. Remove the chicken breasts from the slow cooker and shred them using two forks.
6. In a small bowl, whisk together the cream and cornstarch until smooth. Stir this mixture into the chowder along with the shredded chicken. Cover and cook for 15 to 20 minutes.
7. Remove the bay leaves and discard them. Taste and season with additional salt and pepper, if desired.

---

 **TIPS**

- Cooking the onion first gives a softer, sweeter flavor and is recommended in this recipe.
- For a thicker chowder, mash some of the vegetables before adding the chicken back to the slow cooker or add dried potato flakes 1 tablespoon at a time until desired consistency is achieved.

## TIP

If you don't have an ovenproof skillet, brown the chicken breasts in the skillet and then transfer them to a 9 × 13-inch (22 × 33cm) baking dish. Increase cooking time by 5 to 7 minutes or until the chicken breast reaches an internal temperature of 165°F (74°C).

*Scan for air fryer instructions.*

**Prep Time:** 30 minutes
**Total Time:** 50 minutes
**Serves** 4

_____

### FOR THE FILLING

4oz (113g) **cream cheese**, softened

1 teaspoon **Worcestershire sauce**

½ teaspoon **garlic powder**

¼ teaspoon **salt**

½ cup (57g) shredded **sharp cheddar cheese**

¼ cup (60ml) **pimentos**, drained and chopped

### FOR THE CHICKEN

4 boneless, skinless **chicken breasts,** about 6oz (170g) each

2 tablespoons **olive oil,** divided

1 teaspoon **salt**

½ teaspoon freshly ground **black pepper**

½ teaspoon **smoked paprika**

½ teaspoon **garlic powder**

### FOR THE CORN

3 cups (432g) **frozen corn**, thawed

2 tablespoons **butter**, melted

2 tablespoons **honey**

¼ teaspoon **salt**

¼ teaspoon freshly ground **black pepper**

> **Ingredient Swap**
> Replace the pimentos with **jarred roasted red peppers** or **canned jalapeños** for a spicy kick!

# Pimento Cheese–Stuffed Chicken Breasts with Honey Corn

Don't you just love dinners that seem fancy but are actually really easy to prepare? This is one of those meals: simple yet elegant, and as my mom says, "I'd definitely serve it to company." Tender chicken breasts are filled with a creamy, cheesy pimento mixture and then pan-roasted to perfection in the oven. The juices from the chicken are stirred into sweet honey corn for a next-level side dish. Savory, cheesy goodness—this one will be requested on repeat!

1. Preheat the oven to 400°F (200°C).
2. **To make the filling,** in a small bowl, mix the cream cheese, Worcestershire sauce, garlic powder, and salt. Fold in cheddar cheese and pimentos. Set aside.
3. **To make the chicken,** insert a small knife into the side of the chicken breast at the thickest part. Using the knife, create a pocket by cutting a horizontal opening in the chicken breast about 2 inches (5cm) long and 1½ inches (3.5cm) deep.
4. Fill each pocket with one-quarter of the pimento cheese mixture. Secure each breast by weaving a toothpick to close the opening.
5. Rub both sides of the chicken breasts with 1 tablespoon oil divided between the 4 breasts and evenly season with salt, pepper, paprika, and garlic powder.
6. In a 12-inch (30cm) nonstick ovenproof skillet, heat the remaining 1 tablespoon oil over medium-high heat. Cook the chicken for 2 to 3 minutes on each side or until browned.
7. Place the skillet in the oven and bake for 13 to 17 minutes or until the thickest part of the chicken has an internal temperature of 165°F (74°C).
8. Remove the chicken from the pan and let it rest for 6 to 8 minutes.
9. **To make the corn,** add the corn, butter, honey, salt, and pepper to the skillet along with the juices from the chicken and place it on the stovetop. _(Be careful: the pan handle will be hot from the oven.)_ Increase the heat to medium-high and stir to incorporate any of the juices in the pan, cooking until the corn is heated through, about 3 to 4 minutes.
10. Remove the toothpicks from the chicken and serve with the honey corn.

---

**FOR THE CHICKEN**

1lb (454g) boneless, skinless **chicken breasts**

¼ cup (60ml) **olive oil**

3 tablespoons freshly squeezed **lemon juice**, about 1 large lemon

3 cloves **garlic**, minced

1 teaspoon **dried oregano**

½ teaspoon **salt**

½ teaspoon freshly ground **black pepper**

**FOR THE SAUCE**

¾ cup (170g) plain **Greek yogurt**

⅓ cup (76g) crumbled **feta cheese**

1½ tablespoons finely chopped **fresh mint**

2 teaspoons freshly squeezed **lemon juice**

Pinch of **salt**

**FOR SERVING**

4 **Greek pitas**

1 tablespoon **olive oil**

½ teaspoon **seasoned salt**

2 cups (120g) shredded **romaine lettuce**

1 **Roma tomato**, diced

¼ cup (30g) diced **red onion**

# Grilled Greek Chicken Wraps
## with Feta Mint Sauce

This is a go-to dinner for us all year long and one I often make when we have unexpected guests because everyone loves it. The marinade in this recipe is inspired by the bright flavors in my favorite souvlaki recipe and results in tender chicken with lots of zesty lemon flavor. Served wrap style with fresh, crisp toppings and a savory feta mint sauce, it always gets rave reviews.

1. **To make the sauce,** in a small bowl, combine the yogurt, feta, mint, and lemon juice. Use a spatula to mix well, slightly mashing the feta as you mix. Taste and season with a pinch of salt, if desired. Refrigerate until ready to serve.

2. **To make the chicken,** layer the chicken breasts between two sheets of plastic wrap and use the flat side of a meat mallet to pound to an even thickness of ½ inch (1.5cm).

3. In a large glass bowl or zipper-lock freezer bag, combine the chicken, oil, lemon juice, garlic, oregano, salt, and pepper. Refrigerate for at least 30 minutes or up to 4 hours.

4. Preheat the grill to medium-high heat. Place the chicken on the grill and cook for 6 to 8 minutes per side or until cooked through and the chicken reaches an internal temperature of 165°F (74°C). Transfer to a plate to rest for 5 minutes.

5. **To serve,** brush the pitas with 1 tablespoon olive oil and sprinkle with seasoned salt. Turn the grill down to medium heat. Add the pitas and warm for 1 minute per side.

6. Slice the chicken into ½-inch (1.5cm) slices.

7. Fill each warmed pita with chicken, lettuce, tomatoes, and onion and top with feta mint sauce.

**TO PREPARE IN AN AIR FRYER**

To cook the chicken in an air fryer, prepare the chicken as directed in step 2. Preheat an air fryer to 400°F (200°C) and cook in a single layer for 8 to 10 minutes or until the chicken reaches an internal temperature of 165°F (74°C). There is no need to flip the chicken over.

---

**SERVING SUGGESTIONS**

Make it fun and let everyone build their own wrap. We love to set out bowls of lettuce, cucumber, and tomato, but feel free to add other favorites like sliced olives, diced jalapeño, or chopped bell peppers. Serve homemade or frozen french fries on the side with extra sauce for dipping.

**TIP**

Any style of pita, flatbread, or naan can be used in this recipe.

**HEY! IT'S OKAY TO . . .**

Replace the feta mint sauce with prepared tzatziki. You can also skip the toppings (and the chopping) and add spoonfuls of prepared Greek salad to the pita along with the chicken!

### FEELING FANCY?

The marinade in this recipe makes great souvlaki skewers. Cut 1 pound (454g) chicken into 1-inch (2.5cm) cubes and marinate as directed. Soak wooden skewers in water for at least 30 minutes and thread the chicken onto the skewers. Cook on an oiled grill over medium-high heat, turning skewers frequently, for 10 to 15 minutes or until the chicken is cooked through and reaches an internal temperature of 165°F (74°C).

---

### FOR THE QUINOA
¾ cup (133g) **quinoa**
1½ cups (360ml) **chicken broth**
¼ teaspoon **salt**, plus more
   to taste
1 cup (144g) **frozen corn**, thawed
1 cup (160g) **canned black beans**,
   drained and rinsed
¼ cup (14g) chopped **fresh
   cilantro**
3 tablespoons freshly squeezed
   **lime juice**

### FOR THE CHICKEN
⅔ cup (160ml) **prepared salsa**,
   any variety
2 tablespoons **taco seasoning**
   (for homemade, see page 18)
½ cup (120ml) **water**
1lb (454g) boneless, skinless
   **chicken breasts**

### FOR SERVING (OPTIONAL)
Shredded **lettuce**
Diced **tomato**
Shredded **cheddar cheese**
Sliced **avocado**
**Sour cream**
Sliced **fresh jalapeños**

---

### Ingredient Swap
Replace the quinoa with 3 cups (420g)
of your favorite **cooked grain,** like
rice, farro, or couscous. Stir in the
corn, beans, cilantro, and lime juice
with a little bit of salt and spoon the
chicken over top.

---

# Easy Salsa **Chicken Power Bowls**

These power bowls are a go-to when I'm craving something healthy that really
satisfies and comes together fast. They start with bright and saucy shredded
chicken piled over cilantro-lime quinoa and then are loaded with your favorite
toppings for the perfect customized bowl. Whether it's meal prep for lunches or
a fun family build-your-own bowl night, this is an easy favorite.

1. **To make the quinoa,** rinse the quinoa in a fine mesh strainer and add it
   to a medium saucepan. Add broth and salt. Bring to a boil over high heat,
   reduce the heat to medium-low, cover, and simmer for 15 minutes. Let rest
   covered for 5 minutes; uncover and fluff with a fork.
2. **To make the chicken,** in a 10-inch (25cm) skillet, combine the salsa, taco
   seasoning, and water. Add the chicken breasts to the sauce. Bring to a
   simmer over medium-high heat, reduce the heat to medium-low, and cook
   covered for 15 to 20 minutes, stirring occasionally, until the chicken is
   cooked through and reaches 165°F (74°C) in the thickest part of the breast.
3. Remove the chicken from the pan and shred it with two forks. Add it back
   to the sauce and simmer uncovered over medium heat until slightly
   thickened, about 3 to 4 minutes. Season with salt to taste.
4. Meanwhile, prepare the toppings for serving.
5. Add the corn, beans, cilantro, and lime juice to the quinoa and stir to
   combine. Divide the quinoa among 4 bowls. Top each with one quarter of
   the shredded chicken mixture and add toppings, if using.

### TO PREPARE IN A SLOW COOKER
1. To a 4-quart (3.8L) slow cooker, add 1½ pounds (681g) boneless, skinless
   chicken breasts. Top with 1 cup (240ml) salsa; 10 ounces (284ml) canned
   diced tomatoes with chiles, drained; and 2 tablespoons taco seasoning.
2. Cook on low for 7 to 8 hours or on high for 3 to 4 hours, until the chicken
   is fork-tender.
3. Remove chicken from the slow cooker and shred with two forks.
4. Add the juices from the slow cooker a bit at a time to the shredded
   chicken to reach desired consistency.

---

 **SERVING SUGGESTIONS**
Serve the salsa chicken and
quinoa tucked into warmed flour
tortillas for a meal on the go, or
serve the chicken over a bed of
romaine lettuce. The topping
options are endless—use your
imagination and create a
signature bowl of your own!

 **TIPS**
• Once the quinoa is cooked and
  rested, remove the lid to prevent
  the steam from overcooking it.
• Chicken may need slightly more
  or less liquid. If needed, add
  extra water 2 tablespoons at
  a time.

**Prep Time:** 5 minutes
**Total Time:** 35 minutes
**Serves** 4

---

4 boneless, skinless **chicken breasts**, about 5oz (140g) each

1 teaspoon **poultry seasoning** (for homemade, see page 18), divided

¾ teaspoon **salt**, divided

½ teaspoon freshly ground **black pepper**, divided

¼ teaspoon crushed **dried rosemary**

1 tablespoon **vegetable oil**

4 tablespoons **butter**

½ cup (30g) finely diced **yellow onion**

¼ cup (30g) **all-purpose flour**

½ teaspoon **dried thyme leaves**

1¾ cups (420ml) **chicken broth**

---

**Ingredient Swap**
Replace chicken breasts with 1½ pounds (680g) **boneless, skinless chicken thighs**. Season as directed and cook the thighs in batches for 4 to 5 minutes per side.

# Skillet **Chicken & Gravy**

Who doesn't love a chicken dinner smothered in a rich, savory gravy? While delicious, a full-on roast chicken dinner is a recipe I save for weekends when I have time to cook a leisurely dinner. This weeknight version is a game changer, bringing those slow-roasted flavors to the table in about 30 minutes. Tender, juicy chicken breasts are smothered in a perfectly seasoned gravy that's so good, you'll never believe it came together so quickly.

1. Layer the chicken breasts between two sheets of plastic wrap and use the flat side of a meat mallet to pound to an even thickness of ½ inch (1.5cm). Season with ½ teaspoon poultry seasoning, ½ teaspoon salt, ¼ teaspoon pepper, and rosemary.
2. In a 10-inch (25cm) nonstick skillet, heat the oil over medium-high heat. Add the chicken and cook for 9 to 12 minutes, turning occasionally, until browned and the chicken reaches an internal temperature of 165°F (74°C). Remove from the skillet and set aside, lightly covered with foil.
3. Add the butter and onion to the skillet. Cook just until the onion is tender and begins to brown on the edges, about 3 minutes.
4. Add the flour, thyme, remaining ½ teaspoon poultry seasoning, and remaining ¼ teaspoon pepper. Cook, whisking continuously, until the flour turns brown and is about the color of peanut butter.
5. Gradually add the broth, whisking continuously until smooth after each addition. Bring the gravy to a boil and then reduce the heat to a simmer and cook for 3 to 5 minutes or until thickened.
6. Strain the gravy through a fine-mesh strainer and return it to the skillet. Taste and season with the remaining ¼ teaspoon salt and additional pepper, if desired.
7. Add the chicken to the gravy along with any accumulated juices, and cook for 2 to 3 minutes or until the chicken is heated through.

 **SERVING SUGGESTIONS**
Serve this chicken and gravy over Garlicky Mashed Potatoes (see page 256) with a side of green beans or carrots.

 **LOVE YOUR LEFTOVERS**
Leftover chicken and gravy makes the best hot chicken sandwiches! Chop the chicken into bite-size pieces and stir it into the gravy, adding additional broth or water if needed. Heat on the stove and spoon over lightly toasted bread.

---

2 tablespoons **butter**

1 medium **yellow onion**, diced

2 large **carrots**, diced

1 rib **celery**, diced

8oz (224g) **cremini or white mushrooms**, sliced

1 clove **garlic**, minced

1 teaspoon **salt**

1 teaspoon **dried parsley**

½ teaspoon **dried thyme leaves**

½ teaspoon **poultry seasoning** (for homemade, see page 18)

⅛ teaspoon freshly ground **black pepper**

6 cups (1.4L) **reduced-sodium chicken broth**

2 boneless, skinless **chicken breasts**, about 6oz (170g) each

½ cup (99g) uncooked **long-grain white rice**

# Cozy **Chicken, Mushroom & Rice Soup**

This is one of those meals that everyone is completely amazed by: minimal dishes, minimal steps, and maximum flavor. Ready in under an hour, this fresh soup packs a homemade simmered-all-day kind of flavor. There's no need to precook the chicken—pop it right into the pot and let it simmer in the seasoned broth along with the veggies and rice. Once cooked, shred the chicken and add it back to the pot. Easy peasy!

1. In a 4-quart (3.8L) Dutch oven or a large soup pot, melt the butter over medium-high heat. Add the onion, carrots, celery, and mushrooms, and cook until the onion begins to soften, about 5 minutes. Stir in the garlic, salt, parsley, thyme, poultry seasoning, and pepper. Cook until fragrant, about 1 minute.

2. Add the broth, uncooked chicken breasts, and rice. Stir and bring to a boil over medium-high heat. Reduce the heat to a simmer, cover, and cook for 15 minutes or until the chicken has reached an internal temperature of 165°F (74°C).

3. Remove the chicken from the soup, cover, and cook for an additional 5 to 10 minutes or until the rice is tender.

4. Meanwhile, shred the chicken with two forks. Once the rice is tender, add the chicken back to the pot and let rest uncovered for 3 minutes.

---

**SERVING SUGGESTIONS**

As with most soups, I love bread to sop up any bits in the bowl. Whip up a batch of Garlic Herb Bread (see page 255) for dipping and dunking.

**HEY! IT'S OKAY TO . . .**

Shave a few minutes of prep time by buying presliced mushrooms at the grocery store.

**MAKE AHEAD**

This soup can be prepared ahead of time and refrigerated or frozen. The rice soaks up some of the broth as it sits, so you may need to add additional broth or water. If frozen, there is no need to thaw first; add the frozen soup to a saucepan over medium heat until heated.

---

1 **ear corn**, shucked

3 teaspoons **olive oil**, divided

**Salt** (optional), as needed

12oz (340g) boneless, skinless **chicken breasts**

1 tablespoon **Cajun seasoning** (for homemade, see page 18)

8 cups (340g) chopped **romaine lettuce**

1 cup (160g) **canned black beans**, drained and rinsed

1 **red bell pepper**, diced

¼ cup (30g) finely diced **red onion**

1 cup (195g) halved **grape tomatoes**

½ cup (114g) crumbled **feta cheese**

½ cup (80g) chopped **pitted dates**

1 ripe **avocado**, diced

**FOR THE DRESSING**

⅓ cup (76g) **sour cream**

⅓ cup (67g) **mayonnaise**

3 tablespoons finely chopped **fresh cilantro**

2 tablespoons freshly squeezed **lime juice**

½ teaspoon **onion powder**

¼ teaspoon **smoked paprika**

⅛ teaspoon **salt**

3 to 4 tablespoons **milk**

---

**Ingredient Swaps**

- The dates are one of my favorite parts of this salad, so don't skip them if possible. You can replace them with **dried cranberries** or **raisins** if needed.
- Replace the ear of corn with 1 cup (144g) **frozen corn,** thawed.

# Cowboy **Chopped Chicken Salad**

A take on one of my favorite restaurant salads, this meal is fresh and fabulous! Grilled Cajun chicken is tossed with crisp greens, corn, beans, and dates. We love this dressed with the smoky cilantro lime ranch listed here, but any ranch dressing will do! I serve it with hot chicken for dinner, but it's also a great salad to serve chilled for meal prep.

1. **To make the dressing,** in a small bowl, whisk the sour cream, mayonnaise, cilantro, lime juice, onion powder, smoked paprika, and salt. Add the milk, 1 tablespoon at a time, until the dressing reaches the desired consistency. Refrigerate until ready to serve.
2. Brush the corn with 1 teaspoon olive oil and season with salt, if desired.
3. Layer the chicken breasts between two sheets of plastic wrap and use the flat side of a meat mallet to pound to an even thickness of ½ inch (1.5cm). Rub with the remaining 2 teaspoons olive oil and season with the Cajun seasoning.
4. Preheat the grill to medium-high and add the corn and the chicken breasts to the grill. Cook the chicken for 4 to 6 minutes per side or until the chicken reaches an internal temperature of 165°F (74°C). Cook the corn just until lightly charred. Allow the chicken and corn to rest for 5 minutes. Chop the chicken into bite-size pieces and cut the kernels off the cob.
5. In a large salad bowl, toss the romaine lettuce with ⅓ cup (80ml) dressing.
6. Top with the chicken, corn, beans, bell pepper, onion, tomatoes, feta, dates, and avocado. Drizzle with remaining dressing, if desired.

**TO PREPARE ON THE STOVETOP**

Heat a large skillet over medium heat and add 1 tablespoon olive oil. Add the seasoned chicken breasts and cook for 5 to 6 minutes per side or until the chicken reaches an internal temperature of 165°F (74°C). Use frozen corn kernels (thawed) when assembling the salad.

---

 **SERVING SUGGESTIONS**
Serve with a sprinkle of fresh cilantro, a handful of corn chips or croutons for some added crunch, and fresh lime wedges.

 **MAKE AHEAD**
If making planned leftovers, keep the dressing on the side since a dressed salad does not keep well. The chicken can be served chilled in this recipe. Leftovers make a great wrap in a large flour tortilla.

 **HEY, IT'S OKAY TO . . .**
Skip the homemade dressing and use your favorite bottled ranch. Mix ⅔ cup (160ml) with 2 tablespoons chopped cilantro and ¼ teaspoon smoked paprika.

**Prep Time:** 5 minutes
**Total Time:** 35 minutes
**Serves** 4

---

4 boneless, skinless **chicken breasts**, about 6oz (170g) each
1½ tablespoons **olive oil**

**FOR THE SEASONING MIX**
1 teaspoon **Italian seasoning**
  (for homemade, see page 18)
¾ teaspoon **seasoned salt**
¼ teaspoon **paprika**
¼ teaspoon freshly ground
  **black pepper**

*Scan for instructions to prepare in an air fryer.*

# Perfect **Baked Chicken Breasts**

Perfectly baked chicken breasts are a kitchen staple and with this recipe, your chicken will be tender, juicy, and flavorful every time. Enjoy these chicken breasts as a meal with veggies and rice, use them for meal prep or to top salads, or shred them for casseroles and soups. The possibilities are endless.

1. Preheat the oven to 400°F (200°C). Lightly grease a rimmed baking sheet.
2. **To make the seasoning mix,** in a medium bowl, combine the Italian seasoning, seasoned salt, paprika, and pepper.
3. Add the chicken and olive oil to the bowl with the seasonings and toss well to coat the chicken.
4. Transfer the chicken to the prepared baking sheet and roast for 22 to 26 minutes or until the chicken has reached an internal temperature of 165°F (74°C).
5. Let rest for 5 minutes.

 **VARIATIONS**

Change up the seasonings based on your preference or to complement the dish you're pairing with this chicken. The seasoning mix in this recipe can be replaced with any of these blends.

| Mediterranean Inspired | Homestyle Seasoning | Tex-Mex Blend |
|---|---|---|
| 1 teaspoon **dried oregano**<br>1 teaspoon **seasoned salt**<br>1 teaspoon **lemon zest**<br>¼ teaspoon **dried basil**<br>¼ teaspoon **garlic powder**<br>⅛ teaspoon **dried dill** | 2 teaspoons **dried parsley**<br>1 teaspoon **seasoned salt**<br>½ teaspoon **ground sage**<br>½ teaspoon **dried thyme leaves**<br>¼ teaspoon crushed **dried rosemary**<br>¼ teaspoon freshly ground **black pepper** | 1½ teaspoons **chili powder**<br>1 teaspoon **seasoned salt**<br>½ teaspoon **ground cumin**<br>¼ teaspoon **onion powder**<br>¼ teaspoon **garlic powder**<br>¼ teaspoon **red pepper flakes** (optional) |

 **TIPS**

- Chicken breasts can vary in weight from 5 ounces to 10 ounces (141–284g); smaller chicken breasts will take closer to 20 minutes, while larger chicken breasts will take closer to 26 minutes.
- For best results, use an instant-read thermometer to ensure the chicken has reached an internal temperature of 165°F (74°C).

# Simply Perfect *Sides*

**250**  Dill Pickle Pasta Salad

**252**  The Everyday Salad Dressing

**252**  My All-Time Favorite Yogurt-Ranch Dressing

**255**  Quick Tomato Cucumber Salad

**255**  Garlic Herb Bread

**256**  Skillet Onions & Potatoes

**256**  Garlicky Mashed Potatoes

**259**  Simply Seasoned Garlic Rice

**259**  Creamy Cheesy Crowd-Pleasin' Rice

**259**  Soul-Soothing Buttered Noodles

**262**  Roasting Vegetables in the Oven

**262**  Cooking Vegetables on the Stovetop

**Prep Time:** 15 minutes
**Total Time:** 1 hour 20 minutes
**Serves** 8

---

8oz (227g) **medium shell pasta** (about 3 cups)
½ cup (120ml) **dill pickle juice**
¾ cup (90g) sliced **dill pickles**
⅔ cup (85g) diced **cheddar cheese**
3 tablespoons finely diced **white onion**
2 tablespoons **fresh dill**

**FOR THE DRESSING**
⅔ cup (139g) **mayonnaise**
⅓ cup (80g) **sour cream**
¼ cup (60ml) **dill pickle juice**
¼ teaspoon **salt**
¼ teaspoon freshly ground **black pepper**
⅛ teaspoon **cayenne pepper**

# Dill Pickle Pasta Salad

This is the *original* Dill Pickle Pasta Salad recipe—a recipe I created in honor of my sister Candace, with whom I've exchanged dill pickle–themed gifts for 35 years. Inspired by my lifelong love for (or shall I say obsession with) dill pickles, I first shared this recipe on Spend with Pennies in 2016, and it quickly became a household favorite across the internet. Loved by everyone who has tried it, this pasta salad puts dill pickles in the starring role, adding a zesty flavor and a satisfying crunch to every bite. Best of all, this salad gets even better as it rests, making it the perfect make-ahead side.

1. Bring a large pot of salted water to a boil over high heat. Add the shells and cook al dente according to package directions. Drain well and run under cold water to stop cooking.
2. Toss the drained pasta with ½ cup (120ml) pickle juice and set aside for 5 minutes. Drain and discard pickle juice.
3. To make the dressing, in a large bowl, combine the mayonnaise, sour cream, ¼ cup (60ml) pickle juice, salt, pepper, and cayenne pepper.
4. Add the drained pasta, dill pickles, cheese, onion, and dill to the dressing. Toss well to combine and refrigerate for at least 1 hour before serving.

**TIP**
The dressing will thicken as it rests, so don't worry if it looks runny at first.

# The Everyday
## Salad Dressing

A really great dressing is the secret to a salad that you'll look forward to every meal. With a perfect balance of tangy, sweet, and savory, this simple dressing will convert any leafy green salad from ho-hum into a beautifully fresh, flavorful side dish. Prep a batch on the weekend to enjoy throughout the week.

**Prep Time:** 5 minutes
**Total Time:** 5 minutes
**Serves** 8

3 tablespoons **white wine vinegar**
1 tablespoon freshly squeezed **lemon juice**
1½ teaspoons **Dijon mustard**
2 teaspoons **honey**
½ teaspoon **garlic powder**
¼ teaspoon **salt**
¼ teaspoon freshly ground **black pepper**
½ (120ml) cup **olive oil** or vegetable oil

**Ingredient Swap**
Swap white wine vinegar for **apple cider vinegar**.

1. In a medium bowl, combine white wine vinegar, lemon juice, mustard, honey, garlic powder, salt, and pepper. Whisk until well combined.
2. Very slowly drizzle in the olive oil while continuously whisking.

**SERVING SUGGESTIONS**
This is a deliciously tangy dressing that can be drizzled over almost any tossed salad or chopped vegetable salad. It's also great for dipping bread or using as a marinade.

**TIP**
For a thicker dressing, place all ingredients in a small jar and use an immersion blender to combine.

# My All-Time Favorite
## Yogurt-Ranch Dressing

I can't think of a recipe I make more frequently than this creamy yogurt ranch; I always have a jar in my fridge. It's deliciously dilly and fresh tasting, perfect for drizzling over salads, dunking veggies, or even dipping pizza crust. If you've got extra herbs like basil or chives, they're great added to this recipe.

**Prep Time:** 10 minutes
**Total Time:** 2 hours 10 minutes
**Serves** 8

¾ cup (180g) **plain Greek yogurt**
⅓ cup (67g) **mayonnaise**
1 tablespoon chopped **fresh parsley**
2 teaspoons chopped **fresh dill**
¾ teaspoon **onion powder**
½ teaspoon **garlic powder**
¼ teaspoon freshly ground **black pepper**
⅛ teaspoon **salt**
4 to 5 tablespoons **milk**

**Ingredient Swap**
Replace the fresh herbs with **dried herbs** from your pantry. Use 1 teaspoon each **dried parsley** and **dried dill**.

1. In a medium bowl, whisk the Greek yogurt, mayonnaise, parsley, dill, onion powder, garlic powder, pepper, and salt.
2. Add milk, 1 tablespoon at a time, to reach desired consistency.
3. Refrigerate at least 2 hours before serving.

**VARIATIONS**
- This ranch dressing makes a great dip too; simply skip the milk.
- For buttermilk ranch dressing, replace the milk with buttermilk.

# Garlic Herb Bread

Herby and fragrant with a tender, moist crumb, this loaf is a great addition to almost any meal, and it's perfect for sopping up the last bits of sauce in the bottom of your bowl.

**Prep Time:** 10 minutes
**Total Time:** 1 hour
**Serves** 8

2 cups (240g) **all-purpose flour**
2 tablespoons **dried parsley**
1 tablespoon **baking powder**
1 tablespoon **granulated sugar**
2 cloves **garlic**, minced
1 teaspoon **dried basil**
1 teaspoon **salt**
½ teaspoon **onion powder**
½ teaspoon **dried oregano**
4 tablespoons cold unsalted **butter**, cut into small cubes
1 cup (113g) shredded cheddar cheese (optional)
2 **large eggs**
1 cup (240ml) whole milk

1. Preheat the oven to 350°F (175°C). Grease an 8 × 4-inch (20 × 10cm) loaf pan.
2. In a medium bowl, whisk the flour, parsley, baking powder, sugar, garlic, basil, salt, onion powder, and oregano.
3. Add the cold butter and use a pastry blender or a fork to cut it into the flour mixture until small crumbs form, about the size of peas. Stir in the cheese, if using.
4. In a separate small bowl, whisk the eggs until foamy and stir in milk. Add the egg mixture to the flour mixture and stir just until moistened; do not overmix.
5. Transfer to the prepared pan and bake for 48 to 52 minutes or until a toothpick comes out clean. Cool on a wire rack before cutting.

**VARIATION**
For a quicker baking time, make this recipe as Garlic Drop Biscuits. Preheat the oven to 400°F (200°C). Prepare the batter as directed, but increase the all-purpose flour to 2⅓ cups (280g). Drop 12 heaping tablespoons of dough onto a parchment-lined baking sheet, allowing 1½ inches (4cm) between biscuits. Bake for 11 to 13 minutes or until golden brown on top.

# Quick Tomato Cucumber Salad

This tomato and cucumber salad is a dish I make all year long, and in the summer months, I make it almost daily. While it may seem somewhat simple, it's deliciously fresh and loved by everyone. Best of all, this salad has no rules, so feel free to change it up and add in your favorite fresh vegetables from the crisper or your garden.

**Prep Time:** 10 minutes
**Total Time:** 10 minutes
**Serves** 4

1 **English cucumber**, sliced
2 to 3 large **tomatoes**, diced
½ **red onion**, thinly sliced
1 tablespoon chopped **fresh parsley**, basil, or dill (optional)
2 tablespoons **olive oil**
1 tablespoon **red wine vinegar**
¼ teaspoon **salt**
¼ teaspoon freshly ground **black pepper**

1. In a medium bowl, combine the cucumber, tomatoes, red onion, and fresh parsley or other fresh herbs (if using). Add the oil, vinegar, salt, and pepper. Toss well to combine.
2. If time allows, refrigerate for 20 minutes before serving.

**TIP**
Fresh herbs are optional but really elevate the flavors of this salad. Add 1 tablespoon chopped fresh herbs; use just one type of herb or your favorite combination to equal 1 tablespoon.

# Skillet **Onions & Potatoes**

This dish is one of life's simple pleasures. Boiling the potatoes first makes them soft and buttery inside, while pan-frying creates a crisp crust on the outside. This easy side dish pairs well with anything from bacon and eggs to Skillet Chicken & Gravy (page 240).

**Prep Time:** 10 minutes
**Total Time:** 45 minutes
**Serves** 4

1lb (454g) **thin-skinned potatoes** (red or yellow)
1 tablespoon **olive oil**
1½ tablespoons **butter**, divided
1 medium **white onion**, sliced ½-inch (1.5cm)
1 teaspoon **seasoned salt**
½ teaspoon freshly ground **black pepper**
1 clove **garlic**, minced
Chopped fresh parsley (optional), to garnish

1. Scrub the potatoes and cut them into 1-inch (2.5cm) cubes.
2. Fill a medium saucepan with cold salted water and add the potatoes. Bring to a boil over medium-high heat and cook uncovered for 11 to 14 minutes or until the potatoes are just fork-tender. Drain the potatoes well and set aside.
3. Meanwhile, in a 10-inch (25cm) skillet over medium-low heat, combine the olive oil and ½ tablespoon butter. Add the onion and cook until it begins to soften, stirring occasionally, about 3 minutes.
4. Increase the heat to medium and add the drained potatoes to the skillet. Sprinkle with the seasoned salt and pepper. Cook, stirring occasionally, until the potatoes are tender and golden, about 15 to 20 minutes.
5. Once golden, move the potatoes to one side of the skillet. Add the remaining 1 tablespoon butter and the garlic to the other side of the skillet and cook until the garlic is fragrant, about 1 minute. Stir the garlic butter into the potatoes, taste, and season with additional salt and pepper to taste and a sprinkle of fresh parsley, if using.

# Garlicky **Mashed Potatoes**

Perfectly fluffy mashed potatoes pair with almost any dinner, especially recipes with lots of saucy goodness. Rich and homey with a subtle garlic flavor, this version can be prepared ahead of time, and it reheats well for holidays or busy weeknights. This recipe makes about 6 cups of mashed potatoes.

**Prep Time:** 10 minutes
**Total Time:** 50 minutes
**Serves** 8

3lb (1.4kg) **russet potatoes** or Yukon Gold potatoes, about 6 medium potatoes
8 cloves **garlic**, peeled
¾ cup (180ml) **half-and-half** or light cream
6 tablespoons **butter**
1 teaspoon **salt**, plus more to taste
½ teaspoon freshly ground **black pepper**

1. Peel the potatoes and cut them into large 2-inch (5cm) cubes. Add the potatoes and whole garlic cloves to a large pot of cold salted water.
2. Place the pot over high heat and bring to a boil. Once boiling, reduce the heat to medium-high and boil the potatoes and garlic cloves, uncovered, for 15 to 20 minutes or until the potatoes are fork-tender. Drain well and let rest in the strainer for 5 minutes.
3. Add the half-and-half and butter to the pot and warm over medium-low heat.
4. Transfer the potatoes and garlic to a large bowl and mash with a potato masher. Gradually add the half-and-half mixture and continue mashing to reach a smooth and creamy consistency.
5. Season with the salt and pepper, taste, and adjust seasoning as needed.

**TIP**
The skin on a russet potato is thick and should be peeled. If using yellow or Yukon Gold potatoes, you can leave the skins on for a rustic texture, if desired.

**VARIATIONS**
For extra creaminess, add softened cream cheese or for a little tang, stir in some sour cream.

### MAKE AHEAD

Prepare the recipe as directed and cool
completely. Place them in a sealed container
or covered casserole dish for up to 4 days.
To reheat the mashed potatoes, spread
them evenly into a 1½- to 2-quart (1.4–1.9L)
baking dish and cover with foil. Bake at
375°F (190°C) for 30 minutes. Stir the
potatoes, cover, and bake for an additional
10 minutes or until heated through. Mashed
potatoes can also be reheated in a large
saucepan over medium heat, stirring
frequently. Add additional milk as needed.

# Simply Seasoned
## Garlic Rice

Rice is the perfect side to round out almost any meal. Packed with buttery garlic and herb flavors, this dish uses simple ingredients you probably already have on hand. Not only is it versatile, but it's a side that everyone will agree on!

**Prep Time:** 5 minutes
**Total Time:** 30 minutes
**Serves** 4

1 tablespoon **butter**
2 cloves **garlic**, minced
2 cups (480ml) **beef broth**
1 cup (198g) uncooked **long-grain white rice**
1 tablespoon **dried parsley**
¾ teaspoon **onion powder**
⅛ teaspoon **salt**
⅛ teaspoon freshly ground black pepper

1. In a medium saucepan over medium heat, melt the butter. Add the garlic and cook until fragrant without browning, about 2 minutes.
2. Add the beef broth, rice, parsley, onion powder, salt, and pepper.
3. Bring to a boil over medium-high heat, cover, and reduce the heat to a low simmer. Cook covered for 18 to 20 minutes or until most of the liquid is absorbed.
4. Remove from the heat and let rest covered for 5 minutes.
5. Fluff with a fork and serve.

**TIPS**
- For a bolder garlic flavor, double the garlic to 4 cloves.
- Replace the dried parsley with 3 tablespoons chopped fresh parsley. If using fresh, stir it in just before serving.

# Creamy, Cheesy
## Crowd-Pleasin' Rice

Cheese is my love language, so it's no surprise that this extra creamy and super cheesy rice tops my list. You won't believe how easy it is to turn a handful of basic ingredients into a side dish that just might steal the spotlight. It's the perfect side for anything from fried chicken to The Best Ever Meatloaf (page 190).

**Prep Time:** 5 minutes
**Total Time:** 30 minutes
**Serves** 4

2 cups (480ml) **chicken broth**
1 cup (198g) uncooked **long-grain white rice**
1 teaspoon **onion powder**
½ teaspoon **garlic powder**
¾ cup (85g) shredded **sharp cheddar cheese**
⅓ cup (80ml) **whole milk**
2 tablespoons **sour cream**
2 tablespoons grated **Parmesan cheese**
1 tablespoon **butter**
¼ teaspoon **salt**
¼ teaspoon freshly ground **black pepper**

1. In a medium saucepan, combine the chicken broth, rice, onion powder, and garlic powder.
2. Bring to a boil over medium-high heat, reduce the heat to medium-low, and cover. Cook for 18 to 20 minutes or until most of the liquid is absorbed.
3. Remove from the heat and let rest covered for 5 minutes.
4. Fluff with a fork and stir in the cheddar cheese, milk, sour cream, Parmesan cheese, butter, salt, and pepper.
5. Cook over low heat until the cheese is melted and the mixture is heated through.

8oz (227g) **wide egg noodles**
3 tablespoons **butter**
¼ teaspoon **garlic powder**
2 teaspoons chopped **fresh parsley**
⅛ teaspoon freshly ground **black pepper**
**Salt**, to taste

# Soul-Soothing
# Buttered Noodles

Buttered noodles are one of life's simplest pleasures. This humble dish tastes like a touch of home and can round out almost any meal. Keep them simple with just butter and seasoning to soak up the flavor of your favorite sauces, or dress them up with fresh herbs and a sprinkle of cheese or a splash of lemon juice.

1. Fill a large pot with salted water and bring to a boil over high heat.
2. Add the noodles and reduce heat to medium-high. Cook the noodles al dente, stirring occasionally, according to the package directions.
3. Drain the noodles well, reserving a few tablespoons of pasta water, but do not rinse. (This helps the butter stick.)
4. Heat the same pot over medium heat and melt the butter and garlic powder. Turn off the heat and stir in the noodles, parsley, and pepper. Season with salt to taste.

**TIPS**
- Add 1 tablespoon grated Parmesan cheese, if desired.
- A tablespoon or two of pasta water can be added to the noodles when tossing to reach desired consistency.

# Roasting Vegetables **in the Oven**

Roasting is a simple and tasty way to prepare a wide range of vegetables. Roasted vegetables reheat well or can be added to casseroles or soups. They're also great served chilled as an addition to salads.

**SERVINGS:** Plan for about 1 cup of vegetables per serving as a side dish.

**SEASON:** Add enough olive oil to coat the vegetables along with a generous sprinkle of salt (about ½ teaspoon salt for every 4 cups vegetables, or to taste) and freshly ground black pepper. You can also add spices or herbs from your pantry.

**ROAST:** Roast at 425°F (220°C) unless otherwise noted. Use a large baking sheet to ensure the vegetables have lots of space. Overcrowding will cause the vegetables to steam instead of roast. Two smaller baking sheets can be used if needed.

**COOKING TIME:** The roasting times can vary slightly depending on the size of the vegetables and personal preference for doneness. Check the vegetables at the lower end of the time range to see if they're done to your liking; if not, continue roasting until cooked.

| Vegetable | Preparation | Cooking Time | Notes |
|---|---|---|---|
| Asparagus | Snap off the woody ends and roast whole. | 7–12 min | Thinner spears need 7–8 min; thicker spears need 10–12 min. |
| Beets | Cut off top and bottom and cut in half; wrap in a foil packet on a baking sheet. | 1 hour | Roast at 375°F (190°C). |
| Bell peppers | Remove seeds and cut into 1-inch (2.5cm) strips. | 18–21 min | Pairs well with Italian seasoning. |
| Broccoli | Chop into medium florets. | 14–18 min | Sprinkle with Parmesan cheese before serving. |
| Brussels sprouts | Cut in half if larger than ¾ inch (1.9cm). | 18–23 min | Add ½ teaspoon garlic powder per pound. |
| Carrots, store-bought | Peel or scrub; cut into 1-inch (2.5cm) pieces. | 25–30 min | If carrots are extra thick, cut in half lengthwise. |
| Carrots, baby or garden | Peel or scrub; cut into 1-inch (2.5cm) pieces. | 17–20 min | Check garden carrots early; extra moisture can make them cook quickly. |
| Cauliflower | Dry thoroughly after washing; break into florets. | 18–23 min | Toss with 2 tbsp Parmesan cheese per 4 cups before roasting. |
| Corn on the cob | Remove husk and silk. | 25–30 min | Place in baking dish with ½ cup (120ml) water and cover with foil. |
| Green beans | Trim ends. | 12–16 min | Garden-fresh beans may cook quickly, so check them early. |
| Mushrooms, white or cremini | Wipe clean with a damp paper towel; halve if large. | 14–18 min | Toss with 2 tsp soy sauce, 1 clove minced garlic, and a pinch of salt before roasting. |
| Onions | Cut into ½-inch (1.5cm) wedges. | 20–25 min | Flip after 12 minutes. |
| Potatoes | Cut into 1-inch (2.5cm) cubes. | 30–35 min | Add herbs, if desired. Stir after 20 min; larger cubes need extra time. |
| Sweet potatoes | Cut into 1-inch (2.5cm) cubes. | 25–30 min | Sprinkle with cinnamon, if desired; stir after 20 min. |
| Tomatoes, whole medium | Cut in half. | 14–22 min | Sprinkle with dried basil before roasting or fresh basil after roasting. |
| Tomatoes, cherry | Roast whole. | 15 min | Toss with 1 tbsp balsamic vinegar before roasting. |
| Zucchini | Slice into ½-inch (1.5cm) rounds. | 9–12 min | Thinner slices cook faster; thicker slices need extra time. |

# Cooking Vegetables **on the Stovetop**

The stovetop is a quick and easy way to sauté or steam fresh vegetables with little fuss. Once cooked, add a pat of butter and a sprinkle of fresh herbs or seasonings for a simple side dish.

**SERVINGS:** Plan for about 1 cup of vegetables per serving as a side dish.

**SEASON:** Season the vegetables with a sprinkle of salt (start with ¼ teaspoon for every 4 cups, or to taste) and freshly ground black pepper. You can also add spices from your pantry or fresh herbs.

| Vegetable | Preparation | Optional Seasonings or Additions | Cooking Temperature | Cooking Time | Notes |
|---|---|---|---|---|---|
| Asparagus | Snap off the woody ends and cut into 2-inch (5cm) pieces. | Basil, garlic, lemon zest | Medium-high | Thinner spears need 4–5 min; thicker spears 5–7 min | |
| Bell peppers | Remove seeds; cut into ½-inch (1.5cm) strips. | Oregano | Medium-high | 5–6 min | |
| Broccoli | Chop into medium florets. | Garlic, lemon zest | Medium | 8–10 min | Add 2–3 tbsp water for faster cooking. |
| Brussels sprouts | Trim; halve medium sprouts and quarter large sprouts. | Balsamic vinegar, bacon, garlic butter | Medium | 13–15 min | Add 2 tbsp water for faster cooking. |
| Cabbage | Slice into ½-inch (1.5cm) strips. | Bacon, onion, garlic | Medium | 10–14 min | Cook covered for the first 5 min. |
| Carrots, store-bought. | Peel or scrub, slice ¼ inch (0.6cm) thick. | Brown sugar and butter | Medium | 9–12 min | Add 4 tbsp water and cover for the first 5 min. |
| Carrots, baby or garden | Peel or scrub; halve lengthwise if small, slice ½ inch (1.5cm) thick if large. | Butter and fresh dill | Medium | 7–9 min | Add 1 tbsp water. |
| Corn, whole ear | Remove husk and silk. | Butter | Medium-high | 6–8 min | Add 1 inch (2.5cm) water to the pan; simmer, turning occasionally. |

**COOK:** Use a skillet large enough to spread the veggies without crowding. Add 2 to 3 teaspoons of olive oil to the pan to keep vegetables from sticking. Don't overcrowd the skillet or the vegetables will steam instead of pan-frying.

**COOKING TIME:** The cooking times can vary slightly depending on the size, freshness, and personal preference for doneness. A small splash of water or broth can be added to help firmer vegetables cook quickly. (This is not needed for quick-cooking vegetables.) Check the vegetables at the lower end of the cooking time range to see if they're done to your liking; if not, continue cooking.

| Vegetable | Preparation | Optional Seasonings or Additions | Cooking Temperature | Cooking Time | Notes |
|---|---|---|---|---|---|
| Green beans | Trim ends. | Crumbled bacon | Medium | 6–8 min | Add 3 tbsp water. Garden-fresh beans may cook quicker; check them early. |
| Mushrooms, white or cremini | Wipe mushrooms with a damp paper towel, cut into halves if large. | Garlic, white wine, and soy sauce | Medium until liquid is released, high heat once liquid is released | 8–12 min | A full skillet needs extra time. |
| Onions | Cut into ¼-inch (0.6cm) slices. | Butter | Medium-low | 13–16 min | |
| Peas, frozen green | | Fresh dill | Medium-high | 4–5 min | Add ¼ cup (60ml) water. Drain if needed. |
| Snap peas | Use whole. | Soy sauce and sesame seeds | Medium | 4–6 min | |
| Spinach, fresh leaves | Trim thick stems. | Heavy cream | Medium-high | 2–3 min | Spinach will reduce in volume by 90%; drain before adding cream and simmer until thickened. |
| Tomatoes, cherry | Use whole. | Fresh basil | Medium-high | 3–5 min | |
| Zucchini | Slice into ½-inch (1.5cm) rounds. | Italian seasoning | Medium-high | 5–7 min | Thinner slices cook faster; thicker slices need extra time. Stir frequently. |

# Sweet
## *Endings*

**268**  Creamy Rice Pudding

**271**  Anything Goes Fruit Crisp

**272**  No-Bake Cheesecake

**275**  Magic Lemon Pudding Cake

**276**  Grandpa Z's Banana Cupcakes

**279**  Better-Than-Anything Chocolate Cake

**280**  Chocolate Chip Pecan Cookies

1 cup (198g) uncooked **long-grain white rice**

2 cups (480ml) **water**

3½ cups (840ml) **whole milk,** divided

⅔ cup (133g) **granulated sugar**

⅛ teaspoon **salt**

2 **eggs**

1½ cup (198g) **golden raisins**

2 tablespoons **butter**

1 teaspoon **vanilla extract**

½ teaspoon **ground cinnamon**

⅛ teaspoon **ground nutmeg**

### Ingredient Swap

This recipe can be prepared with **leftover cooked rice.** Skip the rice and water, add 3 cups (600g) leftover cooked white rice to the milk in step 2, and continue as directed.

# Creamy **Rice Pudding**

My husband, Ken, loves all things dessert, and this oh-so-cozy rice pudding recipe is at the very top of his list. It's a dessert my mother-in-law, Ruby, always made for their family on the farm, and I make it often since it's prepared with ingredients I always have on hand. A simple mixture of white rice is cooked in sweetened milk until thick and creamy and is finished with warm spices, a handful of plump raisins, and a pat of butter. It's pure comfort.

1. In a large nonstick saucepan, combine the rice and water. Bring to a boil over high heat, reduce the heat to a simmer and cover. Cook for 18 minutes or until most of the water is absorbed.
2. Stir in 2¾ cups (660ml) milk, sugar, and salt. Bring to a low boil over medium heat, reduce the heat to a simmer, and cook uncovered, stirring frequently, for 18 to 22 minutes until the mixture is very thick and creamy.
3. In a medium bowl, whisk the eggs and the remaining ¾ cup (180ml) milk. Gradually add 2 cups (485g) hot rice mixture to the egg mixture while stirring. (This tempers the eggs, warming them slowly so they don't scramble when added to the saucepan.) Add the egg and rice mixture to the saucepan, stir in the raisins, and cook for 2 minutes more.
4. Remove the saucepan from the heat and stir in the butter, vanilla, cinnamon, and nutmeg.
5. Serve warm and garnish with an additional sprinkle of nutmeg and cinnamon, if desired.

**Serving Suggestions**

This recipe is perfect served right out of the pot, but my husband always likes to add a drizzle of cream over the top.

**Make Ahead**

This rice pudding can be made ahead of time and served chilled or warm. The rice will continue to absorb liquid and thicken as it cools, so add additional milk as needed to create a creamy consistency.

# Anything Goes **Fruit Crisp**

**Prep Time:** 20 minutes
**Total Time:** 55 minutes
**Serves** 6

---

**FOR THE TOPPING**

¾ cup (93g) **rolled oats**

6 tablespoons **butter**, softened

½ cup (96g) packed **light or dark brown sugar**

¼ cup (30g) **all-purpose flour**

½ cup (58g) finely **chopped pecans** or flaked coconut

½ teaspoon **ground cinnamon**

**FOR THE FILLING**

Fruit crisp is a dessert that my mom always served, and I make it for my own family often. Fresh fruit is topped with a buttery oat crumble topping and baked until bubbly. It's simple, delicious, and can be made with almost any kind of fruit, making it a favorite all year long.

1. Preheat the oven to 375°F (190°C).
2. To make the topping, in a medium bowl, add the oats, butter, brown sugar, flour, pecans, and cinnamon. Using a fork or pastry blender, cut together to form crumbs.
3. To a 9 × 9-inch (23 × 23cm) baking dish, add your chosen fruit, sugar, flour, and spices. Toss well to combine.
4. Sprinkle the topping mixture over the fruit and bake for the time shown on the table or until the top is golden brown and the fruit is bubbly.
5. Cool for 10 minutes and serve warm.

| Fruit | Granulated Sugar | All-Purpose Flour | Spices | Baking Time |
|---|---|---|---|---|
| 6 cups (600g) peeled, sliced **Granny Smith apples** | 3 tablespoons | 1 tablespoon | ½ teaspoon **ground cinnamon** or ¼ teaspoon **ground ginger** | 25 to 30 minutes |
| 6 cups (900g) **mixed berries** | ¼ cup (50g) | ¼ cup (30g) | 1 teaspoon **lemon zest** | 35 to 40 minutes |
| 6 cups (700g) **diced rhubarb** | ⅔ cup (133g) | 3 tablespoons | ½ teaspoon **ground cinnamon** | 35 to 45 minutes |
| 6 cups (1kg) peeled, sliced **peaches** | 3 tablespoons | 2 tablespoons | ½ teaspoon **ground cinnamon** | 25 to 30 minutes |

 **SERVING SUGGESTIONS**

Fruit crisp is great served at room temperature or warm and topped with a scoop of vanilla ice cream or whipped cream. If you're serving leftovers for breakfast, add a little bit of yogurt.

 **MAKE AHEAD**

Prepare several batches of the topping mixture and store it in the freezer for up to 4 months. When you're ready for dessert, there is no need to thaw the topping. Sprinkle it over the fruit and bake as directed.

**Prep Time:** 20 minutes
**Total Time:** 4 hours 20 minutes
**Serves** 8

---

### FOR THE CRUST
1½ cups (195g) **graham cracker crumbs**

6 tablespoons **unsalted butter,** melted

¼ cup (50g) **granulated sugar**

### FOR THE FILLING
16oz (454g) **cream cheese,** softened

1 cup (105g) **powdered sugar**

1 teaspoon **vanilla extract**

1 cup (240ml) **heavy whipping cream**

1 teaspoon **cornstarch**

# No-Bake **Cheesecake**

This decadent cheesecake recipe skips the fussy and time-consuming steps of a traditional baked cheesecake. A thick, velvety cheesecake filling is nestled in an easy no-bake graham cracker crust. Since it's made ahead of time, it's a perfect party dessert that's fail proof.

1. **To make the crust,** in a medium bowl, combine the graham cracker crumbs, melted butter, and sugar with a fork.
2. Using your hands or the flat bottom of a measuring cup, press the mixture into the bottom and up the sides—about 1½ inches (4cm)—of a 9-inch (23cm) pie dish or 8-inch (20cm) springform pan. Refrigerate the crust while preparing the filling.
3. **To make the filling,** in a large bowl, beat the softened cream cheese with a hand mixer until smooth and fluffy. Add the powdered sugar and vanilla extract and continue beating until incorporated.
4. In a separate medium bowl, beat the heavy whipping cream on low for 1 minute. Add the cornstarch, increase the mixer speed to high, and beat for an additional 3 to 4 minutes until stiff peaks form.
5. Gently fold the whipped cream into the cream cheese mixture until just combined; the texture should resemble thick whipped cream.
6. Add the filling to the chilled graham crust and use a spatula to spread it into an even layer. Refrigerate the cheesecake for at least 4 hours or overnight.

---

 **SERVING SUGGESTIONS**

Top the cheesecake with fruit, pie filling, or even a drizzle of caramel sauce.

 **VARIATION**

This recipe makes great cheesecake cups for individual servings! Use any small jars or clear cups, spoon the combined crust ingredients in the bottom, pressing it in, and then top with the cheesecake mixture. Chill for at least 2 hours or freeze for later use. The number of servings will vary based on the size of the jars.

 **SOMETHING ON THE SIDE**

Cheesecake with blueberry sauce is my favorite dessert. To make a blueberry topping, in a medium saucepan, combine 4 cups (630g) fresh or frozen blueberries, ½ cup (100g) granulated sugar, ⅓ cup (80ml) water, and 2 teaspoons cornstarch. Bring to a simmer over medium heat and reduce to low. Simmer for 5 minutes. Cool the sauce before spooning over the cheesecake. Prefer strawberry sauce?

*Scan for my Strawberry Sauce recipe.*

**Prep Time:** 20 minutes
**Total Time:** 1 hour 25 minutes
**Serves** 6

---

3 **eggs**, yolks and whites
    separated, at room temperature
¾ cup (150g) **granulated sugar**
3 tablespoons **butter,** melted
¼ cup (30g) **all-purpose flour**
6 tablespoons freshly squeezed
    **lemon juice**
1 cup (240ml) **milk**
1 tablespoon **lemon zest**

# Magic Lemon **Pudding Cake**

This is a retro recipe that I created based on the many similar versions found in my treasured collection of old church and family cookbooks. This recipe magically transforms everyday ingredients into a delicate cake with a delicious sweet-tart lemon sauce. It's easy to make and the results are nothing short of spectacular.

1. Preheat the oven to 350°F (175°C).
2. In a medium bowl, add the egg whites and beat on medium speed with a hand mixer until stiff peaks form.
3. In another medium bowl, combine the sugar and butter with a hand mixer until well combined and sandy looking. Add the flour, lemon juice, and egg yolks, and mix until combined. Stir in the milk until smooth.
4. Gently fold in the beaten egg whites and lemon zest. Whisk lightly until incorporated. Spread the batter into an ungreased 1½-quart (1.4L) baking dish.
5. Place the baking dish into a larger pan—a 9 × 13-inch (23 × 33cm) metal cake pan works well, and fill the larger pan with very hot tap water to a depth of 1 inch (2.5cm).
6. Carefully place the pan with the nested baking dish in the oven and bake uncovered for 50 minutes to 1 hour or until the cake is set on top.
7. Remove the baking dish from the pan of water and rest for 5 minutes before serving.

---

**SERVING SUGGESTIONS**

We like to serve this cake slightly warm or at room temperature with vanilla ice cream or fresh whipped cream.

**TIPS**

- You will need approximately 2 large lemons for this recipe.
- This pudding cake is a very delicate dessert with a delicious custard-like pudding. Baking this dessert in a water bath (bain-marie) helps it to cook evenly and keeps the pudding from curdling. Find 2 dishes that work well together before beginning.
- Use a clean, oil-free bowl and beaters when beating the egg whites. Any oil residue or egg yolk will prevent the egg whites from forming peaks.

---

**FOR THE CUPCAKES**

¾ teaspoon **lemon juice**

¼ cup (60ml) **milk**

2 **eggs**, yolks and whites separated

½ cup (113g) **unsalted butter**, softened

1 cup (200g) **granulated sugar**

2 cups (240g) **all-purpose flour**

2 teaspoons **baking powder**

1 teaspoon **baking soda**

⅛ teaspoon **salt**

1⅓ cups (343g) mashed **ripe banana**, about 3 medium bananas

**FOR THE FROSTING**

4oz (113g) **cream cheese**, at room temperature

3 tablespoons **unsalted butter**, softened

½ teaspoon **vanilla extract**

1½–1¾ cups (158–184g) **powdered sugar**

Pinch of **salt**

# Grandpa Z's **Banana Cupcakes**

My Grandpa Zajac's banana cupcake recipe makes the softest, fluffiest banana cupcakes. I remember the smell of these cupcakes wafting from the kitchen while waiting for them to cool. We would top them with a big smear of homemade cream cheese frosting for the perfect sweet treat. I still have the original recipe, typed out by my grandpa many years ago, and it is absolutely a family favorite.

1. Preheat the oven to 350°F (175°C). Line the wells of 2 to 3 standard-size muffin tins with 18 cupcake liners.

2. **To make the cupcakes,** in a small bowl, combine the lemon juice and milk. Stir and set aside.

3. Using a mixer, beat the egg whites on high speed until stiff peaks form; set aside.

4. Using a mixer and a separate medium bowl, cream together the butter and sugar. Mix in the egg yolks and lemon-soured milk.

5. In another medium bowl, mix together the flour, baking powder, baking soda, and salt. Slowly add the dry ingredients to the butter mixture, mixing continuously until combined. Stir in the bananas.

6. Gently fold in the egg white mixture and fill each muffin well with batter ⅔ full.

7. Bake for 20 to 24 minutes or until the cupcakes spring back when lightly touched.

8. **To make the frosting,** combine the cream cheese and butter with a mixer on medium speed until smooth and creamy. Mix in the vanilla.

9. Add the powdered sugar a bit at a time, scraping the sides of the bowl as needed. Continue beating on medium speed until fluffy. Do not overmix.

10. Spread the frosting over the cooled cupcakes.

---

 **SERVING SUGGESTIONS**
We love these cupcakes with cream cheese frosting but they're also great with your favorite chocolate frosting or vanilla buttercream.

 **MAKE AHEAD**
These cupcakes can be frozen for up to 4 months. Bake as directed, cool completely, and freeze in an airtight freezerproof container. They can be frosted before or after freezing.

**Prep Time:** 15 minutes
**Total Time:** 4 hours 50 minutes
**Serves** 12

---

### FOR THE CAKE

1 (15.25oz / 432g) box **chocolate cake mix**

Ingredients required on the box for a 9 × 13-inch (22 × 33cm) cake

### FOR THE TOPPING

1 (14oz / 397g) can **sweetened condensed milk**

1 cup (240ml) **caramel ice cream topping**

3 cups (216g) **whipped topping**

¼ cup (52g) **English toffee bits**, such as Heath or Skor

# Better-Than-Anything
# **Chocolate Cake**

This recipe was introduced to me by my sister-in-law Wynne, and I immediately fell in love with it. It's quick and easy to prepare with a boxed cake mix, and while this recipe goes by many names, in our family, it's known as "Divorce Cake." When I make it, my husband can't stop eating it. He told me if I kept making it, he'd have to leave me. Twenty-four years later, he's still here . . . I think he stays for the cake.

1. **To make the cake,** prepare and bake a chocolate cake according to the package directions using a 9 × 13-inch (22 × 33cm) baking pan. Remove the cake from the oven and let it cool for 15 minutes.
2. Using the end of a wooden spoon or the thicker end of a chopstick, poke holes into the top of the entire cake. Make your holes about 1 inch (2.5cm) deep. Pour the sweetened condensed milk and the caramel sauce over the cake, allowing it to seep into the holes.
3. Cover and refrigerate the cake for at least 4 hours or overnight.
4. Before serving, spread the whipped topping over the cake and sprinkle the English toffee bits over the topping.

---

 **TIP**

Any variety of chocolate cake mix works well in this recipe. In addition to easy prep, we have found that boxed cake mixes provide just the right texture to allow the toppings to soak into the cake as it rests.

**Prep Time:** 25 minutes
**Total Time:** 40 minutes
**Makes** 28 cookies

---

1 cup (124g) coarsely
    chopped **pecans**
1 cup (227g) **unsalted butter**,
    softened
1 cup (192g) lightly packed **light
    brown sugar**
½ cup (100g) **granulated sugar**
2 **large eggs**, at room
    temperature
2 teaspoons **vanilla extract**
2½ cups (300g) **all-purpose flour**
½ teaspoon **salt**
½ teaspoon **baking soda**
1½ cups (255g) **semisweet
    chocolate chips**
**Flaky sea salt** (optional)

# Chocolate Chip Pecan Cookies

These are literally the perfect cookies in every way. They're crisp on the edges and a little bit chewy in the middle, and they have an amazing buttery, almost caramel-like flavor. They're jam-packed with pecans and chocolate chips in every bite, making them impossible to resist. Best of all, no chilling is required! (Because who wants to wait for cookies?)

1. To a small, dry skillet over medium heat, add the chopped pecans and cook until lightly browned and fragrant, about 4 to 5 minutes. Cool completely.
2. Preheat the oven to 350°F (175°C).
3. In a large bowl or stand mixer, cream the butter, brown sugar, and sugar on medium speed until fluffy, about 2 minutes.
4. Add the eggs, one at a time, beating until well incorporated after each addition. Add the vanilla.
5. In a medium bowl, whisk together the flour, salt, and baking soda. Gradually add to the butter mixture until combined. Fold in the chocolate chips and cooled pecans.
6. Scoop the dough in 2½-tablespoon rounded portions and place on an ungreased baking sheet, 2 inches (5cm) apart, to make 28 cookies. Sprinkle with flaky sea salt, if desired.
7. Bake for 10 to 13 minutes or just until the edges are lightly browned. Let rest on the baking sheet for 1 minute and then transfer to a wire rack to cool.

---

 **TIPS**
- Be sure to measure the flour by gently spooning it into the measuring cup and leveling it with the back of a butter knife. Scooping with a measuring cup will pack the flour into the cup and may result in too much flour.
- Dark brown sugar can be used in place of light brown sugar.

# Acknowledgments

**IT TAKES A VILLAGE**—and when I think about my village, I can't help but feel immense gratitude. This book was more than three years in the making between my vision and the first printed copy, and a multitude of people have brought this dream to reality.

To Ken, my husband, you have always encouraged me to shoot for the stars. Spend with Pennies and this book wouldn't exist without your unwavering support and everything you do behind the scenes. You help me push forward on the days I feel I can't, and you celebrate my wins on the days I can. You're the very best dishwasher, grocery getter, produce picker, sounding board, voice of reason, errand runner, wine filler, dinner date, and taste tester I could ever hope for. Love you all day.

Thank you to my kids, Ayla, Tyler, Maddy, and Kailey, for spending your whole lives taste testing my kitchen adventures, both the wins and the mishaps. You've truly given my life meaning, and this book is a collection of our journey together and beyond. To the little apple of my eye, my grandson Jaxson, my mini taste tester, I promise to always make lots of "pastaroni" for you. To my son-in-law and sometimes sous chef, Chris, and to Colton for sharing in our family meals.

Mom and Dad, you have always made me feel like I could accomplish anything. Mom, this book started fifty years ago with the way you poured your heart into every holiday and every meal for our family, which has extended into how I have raised my own family. Thank you for always guiding me in the kitchen, sharing in my love for food, and still answering my cooking questions. Dad, your entrepreneurial spirit, drive, and ridiculous sense of humor are ingrained within me, and I thank you daily. To Bill and Ruby for being the best in-laws I could have ever asked for, and for your love, support, and inspiration from the day I met you.

To my best friends and sisters Candace and Alesha, I couldn't have done this without your support both now and always. From taste testing to sharing ideas to talking business and the occasional escape from reality, you have been integral in this book.

Alesha, thank you to you and your team for taking such good care of my puppies (and using up their energy) while I spent long hours in the studio, and for always listening to me no matter the time of day. Few people get me the way you do.

Candace, in addition to being my sister, you're the best ever business manager, and I couldn't do any of this without you by my side. Thank you for showing up at a moment's notice, helping me whenever I need it (even if that help comes at 2 a.m.), countless hours of brainstorming, reviewing, recipe testing, and editing. Thank you for being my voice of reason and setting me straight like only a sister could while listening to every crazy idea I throw your way. Even on the most difficult of days, you somehow have a way of making everything magically seem okay. Your dedication and encouragement mean the world to me, and I'm so thankful I get to work alongside you every day.

My studio dream team, Ayla, Nicky, and Leah, without whom this book wouldn't exist. Leah and Nicky, thank you for sharing your insights and ideas, and of course for testing these recipes over and over again (over 1,000 times!) Nicky, your thoughtful approach, quest for perfection, and incredible eye for design have led to so many delicious ideas. I appreciate your calm demeanor in what is an often hectic kitchen and your candor. I'm so glad to have you by my side. Leah, you are a breath of fresh air who got it done, with no meticulous detail left behind, and you have the ability to put the things in my brain on paper in the perfect way. I appreciate you being so thorough, and we all appreciate your sense of humor.

To Ayla, my daughter and content managing queen and SEO guru, thank you for the hours of organizing, editing, reviewing, "mathing" for us, and keeping things on schedule in addition to cooking, testing, and retesting. You kept me levelheaded— thank you for those after-hours and weekend calls. You jumped in and did whatever was needed and contributed in countless ways. You, along with your heartwarming laugh, bring joy to the studio, and I'm so thankful to spend my days with you.

Thank you to the rest of the Spend with Pennies team who kept everything else running smoothly while we have been working on this book: Donnalea, Sam, Shannon, Gaja, Maria, and Catherine. I'm so grateful for all of you. Thank you, Shelby, for keeping things organized and ready every week, and to the best ever recipe testers: Paul, Chris, Shauna, Peyton, Bailey, Tyler, Sydney, and so many more.

To Maria Ribas, my agent, I'm so blessed to have you next to me on this journey. You have believed in me from day one and encouraged me throughout this process. Thank you for sharing your incredible expertise, knowledge, and guidance. It means the world to me.

Thank you to the amazing team at DK Publishing. Ann Barton, my editor, working with you has been an absolute dream. Thank you for your trust in my vision, for your meticulous eye, and your expertise as you led me through writing my first book. You have helped bring my voice, vision, and food to life in a way I could've never imagined.

To Jordan Moore, Michael Sanchez, Cassie Noyes, and the entire extended Raptive team, who have supported me over the years. I appreciate all that you do.

To my incredibly talented food photographer Joanie Simon, the most amazing food stylist Brendan McCaskey, and to Alexa, Audrey, and the rest of the Joanie Simon Media team. Thank you for the weeks and weeks of intense photo shoots, countless hours of planning, reshoots, and for your endless positivity. Your remarkable talent has perfectly captured the essence of my recipes, and I am forever grateful.

Thank you Tracey Jazmin, for flying out and capturing the lifestyle images in this book and beyond. Your talent and ability to make me feel comfortable in front of the camera is unmatched.

To all of my friends who have supported me throughout this blogging career, this book, and beyond. You know who you are. Tanja, thank you for always checking in just when I needed it. Dorothy, you've been such an incredible sounding board and support. Sally, Rachel, Alyssa, Lisa, Jocelyn, Trish, Amanda, Susie, Becky, Aubrey, Chelsea, and Sandra, I'm so grateful for every single one of you. Thank you to those I didn't list, but didn't forget.

To my readers, you are the reason I get to do what I love day in and day out, and this book is for you. I don't have the words to truly express my gratitude to each and every one of you who visit my site and make my recipes. Your comments, feedback, and support mean the world to me. Thank you for sharing your ideas and your stories with me. There is no greater honor than you allowing me to have a place at your family table through my recipes, and for that, I thank you.

# Index

## A

**air fryer recipes**
BLT Baked Chicken Burgers with Chipotle Mayo, 87
Cheesy Beef & Salsa Burrito Supreme, 5
Crispy Chicken & Potato Patties with Creamy Corn, 60
Crispy Oven Chicken with Savory Cheddar Waffles, 88
Crispy Oven Schnitzel Burgers with Zesty Dill Pickle Slaw, 141
Crunchy Pecan Chicken with Honey-Roasted Sweet Potatoes, 157
Easiest Ever Tomato Soup with Cheesy Basil Toasts, 37
Feta Meatballs with Lemon Orzo & Cucumber Salsa, 214
Flaky Fish Tacos with Lime Crema, 98
Grilled Greek Chicken Wraps with Feta Mint Sauce, 236
Hasselback Chicken Cordon Bleu with Skinny Dijon Sauce, 109
Honey Dijon–Glazed Pork Tenderloin with Roasted Sweet Potatoes & Apples, 101
Maple Sesame Salmon Bites with Broccoli & Peppers, 48
My Mom's Hoisin Pork Tenderloin Sammies, 76
Pimento Cheese–Stuffed Chicken Breasts with Honey Corn, 235
Sheet Pan Cheeseburgers with Crispy Potato Wedges, 146
Stuffed Spaghetti Squash with Zesty Turkey Sauce, 102
All-Purpose Meaty Pasta Sauce, 135
Anything Goes Fruit Crisp, 271
**asparagus**
Beef & Asparagus Roll-Ups with Tarragon Sauce, 64
roasting, 262
stovetop cooking of, 264
Avocado Tuna Bowl with Sriracha Mayo, 41

## B

**bacon.** *See also pork*
Bacon-Wrapped Pork Tenderloin with Roasted Brussels Sprouts, 145
BLT Baked Chicken Burgers with Chipotle Mayo, 87
Fast! Homemade Alfredo Sauce (Variation), 128
Lazy Day Bacon & Pea Oven Risotto, 171
Baked Beef Pinwheels, 213
Baked Chicken Spaghetti, 168
**beans**
Cheesy Beef & Salsa Burrito Supreme, 5
Cowboy Chopped Chicken Salad, 244
Easy Salsa Chicken Power Bowls, 239
Hearty Baked Chili with Cornmeal Drop Biscuits, 176
Layered Tex-Mex Tortilla Bake, 222
Tastes-Like-All-Day Quick Ham & Bean Soup, 22
**beef.** *See also ground beef; steak*
Rustic Beef & Veggie Pot Pie, 201
Slow Cooker Pot Roast with Root Veggies & Gravy, 197
Beef & Asparagus Roll-Ups with Tarragon Sauce, 64
Beefed-Up Busy Day Lasagna, 206
**bell peppers**
Maple Sesame Salmon Bites with Broccoli & Peppers, 48
roasting, 262
Sticky Honey-Garlic Drumsticks with Peppers & Snap Peas, 138
stovetop cooking of, 264
The Best Ever Meatloaf, 190
Better-Than-Anything Chocolate Cake, 279
Better-Than-Take-Out Cheeseburger Sloppy Joes, 209
BLT Baked Chicken Burgers with Chipotle Mayo, 87
**bread,** Garlic Herb Bread, 255
**broccoli**
Cozy Chicken, Broccoli & Wild Rice Casserole, 175
Flaky Broccoli Cheddar Chicken Pockets, 83
Maple Sesame Salmon Bites with Broccoli & Peppers, 48
roasting, 262
stovetop cooking of, 264
20-Minute Broccoli Cheese Soup, 30
**Brussels sprouts**
Bacon-Wrapped Pork Tenderloin with Roasted Brussels Sprouts, 145
roasting, 262
stovetop cooking of, 264
**burgers**
BLT Baked Chicken Burgers with Chipotle Mayo, 87
Crispy Oven Schnitzel Burgers with Zesty Dill Pickle Slaw, 141
Sheet Pan Cheeseburgers with Crispy Potato Wedges, 146
**burritos,** Cheesy Beef & Salsa Burrito Supreme, 55
Busy Day Parmesan Mushroom Toasts, 38

## C

**cabbage**
Cabbage Roll Skillet with Garlic Butter Dill Rice, 63
No-Roll Mini-Meatball Cabbage Soup, 97
stovetop cooking of, 264
Cajun Seasoning, 18
**casseroles**
Baked Chicken Spaghetti, 168
Cheesy Herbed-Ricotta Baked Ziti, 179
Chicken Pot Pie–Stuffed Shells with Herb Butter Crumbs, 72
Cozy Chicken, Broccoli & Wild Rice Casserole, 175
From-Scratch Tuna Casserole, 172
Hearty Baked Chili with Cornmeal Drop Biscuits, 176
Layered Tex-Mex Tortilla Bake, 222
Lazy Day Bacon & Pea Oven Risotto, 171
Melt-in-Your-Mouth Pork Steaks in Creamy Mushroom Sauce, 163
Salsa Verde Chicken Enchilada Casserole, 164
Savory Ham & Cheese Bread Pudding, 167
Three-Cheese Creamy Chicken & Mushroom Lasagna, 198
Three-Cheese Scalloped Potato & Beef Gratin, 160
Cheesy Beef & Salsa Burrito Supreme, 55
Cheesy Herbed-Ricotta Baked Ziti, 179

Cheesy Ratatouille Roll-Ups with
Meat Sauce (or Not), 113

**chicken**
Baked Chicken Spaghetti, 168
BLT Baked Chicken Burgers with
Chipotle Mayo, 87
Chicken Pot Pie–Stuffed Shells
with Herb Butter Crumbs, 72
Choose-Your-Own-Adventure
Chicken Stir-Fry, 231
Cowboy Chopped Chicken Salad,
244
Cozy Chicken, Broccoli & Wild Rice
Casserole, 175
Cozy Chicken, Mushroom & Rice
Soup, 243
Crispy Chicken & Potato Patties
with Creamy Corn, 60
Crispy Oven Chicken with Savory
Cheddar Waffles, 88
Crispy Oven Schnitzel Burgers
with Zesty Dill Pickle Slaw
(Variation), 141
Crispy Rosemary Chicken Thighs
with Root Veggies, 52
Crunchy Pecan Chicken with
Honey-Roasted Sweet Potatoes,
157
Easy Salsa Chicken Power Bowls,
239
Egg Roll in a Bowl (Variation), 33
Fast & Fancy Weeknight Shrimp
Piccata (Variation), 42
Flaky Broccoli Cheddar Chicken
Pockets, 83
Grilled Greek Chicken Wraps with
Feta Mint Sauce, 236
Hasselback Chicken Cordon Bleu
with Skinny Dijon Sauce, 109
Herb-Roasted Chicken Pasta
Primavera, 106
Homestyle Roast Chicken Dinner,
187–189
Lemon-Pesto Shrimp Pasta
with Pepper Parm Crumbs
(Variation), 123
Moroccan-Spiced Chicken
Couscous Bowls, 68
My Mom's Hoisin Pork Tenderloin
Sammies (Variation), 76
No-Roll Mini-Meatball Cabbage
Soup, 97
One-Pan Chicken Pomodoro
Skillet, 228
Perfect Baked Chicken Breasts,
247

Pimento Cheese–Stuffed Chicken
Breasts with Honey Corn, 235
Roasted Red Pepper Pasta with
Crispy Parmesan Chicken, 132
Root Beer BBQ Pulled Chicken
Sliders, 29
Salsa Verde Chicken Enchilada
Casserole, 164
Seared Pork Chops with Creamy
Spinach Gnocchi (Variation), 51
Seared Pork Medallions with
Creamy Cracked Pepper Sauce
(Variation), 26
Secret Sauce Orange Ginger Beef
(Variation), 25
Skillet Chicken & Gravy, 240
Skillet Shrimp Fajitas with Corn
Cucumber Salsa (Variation), 105
Slow Cooker Homestyle Chicken &
Vegetable Chowder, 232
Spicy-as-You-Like-It Shrimp
Peanut Noodles (Variation), 131
Sticky Honey-Garlic Drumsticks
with Peppers & Snap Peas, 138
30-Minute Creamy Dijon Chicken,
67
Three-Cheese Creamy Chicken &
Mushroom Lasagna, 198
Weeknight Spinach, Artichoke
& Sundried Tomato Rigatoni
(Variation), 119
Chocolate Chip Pecan Cookies, 280
Choose-Your-Own-Adventure
Chicken Stir-Fry, 231
**chowder.** *See soup*
Clean-Out-the-Fridge Pot Sticker
Soup, 34
Cowboy Chopped Chicken Salad,
244
Cozy Chicken, Broccoli & Wild Rice
Casserole, 175
Cozy Chicken, Mushroom & Rice
Soup, 243
Creamy, Cheesy Crowd-Pleasin' Rice,
259
Creamy Clam Chowder with Mini
Cheddar Biscuits, 194
Creamy Rice Pudding, 268
Crispy Chicken & Potato Patties with
Creamy Corn, 60
Crispy Oven Chicken with Savory
Cheddar Waffles, 88
Crispy Oven Schnitzel Burgers with
Zesty Dill Pickle Slaw, 141
Crispy Rosemary Chicken Thighs
with Root Veggies, 52

Crunchy Pecan Chicken with Honey-
Roasted Sweet Potatoes, 157

**D**
**desserts,** 267
Dill Pickle Pasta Salad, 250

**E**
Easiest Ever Tomato Soup with
Cheesy Basil Toasts, 37
Easy Fried Rice, 56
Easy Salsa Chicken Power Bowls,
239
Egg Roll in a Bowl, 33
**eggs,** Breakfast-for-Dinner Sheet
Pan Chorizo Hash, 154
The Everyday Salad Dressing, 252

**F**
**fajitas,** Skillet Shrimp Fajitas with
Corn Cucumber Salsa, 105
Fast & Fancy Weeknight Shrimp
Piccata, 42
Fast! Homemade Alfredo Sauce, 128
Feta Meatballs with Lemon Orzo &
Cucumber Salsa, 214
**fish.** *See also seafood*
Avocado Tuna Bowl with Sriracha
Mayo, 41
Flaky Fish Tacos with Lime Crema,
98
From-Scratch Tuna Casserole, 172
Lemon Herb-Crusted Salmon with
Garlic Green Beans, 150
Maple Sesame Salmon Bites with
Broccoli & Peppers, 48
Pan-Seared Cod with Fresh Mango
Salsa, 110
Flaky Broccoli Cheddar Chicken
Pockets, 83
Flaky Fish Tacos with Lime Crema,
98
From-Scratch Tuna Casserole, 172

**G**
Garlic Herb Bread, 255
Garlic-Herb Seasoning, 18
Garlicky Mashed Potatoes, 256
Gonna-Want-Seconds Cheesesteak
Pasta, 116
Grandma Mary's Pierogi, 182
Grandma Mary's Rouladen with
Mushroom Gravy, 192–193
Grandpa Z's Banana Cupcakes, 276
**green beans**
Lemon Herb-Crusted Salmon with

Garlic Green Beans, 150
roasting, 262
stovetop cooking of, 265
Grilled Greek Chicken Wraps with
Feta Mint Sauce, 236

**grilling recipes**
BLT Baked Chicken Burgers with
Chipotle Mayo, 87
Cowboy Chopped Chicken Salad,
244
Grilled Greek Chicken Wraps with
Feta Mint Sauce, 236
My Mom's Hoisin Pork Tenderloin
Sammies, 76
Steakhouse Surf 'n' Turf Salad, 94

**ground beef.** See also beef
All-Purpose Meaty Pasta Sauce,
135
Baked Beef Pinwheels, 213
Beefed-Up Busy Day Lasagna, 206
The Best Ever Meatloaf, 190
Better-Than-Take-Out
Cheeseburger Sloppy Joes, 209
Cabbage Roll Skillet with Garlic
Butter Dill Rice, 63
Cheesy Beef & Salsa Burrito
Supreme, 55
Feta Meatballs with Lemon Orzo &
Cucumber Salsa, 214
Gonna-Want-Seconds
Cheesesteak Pasta (Variation),
116
Ground Beef Barley Soup, 218
Hearty Baked Chili with Cornmeal
Drop Biscuits, 176
Hearty Ground Beef Stew with
Rosemary Dumplings, 75
Hearty Homemade Goulash, 225
Herbed Ground Beef & Rice
Stroganoff Skillet, 59
Layered Tex-Mex Tortilla Bake, 222
Lentil Shepherd's Pie, 80
Melty French Onion Meatballs, 221
Mushroom & Swiss–Stuffed Mini
Meatloaf, 217
Must-Make Pizza Meatballs &
Spaghetti, 91
No-Roll Mini-Meatball Cabbage
Soup (Variation), 97
Secret Sauce Orange Ginger Beef,
25
Sheet Pan Cheeseburgers with
Crispy Potato Wedges, 146
Spicy Hoisin Beef with Garlic
Ramen Noodles, 210

Three-Cheese Scalloped Potato &
Beef Gratin, 160
Zucchini Turkey Meatballs
with Roasted Tomato Sauce
(Variation), 153

## H–I

**ham.** See also pork
Savory Ham & Cheese Bread
Pudding, 167
Tastes-Like-All-Day Quick Ham &
Bean Soup, 22
Hasselback Chicken Cordon Bleu
with Skinny Dijon Sauce, 109
Hearty Baked Chili with Cornmeal
Drop Biscuits, 176
Hearty Ground Beef Stew with
Rosemary Dumplings, 75
Hearty Homemade Goulash, 225
Herbed Ground Beef & Rice
Stroganoff Skillet, 59
Herb-Roasted Chicken Pasta
Primavera, 106
Homemade Seasoning Mixes, 18
Homestyle Roast Chicken Dinner,
187–189
Honey Dijon–Glazed Pork Tenderloin
with Roasted Sweet Potatoes &
Apples, 101

Italian Seasoning, 18

## J–K–L

Kailey's Roasted Balsamic Cherry
Tomato Pasta, 12

Layered Tex-Mex Tortilla Bake, 222
Lazy Day Bacon & Pea Oven Risotto,
171
Lemon Herb-Crusted Salmon with
Garlic Green Beans, 150
Lemon-Pesto Shrimp Pasta with
Pepper Parm Crumbs, 123
Lentil Shepherd's Pie, 80

## M

Magic Lemon Pudding Cake, 275
Maple Sesame Salmon Bites with
Broccoli & Peppers, 48

**meatballs**
Feta Meatballs with Lemon Orzo &
Cucumber Salsa, 214
Melty French Onion Meatballs, 221
Must-Make Pizza Meatballs &
Spaghetti, 91
No-Roll Mini-Meatball Cabbage

Soup, 97

**meatloaf**
The Best Ever Meatloaf, 190
Mushroom & Swiss–Stuffed Mini
Meatloaf, 217
Melt-in-Your-Mouth Pork Steaks in
Creamy Mushroom Sauce, 163
Melty French Onion Meatballs, 221
Moroccan-Spiced Chicken Couscous
Bowls, 68

**mushrooms**
Busy Day Parmesan Mushroom
Toasts, 38
Cozy Chicken, Mushroom & Rice
Soup, 243
Lazy Day Bacon & Pea Oven
Risotto (Variation), 171
Melt-in-Your-Mouth Pork Steaks in
Creamy Mushroom Sauce, 163
Mushroom & Swiss–Stuffed Mini
Meatloaf, 217
roasting, 262
stovetop cooking of, 265
Three-Cheese Creamy Chicken &
Mushroom Lasagna, 198
Must-Make Pizza Meatballs &
Spaghetti, 91
My All-Time Favorite Mac & Cheese,
120
My All-Time Favorite Yogurt-Ranch
Dressing, 252
My Mom's Best Ever Pork Roast &
Gravy, 185–186
My Mom's Hoisin Pork Tenderloin
Sammies, 76

## N

No-Bake Cheesecake, 272
**noodles.** See also pasta
From-Scratch Tuna Casserole, 172
Soul-Soothing Buttered Noodles,
260
Spicy-as-You-Like-It Shrimp
Peanut Noodles, 131
Spicy Hoisin Beef with Garlic
Ramen Noodles, 210
No-Roll Mini-Meatball Cabbage
Soup, 97

## O

One-Pan Chicken Pomodoro Skillet,
228
One-Pan Sausage & Penne in
Creamy Rose Sauce, 124
One-Pan Smoked Sausage &
Roasted Veggies, 149

**onions**
Melty French Onion Meatballs, 221
roasting, 262
Skillet Onions & Potatoes, 256
stovetop cooking of, 265

**P–Q**
Pan-Seared Cod with Fresh Mango Salsa, 110
**pasta.** *See also noodles*
All-Purpose Meaty Pasta Sauce, 135
Baked Chicken Spaghetti, 168
Beefed-Up Busy Day Lasagna, 206
Cheesy Herbed-Ricotta Baked Ziti, 179
Chicken Pot Pie–Stuffed Shells with Herb Butter Crumbs, 72
Dill Pickle Pasta Salad, 250
Fast! Homemade Alfredo Sauce, 128
Feta Meatballs with Lemon Orzo & Cucumber Salsa, 214
Gonna-Want-Seconds Cheesesteak Pasta, 116
Hearty Homemade Goulash, 225
Herb-Roasted Chicken Pasta Primavera, 106
Kailey's Roasted Balsamic Cherry Tomato Pasta, 127
Lemon-Pesto Shrimp Pasta with Pepper Parm Crumbs, 123
Moroccan-Spiced Chicken Couscous Bowls, 68
Must-Make Pizza Meatballs & Spaghetti, 91
My All-Time Favorite Mac & Cheese, 120
One-Pan Sausage & Penne in Creamy Rose Sauce, 124
Roasted Red Pepper Pasta with Crispy Parmesan Chicken, 132
Seared Pork Chops with Creamy Spinach Gnocchi, 51
Six-Ingredient, One-Pot Tortellini Alfredo, 45
Spicy Sausage Pimento Mac & Cheese, 79
Three-Cheese Creamy Chicken & Mushroom Lasagna, 198
Weeknight Spinach, Artichoke & Sundried Tomato Rigatoni, 119
Zesty Unstuffed-Shells Soup with Basil Ricotta, 84
**peas**
Lazy Day Bacon & Pea Oven

Risotto, 171
stovetop cooking of, 265
Perfect Baked Chicken Breasts, 247
**pickles**
Crispy Oven Schnitzel Burgers with Zesty Dill Pickle Slaw, 141
Dill Pickle Pasta Salad, 25
Grandma Mary's Rouladen with Mushroom Gravy, 193
Homemade Quick Pickles, 209
Pimento Cheese–Stuffed Chicken Breasts with Honey Corn, 235
**pork.** *See also bacon; ham; sausage*
Bacon-Wrapped Pork Tenderloin with Roasted Brussels Sprouts, 145
Cabbage Roll Skillet with Garlic Butter Dill Rice, 63
Crispy Oven Schnitzel Burgers with Zesty Dill Pickle Slaw, 141
Egg Roll in a Bowl, 33
Honey Dijon–Glazed Pork Tenderloin with Roasted Sweet Potatoes & Apples, 101
Melt-in-Your-Mouth Pork Steaks in Creamy Mushroom Sauce, 163
My Mom's Best Ever Pork Roast & Gravy, 185–186
My Mom's Hoisin Pork Tenderloin Sammies, 76
Seared Pork Chops with Creamy Spinach Gnocchi, 51
Seared Pork Medallions with Creamy Cracked Pepper Sauce, 26
Slow Cooker Sticky Honey-Garlic Ribs, 202
**potatoes**
Crispy Chicken & Potato Patties with Creamy Corn, 60
Garlicky Mashed Potatoes, 256
roasting, 262
Sheet Pan Cheeseburgers with Crispy Potato Wedges, 146
Sheet Pan Steak with Warm Potato Salad & Horseradish Sauce, 142
Skillet Onions & Potatoes, 256
Three-Cheese Scalloped Potato & Beef Gratin, 160
Poultry Seasoning, 18

Quick Tomato Cucumber Salad, 255

**R**
**rice**
Cabbage Roll Skillet with Garlic Butter Dill Rice, 63
Choose-Your-Own-Adventure Chicken Stir-Fry, 231
Cozy Chicken, Broccoli & Wild Rice Casserole, 175
Cozy Chicken, Mushroom & Rice Soup, 243
Creamy, Cheesy Crowd-Pleasin' Rice, 259
Creamy Rice Pudding, 268
Easy Fried Rice, 56
Herbed Ground Beef & Rice Stroganoff Skillet, 59
Lazy Day Bacon & Pea Oven Risotto, 171
Simply Seasoned Garlic Rice, 259
Roasted Red Pepper Pasta with Crispy Parmesan Chicken, 132
Root Beer BBQ Pulled Chicken Sliders, 29
Rustic Beef & Veggie Pot Pie, 201

**S**
**salad dressings**
The Everyday Salad Dressing, 252
Homemade Blue Cheese Dressing, 94
My All-Time Favorite Yogurt-Ranch Dressing, 252
**salads**
Cowboy Chopped Chicken Salad, 244
Dill Pickle Pasta Salad, 250
Quick Tomato Cucumber Salad, 255
Steakhouse Surf 'n' Turf Salad, 94
**salsa**
Easy Salsa Chicken Power Bowls, 239
Feta Meatballs with Lemon Orzo & Cucumber Salsa, 214
Pan-Seared Cod with Fresh Mango Salsa, 110
Salsa Verde Chicken Enchilada Casserole, 164
Skillet Shrimp Fajitas with Corn Cucumber Salsa, 105
**sausage.** *See also pork*
All-Purpose Meaty Pasta Sauce, 135
Breakfast-for-Dinner Sheet Pan Chorizo Hash, 154
Cheesy Herbed-Ricotta Baked Ziti, 179

Cheesy Ratatouille Roll-Ups with
Meat Sauce (or Not), 113
One-Pan Sausage & Penne in
Creamy Rose Sauce, 124
One-Pan Smoked Sausage &
Roasted Veggies, 149
Spicy Sausage Pimento Mac &
Cheese, 79
Zesty Unstuffed-Shells Soup with
Basil Ricotta, 84
Savory Ham & Cheese Bread
Pudding, 167
**seafood.** *See also fish*
Creamy Clam Chowder with Mini
Cheddar Biscuits, 194
Fast & Fancy Weeknight Shrimp
Piccata, 42
Lemon-Pesto Shrimp Pasta with
Pepper Parm Crumbs, 123
Skillet Shrimp Fajitas with Corn
Cucumber Salsa, 105
Spicy-as-You-Like-It Shrimp
Peanut Noodles, 131
Steakhouse Surf 'n' Turf Salad, 94
Seared Pork Chops with Creamy
Spinach Gnocchi, 51
Seared Pork Medallions with Creamy
Cracked Pepper Sauce, 26
**seasoning mixes,** 18
Secret Sauce Orange Ginger Beef,
25
Sheet Pan Cheeseburgers with
Crispy Potato Wedges, 146
Sheet Pan Steak with Warm Potato
Salad & Horseradish Sauce, 142
Simply Seasoned Garlic Rice, 259
Six-Ingredient, One-Pot Tortellini
Alfredo, 45
Skillet Chicken & Gravy, 240
Skillet Onions & Potatoes, 256
Skillet Shrimp Fajitas with Corn
Cucumber Salsa, 105
**slow cooker recipes**
All-Purpose Meaty Pasta Sauce,
135
Beefed-Up Busy Day Lasagna, 206
Easy Salsa Chicken Power Bowls,
239
Slow Cooker Homestyle Chicken &
Vegetable Chowder, 232
Slow Cooker Pot Roast with Root
Veggies & Gravy, 197
Slow Cooker Sticky Honey-Garlic
Ribs, 202
Soul-Soothing Buttered Noodles,
260

**soup**
Clean-Out-the-Fridge Pot Sticker
Soup, 34
Cozy Chicken, Mushroom & Rice
Soup, 243
Creamy Clam Chowder with Mini
Cheddar Biscuits, 194
Easiest Ever Tomato Soup with
Cheesy Basil Toasts, 37
Ground Beef Barley Soup, 218
No-Roll Mini-Meatball Cabbage
Soup, 97
Slow Cooker Homestyle Chicken &
Vegetable Chowder, 232
Tastes-Like-All-Day Quick Ham &
Bean Soup, 22
20-Minute Broccoli Cheese Soup,
30
Zesty Unstuffed-Shells Soup with
Basil Ricotta, 84
Spicy Hoisin Beef with Garlic Ramen
Noodles, 210
Spicy-as-You-Like-It Shrimp Peanut
Noodles, 131
Spicy Sausage Pimento Mac &
Cheese, 79
**spinach**
Seared Pork Chops with Creamy
Spinach Gnocchi, 51
stovetop cooking of, 265
Weeknight Spinach, Artichoke &
Sundried Tomato Rigatoni, 119
**steak.** *See also beef*
Beef & Asparagus Roll-Ups with
Tarragon Sauce, 64
Gonna-Want-Seconds
Cheesesteak Pasta, 116
Grandma Mary's Rouladen with
Mushroom Gravy, 193
Sheet Pan Steak with Warm
Potato Salad & Horseradish
Sauce, 142
Steakhouse Surf 'n' Turf Salad, 94
Sticky Honey-Garlic Drumsticks with
Peppers & Snap Peas, 138
Stuffed Spaghetti Squash with Zesty
Turkey Sauce, 102
**sweet potatoes**
Crunchy Pecan Chicken with
Honey-Roasted Sweet Potatoes,
157
Honey Dijon–Glazed Pork
Tenderloin with Roasted Sweet
Potatoes & Apples, 101
roasting, 262

**T**
**tacos,** Flaky Fish Tacos with Lime
Crema, 98
Taco Seasoning, 18
Tastes-Like-All-Day Quick Ham &
Bean Soup, 22
30-Minute Creamy Dijon Chicken, 67
Three-Cheese Creamy Chicken &
Mushroom Lasagna, 198
Three-Cheese Scalloped Potato &
Beef Gratin, 160
**tomatoes**
BLT Baked Chicken Burgers with
Chipotle Mayo, 87
Easiest Ever Tomato Soup with
Cheesy Basil Toasts, 37
Kailey's Roasted Balsamic Cherry
Tomato Pasta, 127
One-Pan Chicken Pomodoro
Skillet, 228
Quick Tomato Cucumber Salad, 255
roasting, 262
stovetop cooking of, 265
Weeknight Spinach, Artichoke &
Sundried Tomato Rigatoni, 119
Zucchini Turkey Meatballs with
Roasted Tomato Sauce, 153
20-Minute Broccoli Cheese Soup, 30
**turkey**
Cheesy Ratatouille Roll-Ups with
Meat Sauce (or Not), 113
Egg Roll in a Bowl (Variation), 33
Secret Sauce Orange Ginger Beef
(Variation), 25
Stuffed Spaghetti Squash with
Zesty Turkey Sauce, 102
Zucchini Turkey Meatballs with
Roasted Tomato Sauce, 153

**U–V**
**vegetables**
roasting, 262
stovetop cooking of, 264–265

**W–X–Y–Z**
Weeknight Spinach, Artichoke &
Sundried Tomato Rigatoni, 119

Zesty Unstuffed-Shells Soup with
Basil Ricotta, 84
**zucchini**
roasting, 262
stovetop cooking of, 265
Zucchini Turkey Meatballs with
Roasted Tomato Sauce, 153

**IN LOVING MEMORY**
London Brielle (Victoria) Maclellan
2012–2023

*To my sweet niece London. Thank you for taking care of my
puppies throughout the making of this book and for all the love
you have given all of them over the years. Thank you for being an
official taste tester of many of these recipes (and loving mac and
cheese as much as I do). Our lives are forever better for the years
we spent with you. You are forever loved and missed, sweet girl.*